The Country Kitchen

The Country Kitchen

Jocasta Innes

Frances Lincoln

Weidenfeld
& Nicolson

Editor/Designer:
Nonie Niesewand

Art Editor:
Jane Willis

Assisted by:
Piet Saag (design)
Jill Goolden (copy)
Pamela Todd (copy)
Antonia Demetriadi (indexer)

Photographer:
Christine Hanscomb

Illustrators:
Stewart Walton
Tony Kerins
Liz Butler

The Country Kitchen © 1979 by
Frances Lincoln Publishers Limited
Text © 1979 by Jocasta Innes
Artwork and photographs © 1979 by
Frances Lincoln Publishers Limited

First published in Great Britain by
Frances Lincoln Publishers Limited
37–41 Mortimer Street, London W1N 7RJ
in association with
Weidenfeld and Nicolson Limited
91 Clapham High Street, London SW4 7TA

ISBN 0–906459–01–X

Filmset in 'Monophoto' Baskerville by
Keyspools Limited, Golborne, Lancashire
Colour separations by Newsele Litho Limited, Italy
Printed and bound in Italy

Publishers' acknowledgements

Thank you to the team who checked the text:
Miriam Polunin, editor of 'Here's Health' who
read the cereal chapters; Joy Ellery, nutrition
adviser to the Milk Marketing Board for the
dairy information; Dr Geoffrey Burgess, director
of the Torry Research station for the Ministry
of Fisheries who patiently guided us through the
fish chapters; Tony Pike, editor of the Meat
Trades Journal who advised us on the meat cuts
and cures; Geoffrey Kibby of the Natural
History section of the British Museum who
checked our visual guide to identifying mushrooms; Norma MacMillan and Felicity Luard
for editing the American edition.

Thank you to the creative team:
illustrators Stewart Walton and Tony Kerins,
for their step by step drawings and Stewart, in
particular, for the chapter openers; Liz Butler
whose botanical drawings in the fruit and
vegetable chapter will assist country ramblers;
photographer Christine Hanscomb and her
assistant Jean-Luc Bénard who spent many
patient hours creating the beautiful photographs
that head each section; to Dinah Morrison who
enthusiastically cooked so many of the delicious
dishes you see in the book, and Angela Cox who
cooked the sumptuous meat spreads.

Thank you to the following:
Camisa, 61 Old Compton Street, London W1, an
Italian family firm, justifiably proud of their
fresh pasta; Chattels, 53 Chalk Farm Road,
London NW1 for the loan of brewing barrels; the
family business of George and Tony Cooper, fish
smokers and curers who instructed our illustrator
in the skilful business of filleting fish and allowed
us to photograph the fish section at their smokehouse in 5, Dartford Road, London SE17; R. W.
Allen, butchers at 117 Mount Street, London W1
who hung game in autumn for our photography;
F. C. Maddison at 70 Knights Hill, West
Norwood SE27 who made a galantine for our
step by step illustration; C. A. Marett at Gabriel
Machin, 7 Market Place, Henley-on-Thames
who demonstrated the lengthy business of curing a ham for illustration; the Estate Office of
the National Trust at Lanhydrock, Bodmin,
Cornwall who allowed us to photograph there.

Author's acknowledgements

Talking and listening has provided me with so much help in writing this book that I feel a list of acknowledgements should begin with a collective thank-you to all the people whose reminiscences helped to bring the old country ways to life.

My sincere thanks to Angela Cox, most indispensable of assistants, whose North country common sense and genuine love of good food were an unfailing support. I could not have done without the help and advice of George Carter and Peter Stickland, both wise in country ways. Bill Brown told me more about fish than I could have learnt from books. Mark and Rachel Helfer supplied me with Jersey milk which would inspire any amateur cheesemaker and Mr and Mrs Norman Stoate of Cann Mills in Dorset told me all I needed to know about stoneground flour. Among the many friends who helped me with ideas, recipes and encouragement, I would like to thank Lif, Mirdza, Bronnie and Sally. For their forbearance over books missing or overdue, thank you to the charming staff of Wareham Public Library.

Shaping the book for publication was definitely a team effort and here I must thank that vigilant and tactful trio: Pamela Todd, Jilly Goolden and especially Nonie Niesewand, who deciphered illegible notes, revised endless proofs. And finally, thank you to Jane Willis, Christine Hanscomb, Jean-Luc Bénard, Stewart Walton and Tony Kerins for making the book not just useful but beautiful.

Contents

7

The author's kitchen in the country

Your country kitchen

Everyone has a picture of how a country kitchen should look . . . it's a phrase as clustered with associations as a bramble with fruit. Usually it is an old settled place which comes to mind: a flagged floor smoothed into hollows by the passing of countless feet, vast plank table scoured to pale straw colour, round-faced clock companionably ticking and set into the chimney breast, and that tyrant of the old style country kitchen, the cast-iron range whose needs, moods and eccentricities must be faithfully served if bread is not to scorch and kettles refuse to boil. Scrubbed, sanded, scoured, swabbed almost to colourlessness over the years, the gentle austerity of the place is brightened here and there by copper pans big enough to bath a baby in, burnished strings of onions, a bunch of dried herbs, the best china set out against the dark wood dresser. For comfort, a Windsor chair eased by sagging cushions, and beneath it, a scuffed rag rug.

Some features of this imagined kitchen would change from one part of the world to the other, but not the essentials: a certain old fashioned air, the use of honest materials like brick, wood, stone, the sense of an ordered way of life linked to the changing seasons, the good feeling which comes off places where people are generously fed, warmed and cherished, and the squirrelling impulse to store good things away, tucked into pots and jars. But the quintessence of old country kitchens is their smell, a richly complicated experience for the nose in which new bread, frying onions, hot jam, muddy boots, vanilla, wet washing, smoke, herbs, dishwater have all somehow merged their differences over the years.

This archetypal country kitchen is frankly a nostalgic creation. By comparison the typical modern country kitchen is smart, colourful and briskly labour saving. And why not? Stainless steel sinks and drainers are hygienic and practical and you can wipe them down in a moment which certainly was not the case with the old porcelain sink and wooden draining boards. Yet links with the old traditions survive in a contemporary kitchen. Ropes of onions, shallots and garlic still hang by the stove, parsley and chives sprout from pots on a sunny windowsill, the unmistakable smell of working yeast shows that a batch of dough is rising in the big earthenware jar beside the cooker, bundles of dried herbs from the garden are pinned close to the worktop and there is possibly a keg of homebrew propped on bricks in one corner. Not merely decorative accessories chosen to lend a touch of homeliness to streamlined plastic laminates, but signs of a peaceful revolution going on in more and more homes as people discover that they can have the best of both worlds. So they make use of the time and energy saved by modern appliances to rediscover the culinary skills known to their forebears.

First and foremost, the sharpened appetite and relish which comes from eating fresh, homemade, unadulterated food, honest loaves made from flour and yeast, beer and ales of a strength and heartiness since vanished from commercial products, jams, jellies and preserves which still retain the fragrance of summer. Then there is the enjoyable glow with which one chooses a jar of pickled peaches to perfectly complement a plate of cold ham, or home-made pâté. A store cupboard stocked with jars of homemade preserves, jams, jellies, fruit butters and cheeses must be one of the country cook's deepest satisfactions. Quite apart from economy and superlative flavour – straight from the garden to the pan is the rule for the best flavours – homemade preserves look so beautiful, especially the translucent jellies like quince, rowan, apple and mint. I have rediscovered the delights of preserving with old-fashioned recipes that use both fruits of hedgerow and woodland, like the cut gooseberry preserve flavoured with elderflowers to resemble muscatels, and the orchard fruits like the dumpsideary jam. One good thing often leads to another. It is not such a big step from baking bread to making the cheese to eat with it, or from cooking meat in terrines, pâtés and galantines to preserving it by curing and smoking it yourself. Disentangled from the folk lore which is apt to grow up around these old skills, the basic processes prove to be uncomplicated. It is an interesting fact too that brewing, baking, bottling, salting and smoking your own food provide a pleasure as direct, simple and nourishing to the spirit as bread is to the belly.

Nor must you live in the country to enjoy countrified pleasures. Certainly, it is less trouble for country dwellers with a kitchen garden, an orchard and wild foods for the picking to explore new ways of using and preserving them. But one of the most countrified kitchens I ever knew was in the sooty heart of London, a basement room below pavement level that relied on windowboxes and tubs for greenery. Runner beans scrambled up from windowboxes like living sunblinds, the tomato salad came from a plastic grow-bag and was sprinkled with fresh chopped basil from a pot on the windowsill. Stacked in kegs along a wall was an impressive choice of fruit and flower wines, much of it picked on London's wilder heaths and parkland. There is no garden, however small or ill-favoured, where something cannot be coaxed to grow; a morello cherry tree against a shaded wall, herbs in a raised bed to catch the sun, strawberries in pots. Even if you live on the fiftieth floor of a concrete tower, never deny yourself the thrill of growing something edible. Houseplants are decorative and pleasing, but to tend, harvest and finally eat a crop of anything – no matter if it is only a plate of bean sprouts – is a keen delight to that bit of frustrated farmer in us all. More practically, with bulk buying proving an economical way of getting in fruit and vegetables, not to mention meat, cereals and pulses, even the most urbane of urbanites will find it useful to 'put them up' before they perish. It is no more difficult to make epicurean delicacies like damson cheese, spiced beef, apple butter, raspberry vinegar, than it is to fill a few jars with marmalade or jam, but it is a lot more interesting, rewarding and fun.

This book is intended to encourage those cooks who value such things and who have thought they would like to try making sausages . . . or smoking kippers . . . or brewing their own beer . . . or making fruit liqueurs to give away as Christmas presents, if they could only find detailed practical instructions and information on the equipment needed, how long the process takes and whether the product is finally worth the effort and trouble. Nostalgia for the sake of nostalgia has been avoided because gadgets do save time and effort if you can afford them. After all, it is the flavour of your sausage filling that counts, not whether it was pushed into the casing mechanically or by human hand.

Food for all seasons

Spring

Spring sweeps the countryside like a green fire, puffs of white blossom rising behind like smoke. The sharp young greens are a tonic to the eye and to the system, eaten when still acrid with newness. You can taste the old earth minerals in dandelion and hawthorn leaf; use them as our ancestors did in 'sallets', later picking the flowers for wine.

Spring is when the provident cook turns gardener, pricking out, sowing and planting for the year ahead. Sturdy winter vegetables, cauliflowers, brassicas, the worthy root family are making way for catch crops of radishes, the first spinach, lettuce nursed under cloches against spring frosts. As the season advances, sprouting broccoli, or 'poor man's asparagus', makes way for the other sort which you need patience, not riches, to enjoy. Spring fruit is scarce, so value the first young sticks of rhubarb for light fine wine and jam set with ginger and marrow. But the first spring gooseberries, hard, green and acid are the true spring fruit, best for jams, bottling and wine. Gooseberry wine is like a good hock.

Early spring sees the end of the white fish season, a good time to buy halibut, cod for drying and salting, herring for pickling and smoking. By mid-spring, the breeding season is well under way so game is taboo apart from the odd rabbit. However, as the months pass, lobster and crab – 'game of the sea' – take over from oysters, mussels and scallops.

Summer

Everywhere summer oozes richness: cattle, fed on lush grass yield the year's richest milk for cheesemaking, or to eat as clotted cream with the season's soft fruit, first gooseberries then strawberries, currants, loganberries and raspberries, best eaten fresh before making into the delectable jams, jellies, syrups and cordials. Elder blossom makes a fragrant wine.

Even the fish of the season are sappy, rich with oil like mackerel and trout. Freshly caught fish can be smoked in the simplest metal box to eat later with all the crisp salad vegetables, lettuce, cucumber, peppers, early tomatoes or pound shrimp with butter and pot it for spreads. The best meat is young – veal, lamb, chicken, duckling – good to make up into refined pâtés and galantines. Venison is back in midsummer, buck not roe, as the herds are being culled. It is excellent home-cured to eat with a sharp currant or rowan jelly, or made into hearty sausages.

As summer draws to a close, a glut of vegetables – courgettes, marrows, watermelon, tomatoes – sets one rooting among pickle and chutney recipes. Green beans should be salted down each week for winter use; tomatoes bottled for pasta sauces. Collect herbs to dry and store, or to flavour your pickles. Late summer brings cherries, plums, apricots, peaches, all excellent dried, or bottled to make lavish preserves, fruity wines and unbeatable home-made liqueurs, like cherry shrub which uses brandy as a preservative for fresh cherries.

Autumn
This is the season that sees the most bustle and stir in country, and countrified, kitchens. Crops are harvested daily. Begin with a glut of late vegetables by plaiting, for drying into coppery strings, onions, shallots, garlic. A profusion of late plums, pears, damsons, quinces can be made into jams, preserves, fruit cheeses and butters to eat later.

By mid autumn, the wild fruits, berries and nuts, are ready for picking – blackberries, sloes, crab apples, elderberries, rosehips. These yield some of the freshest tasting, most evocative preserves and wines. Wild cob nuts and sweet chestnuts will be just right for Christmas eating.

Field mushrooms and puffballs, most mysterious earth fruit of all, are there for the persevering rambler. Surplus mushrooms – excepting puffballs – can be dried to add savour to winter soups and casseroles. For winter pulses, dry beans, peas and store them in a cool place.

Traditionally, autumn is when the family pig was killed to make hams, bacon, brawns, sausages and blood pudding to be stored for winter use. It is still practical to cure and smoke hams and sausages now so they can mature and mellow during the winter when there is least danger of bacteria spoiling your handiwork. Also, with Christmas in mind, meat can be put up in various ways. A good time too to smoke herring, which is plentiful now.

Winter
Stormy, sodden or frosted with stars, winter nights are long enough to oppress the spirit, and it needs human resourcefulness to make them homely with such comforts as bright fires, good food and warming drinks. Nothing is more fortifying than a steaming mug of spiced, mulled elderberry wine or a hot raspberry cordial to drive away the cold.

It is now that the provident cook really scores with so many good things put by. Some industrious cooks may find time to pickle the first hard cabbages in brine to eat with Christmas goose, or begin fermenting their parsnip wine. Now is a good time to make sausages, bland or spicy, to dry, freeze or smoke. Game is back and plentiful for layering into terrines, flavoured with port and brandy, spices and herbs, or for eating spiced, cured or pickled.

Stored fruit and vegetables, fresh and dried, need checking to weed out mouldy ones. As winter hardens, your stores are raided in earnest to flavour the heartening soups and casseroles and add variety to meals threatened by monotony. As the last stored apples come to an end, all the citrus fruits reach their peak in time for marmalade making, row upon row of tawny pots to last the year's breakfasts.

Just when spring seems further away than ever, snowdrops pierce the frozen ground, a glow surrounds the budding elms and the whole cycle, sowing and reaping, birth and death, nature's gifts and man's industry is poised to begin again.

Cereals

The staff of life

All the maincrop cereals so vital to feeding the world's hungry millions belong to the botanical family of *Graminaciae*, grasses, along with reeds, rushes and lawns. Corn (a word for the seed of grass) in the old days signified grain in general, meaning oats to the Scots, wheat, rye or barley to the English, maize or sweetcorn in America. It might be eaten whole, boiled up into porridge, roughly crushed into groats to make a more digestible gruel, split into flakes, ground into flour of varying degrees of fineness. Often the grain could be fermented to make alcoholic drinks, both mild and potent. Before factory milling and cheap transport brought 'fine whete' flour within everyone's reach, dishes of strong local character were invented to use the corn, or cereal ... consider the way Mexicans, early Americans and Italians variously explored the possibilities of cornmeal, mixing it with hot chilies, or molasses or cheese with utterly different results.

It may come as a surprise to learn that the Western world still relies to a large extent on basic cereals – wheat primarily, also rice and oats. Nutritionists' surveys indicate that cereals account for one *quarter* of the daily calorie intake in the average Western diet. The significance of this, from the health point of view, only becomes clear once you realize how much cereals, in particular wheat and rice (the most widely eaten), vary in food value according to whether they have been refined, polished, bleached or otherwise commercially processed.

In their unrefined state all the cereals are valuable foods, providing good protein, a rich source of B vitamins and many essential minerals. Wheat germ is the richest natural source of vitamin E, which is involved in the health of muscles, skin and all tissues. When wheat grain is milled to produce refined white flour most of the B vitamins, in the outer husk, are removed and *all* the wheat germ, because wheat germ oil can turn flour rancid if it is stored for any length of time. True, two of the lost B vitamins, plus calcium and iron, are partially restored, but who knows whether the lost vitamin E may not count for more in the subtle biochemistry of the human body? Similarly with rice, the nutrients are concentrated in the brown husk, which is entirely removed to produce polished white rice.

It is not just what commercial processing takes out, but what it puts *in* which needs thinking about. The wheat grains used to make flour have been subjected to all manner of interference, from sprays used on the growing crop, through bleaches used to brighten white flour, to 'improvers' used to achieve the standard commercial loaf.

Without becoming too diet conscious, it seems sensible to make sure that the cereals which form a large part of your family's diet should be as rich in all their natural nutrients as possible.

Begin with bread, which is the cereal food most people, especially children, eat in largest quantities. Half the battle is won if you switch from white to wholemeal bread, by which I mean bread made from stoneground, compost grown, wholemeal flour. Wholemeal flour delivers all the goodness in wheat intact, while stoneground ensures an even distribution of the precious wheat germ oil. Buy your own flour by the sack from a reputable miller and make and bake the bread yourself. This is both economical and satisfactory. If the family are gluttons for white loaves, begin with a half and half mixture of wholemeal and strong white flour, and step up the wholemeal content gradually. Reluctant children can be tempted by adding enough sweetener – molasses, malt or honey – to make a slightly sticky loaf. The chewy texture of wholemeal bread is due to the bran content, which, in many doctors' opinions, is one of its most important contributions to health. A generous dollop of bran daily is one of the best ways of adding roughage.

Try making some of the simpler biscuits, cakes, and tea breads with wholemeal flour mixed with white. All sorts of things can be added to make them more nourishing as well as more delicious: nuts, seeds, dried fruit, cracked wheat, eggs, honey, fats. These not only bring their own quota of protein, calcium and iron but also help the body to assimilate the cereal nutrients more efficiently. Yeast is a potent source of B vitamins and much else. Keep an airtight tin of wheat germ handy too, and add a spoonful wherever its faintly nutty taste seems appropriate.

Perhaps the most flexible, popular health food of our time is muesli. Health conscious people have discovered that the basic formula of rolled oats and raw grated apple is endlessly adaptable. You can add fresh fruit in season, or dried milk powder, wheat germ or a little bran. It can be eaten with milk, cream, yogurt, and sweetened with honey or condensed milk. Some people like a savoury version with grated cheese and herbs. But the most instantly popular variant is 'granola', which uses your favourite basic muesli mix, turned over with a little corn oil and honey and toasted in a low oven till slightly crisped and golden.

Rolled oats are the cereal richest in minerals and oils and old fashioned porridge needs no introduction. Any food with vitamin C eaten with the oats helps to make use of the iron more effectively. So give your children a glass of orange juice with their porridge and eggs for a warming, impeccably nutritious winter breakfast, or try hot oat cakes eaten with fresh butter, followed by fresh fruit.

According to nutritionists, the best way to get full protein and vitamin value from cereal is to eat as many different types as possible during the course of the day. So, muesli for breakfast, wholemeal bread with lunch, nut bread for tea, rice with supper, and so on. Keep a supply of the less conventional cereal foods such as millet, buckwheat, cornmeal, brown rice and barley on hand and experiment with different ways of using them. Be tactful; if you overdo the health side of things you run the risk of making healthy eating seem downright dull and penitential. Instead, try brown rice in soups, cold and well seasoned as a basis for salads or fried up with soy sauce, prawns and spring onions, Chinese style. Buckwheat is delicious when cooked in any of the traditional Russian ways, with mushrooms, hard boiled eggs and sour cream. Millet can be used to make light and delicious gnocchi. Rye mixed with wholemeal flour makes a sophisticated dark bread, with a sour flavour which contrasts particularly well with good cheese, radishes and pickles. Add barley to soups, stews and casserole dishes, or use it instead of rice with game dishes. Try substituting cooked barley, millet or buckwheat, well seasoned, for rice in stuffings for vegetables and poultry. Chase up traditional peasant recipes which rely on cereals and try them out.

Bread

'The smel of new breade is comfortable to the heade and to the herte'
Anon 1400

How one's heart goes out across the centuries to the unknown person who felt it worth recording such a touchingly simple truth. For he – or she – was quite right: the smell of new bread is incomparable; rich, warm and yeasty, it makes the kitchen a place of true comfort.

Bread making is one of those basic skills, like being able to light a fire or ride a bicycle, which everyone should master. When bread strikes loom, or public holidays strip shop counters bare, it is a relief to know you have only to reach for the flour and the dried yeast to fill the gap. Baking your own bread regularly saves money and it is reassuring that the loaves contain only what you have put into them. Freshly baked loaves, buns and croissants can be frozen successfully, so deep freeze owners can organize one massive baking session every fortnight. The rest of us can get by with baking once a week and wrapping the loaves in foil or greaseproof paper, to keep them from drying out.

The best argument for making bread is simply that it is altogether pleasurable. The sensuous glee to be found in working up a sticky flour and water mess with your fists is capped only by the wonder of the rising dough, puffing itself up steadily in the warm, sleek as a mushroom. Finally, there is the crowning moment when the oven door is opened and out come the steaming loaves, so rounded, golden and immaculate it is hard to believe they could be the work of your own hands.

Compared with precision cookery, which depends on timing and judgement to come out right (béarnaise sauce, soufflés, batters) making bread is easy. It uses few ingredients and the simplest equipment and once you have had a couple of trial runs, you will find that the stages follow upon each other as inevitably as ABC. If you are in a hurry the process can be speeded up so that the bread is on the table in one and a half hours flat. Alternatively the raising period can be extended by anything up to forty-eight hours by leaving the dough to rise in progressively cooler temperatures often with better results. Begin with a foolproof recipe like the one for daily bread, but don't be afraid to experiment with more elaborate ones – they may look complicated but this is simply because they contain more ingredients – the basic formula of yeast, flour and liquid still remains. You can add honey, malt, treacle for sweetness, wheat germ for extra vitamins, seeds, herbs, spices for relish, and shape the loaves in many ways.

At the bakehouse oven, the miller's loaf and rising daily bread. In the flour sieve (foreground) hot cross buns and (clockwise) glazed Swedish Christmas bread in both ring and stick shapes, Chinese sesame seed buns, unleavened chapattis, two sticks of rye bread and, centre, Irish soda bread.

Flour

Wheat flour is the universal choice for regular baking because it makes lighter bread. Hard wheat (mostly winter wheat grown in Canada) is richest in gluten, the protein substance which gives dough enough strength and elasticity to expand and contain the furiously multiplying yeast cells (and to remain that way after oven heat has killed off the yeast). Milled, 'hard' wheat gives a strong flavour which absorbs more liquid, makes a springier dough and bakes into a larger loaf. Soft wheat flour, usually milled from a local crop, is less absorbent and results in a denser, shorter textured crumb. The colour, texture, nutritional content and flavour of wheat flour are established by the degree to which it has been milled and refined (that is, sieved and bolted) to remove bran or wheat husk. As milling proceeds, the flour becomes milder and paler.

Wholemeal: ground from the whole grain, germ, endosperm and husk. It makes a dark, chewy, strongly flavoured bread that is close in texture.

Wheatmeal: falls between wholemeal and strong plain bread flour. It is wholemeal with a varying proportion of the bran or wheat husk sieved out – extraction rate varies from 81% to 90%. However, it retains a wheaty flavour and makes softer, lighter bread and more spicy solid types of cakes, buns or biscuits. It is also obtainable stoneground, compost grown.

Strong plain bread flour: is available bleached (white) or unbleached (creamy). This flour contains an extra high proportion of hard wheat and gluten, and rises well, making a loaf of elastic, spongy texture and good flavour. Use it wherever springiness matters: pizzas, baps, buns, cakes, puff and flaky pastry, Yorkshire puddings and batter in general.

Household flour: whiter than white, bleached, bran free, 'soft' and satisfactory for general cooking, thickening sauces, making cakes, biscuits and quick tea breads (self-raising flours make these even quicker).

Many people keep a supply of wholemeal and strong plain bread flour, mixing the two wherever a wheatmeal effect is needed. It is economical to buy wholemeal or wheatmeal flours in bulk from a miller who grinds – stone-grinds usually – his own on the premises. It is also possible with the aid of an electrical gadget or a hand operated mill to mill your own flour in small quantities. All flour should be stored in a cool, dry place. Plastic dustbins with lids are clean, neat and mouseproof, if not things of great beauty.

Finally, a brief word about other cereal flours:

Rye, on its own, or mixed with white flour, gives a sharp flavour which is ideal for sour dough techniques and for snacks of the smorgasbord variety. It contains less gluten than wheat flour.

Barley flour is hard to come by (try health food shops) but a couple of ounces mixed into a wholemeal dough will give a distinctive, nutty taste to your bread.

Oat flour, or fine meal, is also hard to find outside traditional oat growing areas, but a handful of medium oatmeal (not the porridge type) can be added to wholemeal bread for a pleasant change in flavour. It can also be used to make oatcakes which taste delicious eaten with cheese.

Yeast

The yeast you buy, whether fresh or dried, is made by cultivating and processing selected strains of wild yeast, colourless, microscopic fungi present in the air about us. In a moist, warm environment and fed with a little sugar, yeast starts multiplying furiously, converting sugar into carbon dioxide and, ultimately, alcohol. The word yeast is derived from the Sanskrit *yas*, to seethe, which neatly describes what you see when you peer into a bucket of homebrew. Scrape the sludge off the bucket and mix a cupful into your next batch of bread. It raises the dough slowly and leaves a slight 'hoppy' bitterness which makes an appealing change.

Hoping to settle the controversy about the respective merits of fresh and dried yeast, I made up a loaf using each. The fresh-yeast dough made a spectacular start, doubling in size faster than its fellow, and maintaining its lead when they went into the oven together, on the same shelf. Unexpectedly, things levelled out during the baking, and there was less than 6 mm ($\frac{1}{2}$ inch) in height between the cooked loaves, the fresh-yeast loaf being fractionally lighter textured and perhaps a little sweeter tasting than the other. From this I concluded that fresh yeast is slightly stronger but you can still make excellent bread from the dried. Fresh yeast will keep for a week stored in a screwtop jar or polythene bag, in a cool place; the potency of dried yeast will decline once the tin has been opened. When baking, remember you will need to use twice as much fresh yeast as dried, because dried yeast is concentrated and so more powerful. Two other factors affect the amount of yeast needed: the density of the dough (wholemeal flour needs more yeast, as do fancy breads enriched with fruit and nuts) and the length of time allowed for raising it. The longer you leave it the more dough a given amount of yeast will raise, producing lighter bread every hour.

Activating yeast

Yeast cells respond to a little encouragement so warm the flour, bowl and the liquid before use. Never knead the dough in a draughty place. Salt inhibits yeast, though improving bread flavour and crisping the crust, so use *less* salt for quick breads. Sugar boosts yeast growth – a pinch is enough to reactivate fresh yeast. Or you can crumble the yeast into the liquid or rub it straight into the flour. To reactivate dried yeast, add a pinch of sugar to a small cupful of warm water, stir in the yeast granules and leave for ten minutes until frothy.

Yeast culture

Thrifty souls might like to try keeping their own yeast culture going between baking sessions. Keep aside a small piece of dough when next baking and store it in a screwtop jar in a cool place. Look at it every few days and sprinkle on a little sugar if it shows signs of wilting. Before your next bake, bring it back into the warm, add a little warm water and sugar to it and sprinkle a little flour on top. At bedtime transfer it into a bowl, add a few ounces of flour, mix together and leave overnight to prove. It can now be kneaded into the rest of the flour as if it were ordinary yeast. Remember to subtract the flour you used and to keep a little back for the next time. This method does not work every time but is worth trying.

Bread making

Flour, water and yeast are mixed to a dough which is kneaded to distribute the working yeast and force in air and then left for a varying period to allow the yeast cells to expand and develop. The dough is then punched down, or knocked back, and rapidly kneaded again before being shaped into loaves or filled into tins. These are left to rise once more for a short time before they are cooked. Some simpler bread recipes cut out the knocking back and second raising stage which saves time but results in a less uniform texture. Thanks to modern technology, there are now a number of gadgets designed to do some of the work of kneading, and yeast boosters like ascorbic acid to speed up the raising time, but, essentially, the old methods stand unaltered.

Mixing and kneading

Tip a measured amount of flour and salt into a mixing bowl and warm slightly. The water or milk used for mixing should also be hand-hot. Start with a little more liquid than the recipe requires to save having to fumble about with sticky hands if the flour proves unexpectedly absorbent, but add it gradually and have the flour bag handy to dust the table top and your hands if the dough becomes too sticky to manage. All the ingredients for fancy bread recipes should be measured out into bowls and close at hand to save confusion. The reactivated yeast should also be ready, frothing in a measuring jug.

Make a well in the warmed flour, tip in the yeast and some of the liquid. Use your hand to draw the flour into the liquid, stirring it round and adding water cautiously until the bulk of the flour feels moist and is beginning to stick together. Use both hands now to collect the sticky mess into a lump and roll it around to collect the last of the loose flour. Add a little more water if needed. It is possible to do all the kneading in the bowl but I prefer a flat table top, the surface lightly floured to prevent sticking. Smack down the dough lump, push it down and away from you with the flat of both hands, fold it back towards you and push it away again. This traps the air and the rhythmic back and forth motion soon becomes instinctive. If the dough remains obstinately sticky, after a minute's kneading, shake a handful of flour over it. If you can spare the time, knead the dough for between ten and twenty minutes or until the dough springs up smoothly leaving a print which fills up in a second when poked with a finger. Once-raised, or quick breads, benefit from an extra long kneading which compensates for the shorter time spent developing the yeast.

Electric mixers with dough hooks

If you are using one of these to make bread, put the yeast and liquid in the bowl, tip in the dry ingredients, set to lowest speed and mix for a couple of minutes until a dough is formed. Increase the speed slightly and mix for another two or three minutes to knead the dough. Most mixers will not hold more than 450 g (1 lb) of flour at a time but they make dough so quickly, you can make two or three batches in less time. Add the liquid gradually in an electric mixer, as you may find the dough needs less liquid than normal.

Making plain white bread: first stage

This quantity of dough divides conveniently into one large loaf and one smaller one which can be mixed with fruit and eggs to make a sweet tea bread.

1. In a measuring jug, mix 2 teaspoons dried yeast and 1 teaspoon sugar or honey with a little warm water and leave it till it foams. Sift 675 g ($1\frac{1}{2}$ lb) flour with 2 teaspoons salt into a warmed bowl then tip onto a floured working surface, make a well in the centre and tip in the yeast mixture. Use your hands to draw the flour into the liquid. Keep adding warm water a splash at a time (up to 450 ml, $\frac{3}{4}$ pint), till the liquid binds the flour.

2. Draw in all the flour till a doughy lump forms which feels firm and does not stick to the surface. Roll it around to collect the last of the loose flour.

3. Begin kneading. Using both hands, push the dough down and away from you with the flat of both hands. Kneading must push air into the dough, unlike kneading clay for pottery which drives air out.

4. Fold it back towards you and push it away again and so on in a rhythmic back and forth motion that traps in the air. After a few minutes you will notice the dough changing from an inert lump, acquiring smoothness, even texture. It is shaping up.

5. Knead the dough for anything between 10 and 20 minutes – the longer you knead, within reason, the lighter the bread – till the dough springs elastically, leaving a print which fills up in a second when prodded gently with a finger.

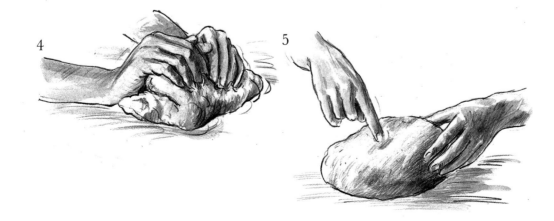

Raising and knocking back

Smear a drop of oil over the dough (to stop a crust forming) and either put it back in the mixing bowl under a clean, thick cloth or into a lightly tied and oiled polythene bag. For rapid raising, place it somewhere warm, near a cooker with the oven turned down to the lowest setting for instance, or to one side of a solid old fashioned range if you are lucky enough to own one, or in an airing cupboard. Never allow it, or the container, to touch anything hot because this will check, if not destroy, the budding cells. What you are aiming for is an even warmth.

For slower raising, two to four hours, leave the dough at room temperature, covered or wrapped as before. For an overnight raising, place the dough in a cool place like a larder. For a 48 hour raising, leave it in the lower half of the fridge.

Wheat flour has risen sufficiently when doubled in size; rye and barley, however, will always rise less, even when mixed with wheat flour. Never leave dough rising in a warm place for hours on end because yeast tends to die back gradually when it has reached its capacity. This will result in hard, bitter tasting bread. If, for some reason, you have to break off in the middle of the rapid raising routine, remember to shift the dough into a cooler spot first. If already well risen, quickly knock it back, shape it and leave to prove at room temperature.

Knocking back, or punching down, means exactly that. Punch the puffy surface of the dough, which collapses like a burst paper bag, scrape it up into a lump and knead quickly for a minute or two. Shape the dough into loaves by hand, or pat into well greased or oiled tins, not more than half full as the dough will double in size again before cooking. Leave to rise.

Once-raised bread is put straight into tins, or onto a greased baking sheet, after the first kneading and put into a hot oven as soon as it has doubled in size.

Cooking

Always preheat the oven for five minutes to the given setting as bread dough needs to be started off at a brisk heat to kill the yeast and set the loaves.

The cooking time varies with the size of the loaves – about 40 minutes for 450 g (1 lb) loaves, an hour or more for larger loaves. When the tops are crisp and hard and the loaves make a hollow sound when tapped, the bread is cooked. If in any doubt, take them out of their tins and return them to the oven, upside down, for five minutes. Brush a little melted butter over the loaves while still hot to give an attractive glazed finish. If you want to press seeds, nuts or cracked wheat over the top, take the loaves out ten minutes before they are done, brush with beaten egg, or milk, press the seeds on top and replace them in the oven. The seeds can scorch if you do this at the start.

Storing

Always allow the loaves time to go quite cold on a wire rack, before storing. Warm bread will go mouldy if imprisoned. Wrap the loaves in foil or greaseproof paper for longer storing. If any mould appears, either scald the bin or box or swab it out with a sodium metabisulphite solution (see wine making).

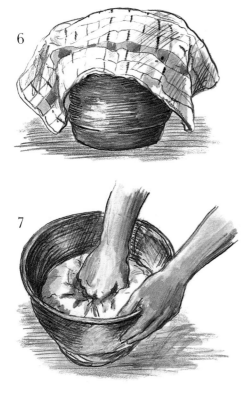

Making plain white bread: second stage

6. Put the dough in a mixing bowl, smear a drop of oil over it to stop a crust forming, and put a thick clean cloth over the bowl. Choose a raising time which suits your schedule: for rapid raising set the bowl near the oven, for overnight raising, leave in a cool place, or for really slow raising – 48 hours – put the dough in the fridge.

7. Depending on the raising time you have chosen, the loaf is ready for knocking back when it has doubled in size. Quickly knock it back by punching it with your fists.

8. Scrape it up in a lump and knead the dough on a floured working surface for a minute or two. Take two-thirds of the dough for a cottage loaf and keep back one-third for a fruit loaf.

9. To shape the cottage loaf, lightly roll out a piece of dough, make a division with the edge of the hand. The whole is then lifted, set on end and in the lifting the top bit is twisted slightly to make the divide more marked. Top and bottom sections are then let down into each other and a central punch secures them. Place the loaf on a greased baking sheet in the oven for 10 minutes at 220°C (425°F, Mark 7), then turn down to 190°C (375°F, Mark 5) for 30 to 40 minutes.

10/11. Add 50 g (2 oz) sultanas, 40 g (1½ oz) currants, 12 g (½ oz) candied peel, 1 tablespoon brown sugar and a pinch of allspice to the remaining piece of dough, place it in a 1 litre (1½ pint) loaf tin, already warmed and greased, and leave it to rise for a further 30 minutes. Cook according to fruit loaf recipe (p. 30) until the bread is firm and has shrunk away slightly from the sides of the tin.

Plain breads

Use wholemeal, for health and flavour, and strong plain bread flour for bounce and texture. Some bread recipes call for fat or milk as these give a richer, moister dough with good lasting qualities.

Daily bread

As the name suggests, this is a good loaf for everyday eating. It requires only one raising made up for by generous kneading.

1 kg (2 lb) wholemeal flour
450 g (1 lb) strong white bread flour
1 level tablespoon salt
25 g (1 oz) dried yeast
900 ml (1½ pints) warm water
1 teaspoon sugar or honey

Mix the two flours and salt together in a large bowl and put to warm slightly. Dissolve the honey or sugar in a small cupful of warm water, stir in the yeast and leave for 10 minutes till frothy. Add the yeast to the flour and mix adding the rest of the water bit by bit till the dough forms a lump and leaves the sides of the bowl clean. Transfer to a floured board or table and knead for at least 15 minutes. Place in greased tins or shape into loaves on a greased baking sheet. This amount will make two large (1 kg/2 lb) loaves or four smaller ones. I usually make one big loaf to wrap and keep, and two smaller ones to eat during the next day or two. Slip the loaves into a large oiled polythene bag and leave to rise for 45 minutes to one hour in a warm place or two to three hours at room temperature. When the loaves have doubled in size put them into a preheated hot oven (220°C, 425°F, Mark 7) for 10 minutes then turn down to 190°C (375°F, Mark 5) and cook for another 30 to 50 minutes, depending on the size of the loaves. Turn out and leave till cold.

The miller's loaf

This wholemeal bread recipe comes from the miller who supplies my stoneground flour. His family have been millers since the early 19th century – the mill is still driven by water – and having experimented with a number of different flours they stick with plain wholemeal flour 'for flavour'. The fat makes a much moister loaf.

2 teaspoons of sugar or honey
900 ml (1½ pints) water
50 g (2 oz) fresh or 25 g (1 oz) dried yeast
50 g (2 oz) margarine or lard
1.35 kg (3 lb) wholemeal flour, preferably stoneground
1 level tablespoon salt

Stir the sugar or honey into a little of the measured water, crumble fresh yeast on top (or sprinkle dried) and leave to froth up. Meanwhile work the fat and salt into the warmed flour with your fingers, as if making shortcrust pastry. Combine the yeast mixture with the flour, adding about three-quarters of the remaining water and start mixing. Add the rest of the water slowly till the dough begins lumping together nicely – it should be on the soft side, but not sticky. Sprinkle on more flour if tacky.

Transfer to a floured table and knead for 5 to 10 minutes. Leave to rise under cover, or in a polythene bag, in a warm place until the dough has doubled in size – about one hour. Knock back, knead for three minutes and divide into pieces that half fill your loaf tins. Shape the dough into loaves on baking trays. Leave, covered with polythene, in a warm place till the dough has doubled in size again. Put the loaves into a hot oven (220°C, 425°F, Mark 7) for 15 minutes then turn down to 190°C (375°F, Mark 5) and cook for a further 30 to 45 minutes, depending on the size of the loaves. Turn out onto a rack and leave till cold before storing.
Note: For a stronger version, add 1 tablespoon of molasses (rich in iron too) at the stage when you stir the sugar into the water before adding the yeast.

Swedish rye bread

A simplified rye bread, this has the typical rye tang, but is nothing like so sour or dark as the sourdough recipe using wild yeast that follows. Also it is made in one operation, though with more than the usual number of raisings.

Do not expect this bread to rise dramatically

after proving the dough – rye flour dough only increases by one-third – because rye flour has little gluten, a protein substance that gives dough enough energy and strength to expand.

300 ml (½ pint) scalded milk
150 ml (¼ pint) water
2 teaspoons honey or sugar
3 teaspoons dried yeast
225 g (8 oz) rye flour
400 g (14 oz) strong plain bread flour
2 teaspoons salt
1 tablespoon caraway seeds (optional)

Scald the milk by heating it till it rises up the pan, then leave it to cool till lukewarm. Into warm water stir the honey or sugar, then the yeast and leave till frothy. Mix the flours and salt together and warm slightly. Add the yeast to the flour, then add the milk, gradually working up to a moderately stiff dough. Mix in the caraway seeds. Turn the dough onto a floured surface, knead for 10 to 15 minutes. Leave in a bowl or bag to rise till it has doubled in size. Knock back, then leave to rise again till it has doubled in size. (This extra knocking/raising is to get the most from the rye flour, but can be skipped.) Knock back a second time, knead for a few minutes till firm then fill into oiled tins. Leave to rise once more, then bake in a moderate oven (190°C, 375°F, Mark 5) for 40 minutes.

Sliced thinly, this loaf makes the ideal base for open sandwiches of the smorgasbord variety.

Naturally fermented rye bread

Try this once, if only for a graphic demonstration of how to make a sour, dark, well-risen loaf using the mysterious powers of wild yeast. The recipe was given to me by a Latvian friend and makes the most distinctive continental rye bread I have ever tried. It tastes delicious with cheese and pickles or, more unexpectedly, toasted with honey. It takes five days to get a strong wild yeast culture.

675 g (1½ lb) wholemeal flour
225 g (8 oz) rye flour
450 ml (¾ pint) water
salt and sugar
450 ml (¾ pint) warm water

Measure out approximately 100 g (4 oz) of each flour into a small bowl, mix together with a pinch of salt and sugar and enough warm water to make a sloppy dough. Leave, uncovered, in a warm place to ferment for three days. Add the same amount again of both flours, plus enough water to make a slack dough and another small pinch of salt and sugar. Leave for two days uncovered. Transfer to a large bowl and mix in the remaining 450 g (1 lb) of wholemeal flour and 1 teaspoon of salt. Add enough warm water to make a firm but pliable dough. Knead on a floured surface till smooth and springy, shape into French type loaves pointed at both ends and slip onto a greased baking sheet. Then place them in an oiled polythene bag and leave to rise. This can take all day, but they will rise steadily by about a third to a half. Bake in a fairly hot oven (190°C, 375°F, Mark 5) for 45 minutes or till the loaves sound hollow when tapped.

Note: Add 1 tablespoon of caraway seeds with the last lot of flour for extra pungency. If you want to press seeds, nuts or cracked wheat over the top, take the loaf out of the oven ten minutes before it is done, brush with beaten egg or milk, press on seeds and replace in the oven.

Semolina bread

Semolina (a coarse phase of milling wheat flour) gives a close, firm bread nicest eaten warm with butter. Unless cooked in round cakes, the middle remains raw.

1 teaspoon honey
300 ml (½ pint) warm water
2 teaspoons dried yeast
450 g (1 lb) fine semolina
a pinch of salt
1 tablespoon oil

Dissolve the honey in a little of the warm water, then stir in the yeast and leave to froth. Mix the semolina, salt and oil in bowl. Add the yeast mixture, stir, then add more warm water and mix to make a short dough.

Shape into two round flat cakes, score the tops lightly and leave to rise in a warm place in an oiled polythene bag. When well risen, bake for approximately half an hour in a hot oven (205°C, 400°F, Mark 6).

Emergency and unleavened breads

A speedier raising agent like baking powder, or bicarbonate of soda with buttermilk and cream of tartar will cut down on raising time. Unleavened breads are mostly quick to prepare and are excellent blotting paper for all spicy, juicy, seasoned dishes.

Soda bread
This Irish recipe is the most distinguished of hasty loaves. It is as delicious hot with butter and sharp fruit jelly as it is cold with cheese. Use wheatmeal flour if you can.

450 g (1 lb) wheatmeal or strong plain flour or household flour
1 teaspoon salt
1 teaspoon cream of tartar
1 teaspoon bicarbonate of soda
25 g (1 oz) margarine or lard
300 ml (½ pint) buttermilk or sour milk

Note : Fresh milk can be soured by stirring in 1 teaspoon of lemon juice or vinegar.
Sift the dry ingredients (flour, salt, tartar, bicarbonate of soda) into a bowl, rub in the lard or margarine, make a well in the middle and pour in the liquid a little at a time, mixing till a soft dough forms. Turn onto a floured board, knead lightly for a minute, pat out into a round about 4 cm (1½ in) thick and place on a greased baking sheet. Cut a cross on top with a sharp knife and bake in a hot oven (205°C, 400°F, Mark 6) for 35 minutes. Eat hot, warm or cold.

Sesame seed buns
Chinese in origin, these are easy to make and excellent to serve up at an impromptu party.

450 g (1 lb) strong plain flour
a pinch of salt
1 teaspoon baking powder
200 ml (⅓ pint) water
1 tablespoon oil, sesame oil preferably
2 teaspoons sugar
4 tablespoons sesame seeds

Sift the flour and baking powder together into a bowl. Stir in the sugar, salt and water with a wooden spoon. Collect into a ball with both hands, knead quickly till smooth, then roll out into a salami sized sausage. Cut into 5 cm (2 in)

slices and pat flat into rounds. Moisten one side of each round with water, turn and press with the damp side facing down into a plate of sesame seeds. Heat a large, heavy frying pan, or griddle, and wipe over with a film of sesame seed oil. Put the buns in, plain side downwards, and cook for about 5 minutes or till lightly browned. Move to the grill, and place underneath *moderate* heat for a few minutes, till the seeds start to toast. Serve hot.

Pitta bread
This needs ascorbic acid (vitamin C) and fresh yeast but is the quickest route to properly leavened bread. Rolls or *pittas* made this way are best eaten hot. Yeast battens onto vitamin C, as any winemaker knows, cutting raising time to a minimum.

1 25 mg ascorbic acid tablet
300 ml (½ pint) warm milk
25 g (1 oz) fresh yeast
25 g (1 oz) margarine or lard
450 g (1 lb) strong white bread flour or household flour
1 teaspoon sugar
1 teaspoon salt
1 egg to brush over tops (optional)

Crush the tablet and stir into the milk with the crumbled yeast. Rub fat into the flour, mix in sugar and salt, make a well in the middle and add the yeast mixture. Stir, adding the rest of the milk gradually to make a firm dough. Turn onto a floured surface and knead well for about 10 minutes till smooth and springy. Leave to rise in a bowl in a warm place. Knead again for a minute, then divide into twelve pieces. Shape these into round balls or flattened ovals (*pittas*) and arrange well apart on a greased baking sheet. Put them all into an oiled bag and leave to rise in a warm place till doubled in size. Brush with beaten egg, and bake for 10 to 15 minutes (205°C, 400°F, Mark 6).
Note : Poppy seeds can be sprinkled over the egg glaze.

Baking powder bread

Use this dough to make speedy buns for hungry people.

450 g (1 lb) household flour
2 heaped teaspoons baking powder
25 g (1 oz) butter or margarine
1 teaspoon salt
450 ml (¾ pint) warm milk

Sift baking powder with flour, add salt, rub in fat. Stir in warm milk, mixing quickly with a wooden spoon. Turn onto floured board, shape into a round, cut a cross on the top and bake in a hot oven (205°C, 400°F, Mark 6) for 30–40 minutes.

Corn pones

Cornmeal is the basis of many endearingly homely types of bread like this 'low down corn pone' to quote Huckleberry Finn in Mark Twain's novel of the same name.

450 g (1 lb) cornmeal
1 teaspoon baking powder
1 teaspoon salt
300 ml (½ pint) warm water and milk mixed
2 tablespoons finely chopped onions (optional)

Sift the cornmeal and baking powder into a bowl, add salt. Stir the liquid gradually into the flour, adding a little onion as you go. The dough should be soft but not sloppy. Turn onto a floured surface, flour both hands and shape pieces of dough into 'pones', oblong cakes about the size of a small envelope, and 2 cm (¾ in) thick. Put onto a greased baking sheet, brush tops with milk and bake in moderately hot oven (205°C, 400°F, Mark 6) for 20 to 30 minutes, or till golden brown. Eat hot, dripping with butter.

Chapattis

The simplest Indian bread, unleavened and earthy tasting with a pleasantly dry homespun texture.

The only problem in making chapattis is to judge the cooking heat so that they cook but do not scorch and smoke out the kitchen. They can be buttered on one side for a richer flavour before wrapping.

225 g (8 oz) wholemeal flour
225 g (8 oz) strong plain bread flour
1 teaspoon salt
300 ml (½ pint) water

Mix the flours together with the salt. Add the water bit by bit to make a stiff but workable dough. Knead thoroughly till pliable, adding a drop more water if necessary. Cover with a damp cloth and leave for a couple of hours. Knead again. Pinch off egg-sized lumps, roll between palms into round balls, flatten on a floured surface and roll out very thinly to about the size of a side plate. Heat a heavy cast iron pan over a moderate flame, put in a chapatti, and cook for a minute until brown spots appear underneath. Turn over and repeat, pressing it gently with a cloth to make it puff up. As each chapatti is done, put into a clean cloth, wrapping them to keep hot and soft.

Simit

Unleavened bread shaped in decorative rings, sprinkled with sesame seeds. In Turkey they are peddled through the streets slung on poles.

225 g (8 oz) plain white flour
1 teaspoon salt
50 g (2 oz) margarine
1 tablespoon oil
1 tablespoon milk
1 tablespoon water
1 egg
approx 25 g (1 oz) sesame seeds

Mix the flour and salt in bowl, make a well in the middle. Melt the margarine over gentle heat, mix with oil, milk, water and beaten egg and stir this into the flour. Mix to a dough – it will feel slippery but can be worked quite easily. Knead for a minute or two. Shape with floured hands into rings about the diameter of a saucer, arrange on a greased baking sheet. Brush over with milk and sprinkle with sesame seeds. Bake in a hot oven (205°C, 400°F, Mark 6) for about half an hour or till golden brown.

Simit makes a delicious breakfast bread and because of its quick mixing, kneading and baking can be made in time for an early morning start.

Fancy breads

Traditionally a fancy bread would be made with odd bits of dough left over from the weekly bread baking. By adding an egg, sugar and a handful of dried fruit the plain dough became a sweet loaf or small buns for the family tea.

Christmas bread

Traditional fare over the Christmas period, this fragrant but not over-sweet bread is made with a mixture of rye and plain flour, moistened with stout. In Sweden this bread is flavoured with cardamom, a deliciously scented spice, that has been popular in Scandinavia since the Vikings.

1 teaspoon sugar
150 ml (¼ pint) milk or water
1 rounded tablespoon dried yeast granules
25 g (1 oz) butter or margarine
300 ml (½ pint) stout
150 ml (¼ pint) golden syrup or corn syrup
350 g (12 oz) rye flour
350 g (12 oz) strong plain bread flour
finely grated rind of 1 large orange
1 level tablespoon caraway seeds or seeds from 8
  cardamom pods
a pinch of salt

Dissolve the sugar in warm milk or water, stir in the yeast and leave for 10 minutes till frothy. Melt the butter, beat in the stout and continue beating till lukewarm, then beat in the syrup and blend till smooth. Sift both flours together, and divide into three bowls, so that you have 350 g (12 oz) in one, 200 g (7 oz) in the next, 150 g (5 oz) in the last.

Add the stout mixture to the 350 g (12 oz) bowl of flour, beat well, add the yeast mixture and beat again till thoroughly blended. Now add the grated orange rind and caraway or cardamom seeds, a pinch of salt and beat in the 200 g (7 oz) of flour a little at a time. When the dough is thoroughly blended, with a shiny appearance, leave to rise under cover or in an oiled polythene bag till almost doubled in size. Shake the last lot of flour over the work top and tip the dough out on top, kneading it so as to pick up all the loose flour. Divide in half and shape into two long French type loaves on a greased baking sheet. Cover again with polythene and leave till well risen. Bake in a moderate (180°C, 350°F, Mark 4) oven for 45 minutes. After 30 minutes glaze the tops of the loaves quickly with syrup or honey diluted with a little water. When cooked, cool on racks, re-glaze the tops, and, when cold, wrap in clean dishtowels to keep the crust soft till the bread is eaten.

Fruit loaf

This delicious sweet bread is a traditional Celtic recipe, known as Bara Brith in Wales and Barm Brack in Ireland.

2 tablespoons soft brown sugar
300 ml (½ pint) lukewarm milk
15 g (½ oz) dried yeast
450 g (1 lb) strong plain bread flour or wheatmeal flour
  or a mixture of both
100 g (4 oz) sultanas
75 g (3 oz) currants
25 g (1 oz) candied peel
50 g (2 oz) margarine or butter
a pinch of allspice
a pinch of salt
1 egg

Dissolve a little of the sugar in half the milk, add the yeast, stir and leave for 10 minutes till frothy. Warm the flour slightly in one bowl and the fruit and peel in another. Rub the fat into the flour, then stir in fruit, peel, spice, sugar and salt and mix well. Whisk the egg. Make a well in the flour, add the yeast mixture and the egg, then as much of the warm milk as is needed to make a soft dough. Cover and leave to rise in a warm place for two hours.

Turn out onto a floured board and knead for 5 minutes. Put into a greased, *warmed* loaf tin of 1.8 litre (3 pint) capacity and place in an oiled polythene bag to rise for 30 minutes. Bake in a moderately hot oven (205°C, 400°F, Mark 6) for 20 minutes; lower heat to 160°C (325°F, Mark 3) and cook for a further 20 to 30 minutes, or till the bread is firm and has shrunk away slightly from the sides of the tin. Turn out and brush the top with a spoonful of honey to glaze. Eat cold.

Shaping your loaf

1. Naturally fermented rye bread: like French-type loaves, made by rolling out the dough to the length required with the palms of your hands. If you want a crusty loaf, score it like this to get as much crust as possible. Also bake one smooth and plain to keep longer.

2. Hot cross buns: light, spicy fruit dough divided after kneading into a dozen marbles, set out on greased baking sheets and marked on top by a knife with the shape of a cross – traditionally eaten on Good Friday – then left to rise again for half an hour, then baked for 15 minutes at the top of a hot oven. When cool, the buns are glazed with sugar dissolved in milk.

3. Onion and herb bread: plain bread can be dressed up for savoury loaves. Add herbs to a plain dough, punch it into a round flat shape, brush with beaten egg, then top with thin slices of overlapping fried onion rings, sprinkled with sea salt and bake.

4/5. Swedish Christmas bread: a fancy shape for a fruit bread, with two twists of bread dough pinched together at the top then twisted around each other loosely. Coiled into a greased Savarin or ring mould, the dough is left to rise for half an hour, then baked.

6. Plain white bread: roll out a long strip of bread, cut two vertical lines almost to the top to separate the dough into three strands. Plait these and pinch the dough ends top and bottom before baking. This suits plain white bread and ten minutes before baking time is up, take out of the oven, brush with beaten egg and sprinkle with poppy seeds.

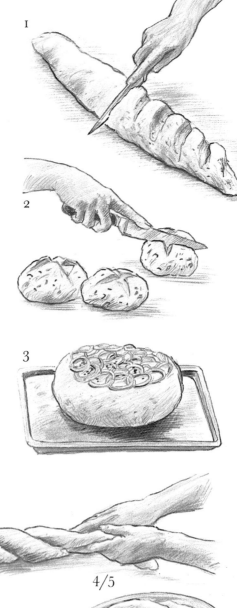

Apple bread

Serve this German version of the fruit loaf, with the added juiciness of a paving of sliced apple on top, as a pudding, warm with cream.

350 g (12 oz) strong plain bread flour
a pinch of salt
1 heaped teaspoon sugar
300 ml (½ pint) milk
15 g (½ oz) dried yeast
50 g (2 oz) margarine or butter
1 egg
50 g (2 oz) sultanas or seedless raisins
3 or 4 sharp dessert apples
Castor sugar and powdered cinnamon to sprinkle on top

Sift together the flour and salt and set to warm slightly. Stir a little sugar into the milk, add the yeast, mix, and leave for 10 minutes till frothy. Melt the butter over a gentle heat. Make a well in the flour, stir in first the yeast, then the well whisked egg, and finally the melted butter. Beat well with a spoon and leave in a warm place to rise till doubled in bulk. Turn onto a floured board and knead for a few minutes, or till smooth, then work in the raisins or sultanas and knead again to distribute them evenly. Press the dough down into a well greased 20 or 23 cm (8 or 9 in) cake tin. Peel, core and thinly slice the apples. Press the slices into the dough.

Brush over the surface with water, sprinkle thickly with castor sugar and a little cinnamon and leave for 20 minutes in an oiled polythene bag to prove. Bake in moderate oven (180°C, 350°F, Mark 4) for 45 minutes. Serve warm with single cream.

Onion and herb bread

Plain bread dough can, of course, be dressed up for savoury, as well as sweet, loaves. If your tastes incline that way, try this simple but tasty bread using 450 g (1 lb) of dough made according to the plain white bread recipe.

450 g (1 lb) white bread dough (see p. 23)
1 teaspoon dried white thyme, marjoram or dill seeds
2 onions
margarine or oil for frying
1 egg
a pinch of sea salt

At the knocking back stage, mix the dried herbs well into the dough. Leave to prove for 20 to 30 minutes. Meanwhile, fry thinly sliced onion rings in a little oil or margarine till softened, drain on kitchen paper. Just before baking, brush the top of the loaf with beaten egg and spread with overlapping onion rings, pressing them down slightly. Sprinkle sea salt all over. Bake as for plain white bread, but check after 20 minutes to see if onions are browning. If so lay a piece of buttered or oiled paper on top. Can be eaten hot or cold.

Note: You can of course vary the selection of herbs according to what you happen to have in your storecupboard.

Hot cross buns

These are made and eaten, by ancient custom, on Good Friday to mark the crucifixion. They only need to be made without the cross mark on top to become light spicy fruit buns to eat any day of the year.

150 ml (¼ pint) milk
1 teaspoon sugar
7 g (¼ oz) dried yeast
350 g (12 oz) strong plain bread flour or plain household flour
1 teaspoon salt
25 g (1 oz) butter or margarine
1 teaspoon mixed spices (powdered ginger, cinnamon, cloves and nutmeg)
50 g (2 oz) sugar
100 g (4 oz) currants
1 egg

Warm the milk slightly, stir in a teaspoon of sugar and sprinkle the yeast onto it. Leave it for 10 minutes, till frothy. Sieve the flour and salt, rub in the fat and stir in the spices, sugar and fruit. Mix in the well beaten egg and the yeast mixture. Beat till smooth, adding a little more milk if needed – the dough should be soft. Turn onto a floured board and knead till springy and smooth. Leave the dough inside an oiled polythene bag at room temperature till doubled in size. Knead again lightly till firm, then divide into 12 pieces and set these out – not too close – on greased baking sheets. Mark a cross on top with a knife, then leave about half an hour to rise again.

Touch up the crosses and bake in a hot oven (220°C, 425°F, Mark 7) near the top for about fifteen minutes. If they seem in danger of scorching, lower the oven heat a little after 10 minutes. Glaze the tops by brushing with 1 tablespoon of sugar dissolved in 1 tablespoon of milk.

Note: For extra light buns, leave the dough to rise overnight in a cool place before you add the sugar, spices and fruit. The next day, add them and proceed with a second raising and the rest of the steps, as above.

Croissants

Anyone who makes their own puff pastry will find no difficulty producing excellent croissants, essentially rolls made with a leavened puff pastry. Nothing is more delicious, and you can make a dozen for the price of two in the shops. Better still, if you have a freezer, make three times that number in one session and freeze the surplus.

1 teaspoon sugar
300 ml ($\frac{1}{2}$ pint) less 4 tablespoons warm water
15 g ($\frac{1}{2}$ oz) dried yeast
1 egg (plus 1 egg yolk for glaze)
25 g (1 oz) lard
450 g (1 lb) strong plain flour
2 level teaspoons salt
175 g (6 oz) margarine

Dissolve the sugar in water, stir in the yeast and leave for 10 minutes till foaming. Add the egg, well beaten, to the yeast mixture. Rub the lard into the flour and salt. Mix in the yeast mixture, knead for between 5 and 10 minutes, till smooth. Roll the dough out on a lightly floured surface to make a rectangle of approximately 50 × 20 cm (20 × 8 in) and 18 mm ($\frac{3}{4}$ in) thick. Take a third of the margarine, break it up into small pieces and dot the pieces evenly over two-thirds of the dough rectangle. Fold the plain third over towards the centre, then cover with the remaining 'dotted' third and press the edges down with the rolling pin to seal.

Repeat this twice, rolling out the strip to the same size, dotting it with margarine, folding and sealing. By now you will have used up all the margarine. Put the dough in the fridge for an hour, then do three more rollings and foldings but without adding any fat. Return to the fridge for 30 minutes to 1 hour, or till firm and cool.

Roll out on a lightly floured surface to make a sheet 60 × 38 cm (29 × 15 in), trim the edges and cut into 15 cm (6 in) equilateral triangles. Roll the triangles up from base to point, bending them into the characteristic horseshoe shape. Place them on greased baking sheets, brush with egg glaze and leave uncovered to prove for 30 minutes in a warm place. Brush again with egg glaze and bake in a hot oven (220°C, 425°F, Mark 7) for about 20 minutes.

For freezing, cook the croissants till they are light brown, otherwise leave 2 to 3 minutes longer, till golden brown.

To freeze. Cool, pack in rigid containers, store for up to 2 months.

To unfreeze. Place the croissants in a moderate oven (180°C, 350°F, Mark 4) and bake for 15 minutes.

Croissants, rolls made with leavened puff pastry, are shaped by cutting the dough into 15 cm (6 in) equilateral triangles. Roll up the triangles from base to point, bending into the horseshoe shapes. Place on ungreased baking sheets, brush with egg glaze and leave to prove for 30 minutes. Brush again with egg glaze, bake in a hot oven (220°C, 425°F, Mark 7) for 20 minutes.

Cakes & Biscuits

'... her mistress ... now sat in state,
pretending not to know what cakes were sent up,
though she knew, and we knew, and she knew that we knew,
and we knew that she knew that we knew,
she had been busy all morning
making tea-bread and sponge-cakes.'
Cranford   Elizabeth Gaskell   1853

Baking cakes and biscuits and suchlike confections has always provided good cooks with a chance to shine. Indeed, the best of them made quite a name for themselves in their day. Mrs Macnab, for instance, a 19th-century Ballater farmer's wife, was so famous for her fine baking that she enticed royalty to tea from nearby Balmoral, bringing with them such distinguished guests as King Frederick of Prussia. What drew the royals was not some rococo gâteau, sumptuously iced and oozing cream, but a plain – though perfect – scone. I came across an almost identical recipe recently, described as 'Queen Victoria's favourite scone' which suggests that the formidable little lady was as quick as the next housewife when it came to wheedling a good recipe out of a friend. Refined simplicity is the hallmark of the best traditional recipes, which brings them right into line with contemporary tastes in food. I find children who are not concerned with 'eating for health' will devour a plateful of the plainest home-made water biscuits with a sprinkling of sea salt. But simplicity is not a rigid rule as birthdays would not be the same without a sticky chocolate cake. Therefore I have included a recipe for this and one or two more fanciful confections for special occasions. To enjoy really delicious cakes you simply have to make them yourself – all but the most expensive commercial confectionery proves sickly and synthetic tasting. None of the recipes in this section should prove too difficult, even for beginners, but remember that cake, scone and biscuit making is something of an exact science. All the minor details like accurate measuring, the right oven setting, conscientious whisking and creaming really do *matter*. Make cakes when you are in a calm, confident frame of mind and have the kitchen to yourself for a couple of hours. If the worst happens and the sponge sinks in the middle, do not rage or panic – cut out the gooey bit, fill it with whipped cream and dish it up as a pudding.

Late summer blackberry picnicking: shortbread wedges made with ground rice to give a light, short texture, ideal for picnics as it keeps well in a tin, caraway tea bread, sliced and eaten with butter, and blackberry cordial to mix with sparkling soda.

Baking

Cakes

A firm grasp of the basic principles helps in cake making. The object of the laborious whisking and creaming is to force as much air into the batter as possible and so make the cake rise. Most recipes, though not all, also require a raising agent like baking powder (self-raising flour has its baking powder built in) or bicarbonate of soda plus cream of tartar. These agents react with liquid and heat to produce a gas, carbon dioxide, which expands and makes the cake rise as it cooks. But don't expect them to raise your cake unaided. Probably the commonest mistake in cake making is to imagine that you can cut down on the creaming or whisking if you double up on the baking powder. As a result the cake rises like a hot air balloon, then drops like a balloon with a puncture, and you are left with something dry, crumbly and heavy. *Moral*: get an electric beater, or stick to scones, buns and tea breads which do not need beating.

Always make sure before leaping into action that everything you will need in the way of equipment and ingredients are close to hand, and, if possible, ready for use: tins greased, oven preheated, eggs separated.

For light mixtures sieve the flour with the baking powder *three* times, to aerate it. Use castor sugar for whisked, creamed mixtures because it melts readily, use granulated sugar only for the rubbed-in sort. A metal spoon should be used to fold flour into a whisked sponge as a wooden spoon will squash those vital air bubbles. The secret of a foolproof sponge is to use extra egg yolks as they emulsify the mixture better and keep it stable during cooking. One or two tablespoons of hot water mixed into a well whisked – especially electrically whisked – batter at the last minute will make a moister cake. If you want the flavour of almonds, use the whole variety, lightly toasted then chopped. However, bought ground almonds can be added to rich fruit cakes to prevent the fruit from sinking. If you are using cocoa to flavour cakes, mix a little boiling water into it first to take the raw taste off. Spirits, which are expensive, are best poured over the cooked cake, not mixed into the batter. That way you keep all the flavour and bouquet (heat volatilizes alcohol) and the alcohol helps preserve the cake.

Baking times

Baking times vary according not only to the recipe, but the size and shape of your container and the idiosyncrasies of your oven. Deep cakes keep better but need longer cooking at a lower setting. Don't open the oven door before the end of the recommended cooking time as a rush of cold air may make the cake sink. To test if a cake is done press lightly with a finger, and it will spring back when ready. If in doubt insert a skewer or knife down the centre; if it comes out clean, the cake is ready. Leave it to cool in the tin for five minutes before turning out on a wire rack.

Biscuits

For crisp, short (like shortcrust) biscuits use block not tub margarine, so they do not spread everywhere, and an ounce or two of ground rice or cornflour in place of some of the wheat flour. If the mixture is crumbly, bind it with an extra egg yolk. Again, do not handle them too much, or the fat will soften, resulting in leathery biscuits. Do not store biscuits in the same tin as cakes, or they will absorb moisture and soften.

Equipment

A hand-held electric beater takes the ache out of cake making and is more useful than the fixed kind because it can be moved from the work top to the stove for different purposes. A fine meshed sieve – wire or plastic – is essential. Kitchen scales – spring balanced or the old fashioned kind with separate weights – are necessary for most recipes, though with simple mixtures such as scones and shortbread, you can gauge with a marked measuring beaker or jug. Save time by weighing out the dry ingredients beforehand. One large bowl and several smaller ones are essential for mixing and separating eggs. Standard measuring spoons are helpful, though domestic cutlery – teaspoons, tablespoons – can be used instead. Wooden spoons are required for beating and creaming. The non-stick variety of cake tin though more expensive does save time otherwise spent greasing and flouring. For deeper cakes, tins with detachable bottoms are useful. Grease the tins by brushing them over with a pastry brush dipped in oil or melted lard. Tip a little flour in the tin as a further guard against sticking and shake till evenly coated. Tin ring moulds, plain or fancy, add glamour to brioche-type cakes. Biscuits and cookies may be cut with a cup or glass, but children love the more amusing cut-out shapes and these are available in tin or rigid plastic. Foil is essential for wrapping cakes for long storage (fruit cakes and Christmas cakes) but use a layer of greaseproof first, then foil, or the acid in the fruit will eat through the foil and leave you wondering whether mice have got there first. Store cakes and biscuits in *separate* airtight tins or plastic containers with lids. Light spongy cakes do not keep well so eat them fast.

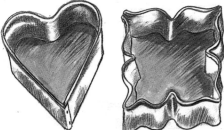

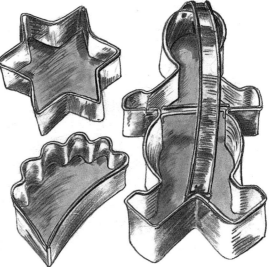

Tin biscuit cutters like these can be used with a short crisp biscuit mixture like Dutch butter cookies to cut fancy shapes before baking: just press the mix into the tin to bake, and cool biscuits before turning out and icing. Roll the mixture thinly to make the crinkle-edged biscuits, more thickly to decorate a Christmas tree with hearts and star shapes.

Cakes and tea breads

A clutch of plainish cakes for everyday eating and a few lavish ones for birthdays or to round off a dinner party. Beginners should tackle the tea breads first as the essence here is a simple loaf whereas the fluffier cakes require conscientious whisking.

Caraway tea bread

A traditional feature of nursery teas, this is far too good to disappear along with nannies and starched tablecloths. Tea bread in this case means a plain cake which should be baked in a loaf tin, to be sliced and eaten with lots of butter. The caraway seeds – beloved of Victorian cookery – give it a unique flavour.

350 g (12 oz) plain household flour
2 teaspoons baking powder
175 g (6 oz) castor sugar
75 g (3 oz) butter or margarine
150 ml (¼ pint) boiling milk
1 egg
3 teaspoons ground caraway seeds

Sieve the flour and baking powder twice, add the sugar and lightly rub in the butter or margarine. Mix scalded milk, which has been left to cool a little, with well beaten egg and ground caraway seeds. (To achieve the best flavour, lightly heat the seeds in a frying pan for a minute, then pound in a mortar or whizz in an electric coffee grinder.) Stir the milk and egg mixture into the dry ingredients, beat till well mixed, turn onto a floured board and knead quickly into a loaf tin approx. 20×10 cm (8×4 in) and bake on the middle shelf of a fairly hot oven ($190°C$, $375°F$, Mark 5) for 60 minutes, or till it feels firm on top. If in doubt, cover the top with buttered paper to prevent scorching, and cook for 10 minutes.

Mrs Macnab's featherweight scones

Mrs Macnab was a 19th century Ballater farmer's wife famed for her fine baking.

450 g (1 lb) plain household flour
1 teaspoon salt
1 scant teaspoon bicarbonate of soda
2 scant teaspoons cream of tartar
50 g (2 oz) butter
1 egg
300 ml (½ pint) sour milk or buttermilk

Note: Use fresh milk soured by stirring in ½ teaspoon lemon juice, or milk which has just 'turned' naturally, but *not* milk three days old and bitter tasting. Buttermilk, if you can get it, is best of all as the acid in it reacts with the raising agents to produce a lighter texture.

Sift the flour with the soda, cream of tartar and salt. Repeat once. Rub in butter. Stir in the well beaten egg, then the sour milk or buttermilk. Keep stirring till the dough collects in a lump, then turn onto a floured surface and knead for a few seconds till smooth. Break off little pieces and flatten them with your knuckles on a greased baking sheet to form a roughly round shape. Do *not* roll. Prick with a fork. Bake in a hot oven ($220°C$, $425°F$, Mark 7) for 8 to 10 minutes, or till just coloured on top. Wrap them in a clean cloth to keep warm and soft.

Nutcake

A characteristically sophisticated Austrian confection, rich but not sickly thanks to the stiffening of chopped nuts. Walnuts, hazelnuts or almonds (or a mixture) can be used with varying effect. Observe that the cake uses no flour, only breadcrumbs.

50 g (2 oz) dry white breadcrumbs (see below)
2 tablespoons rum
150 g (5 oz) castor sugar
5 eggs, separated
150 g (5 oz) chopped nuts
300 ml (½ pint) whipping or thick cream

Make the breadcrumbs by whizzing up stale bread in a grinder. Put them in a low oven for a few minutes to dry out. To make the cake, first mix half the rum with the breadcrumbs. In a bowl over a pan of hot water whisk the sugar and egg yolks till thick, creamy and a trail of the mixture dropped on top holds its shape for a few seconds. Whisk the egg whites till stiff then, using a metal spoon, gently fold the egg whites, breadcrumbs and nuts into the fluffy whisked yolk mixture, trying not to crush the mixture as you blend. When well blended turn gently into a greased, floured 20 cm (8 in) cake tin and bake in a fairly hot oven 190°C (375°F, Mark 5) for between 45 minutes and one hour. Test with a skewer down the middle – if it comes out clean, the cake is done. Cut in half and sandwich with slightly sweetened whipped cream flavoured with 1 tablespoon of rum and the same amount of chopped nuts. Serve this up as a sweet course, accompanied for a lavish effect by a dish of peaches or apricots preserved in brandy.

Mary Ball Washington's gingerbread

We owe this most sumptuous of dark, spicy, sticky gingerbreads to the mother of the famous President of the United States of America. One or two slight modifications like nutmeg in place of mace tone it down a little for modern palates, but essentially it is just as it was served up to an appreciative Marquis de Lafayette close on two hundred years ago.

100 g (4 oz) butter
100 g (4 oz) soft dark brown sugar
350 g (12 oz) plain household flour
1 teaspoon cream of tartar
150 g (5 oz) sultanas
150 ml (¼ pint) warm milk
4 tablespoons sherry
2 tablespoons ground ginger
2 teaspoons powdered cinnamon
3 teaspoons freshly grated nutmeg
225 g (8 oz) golden syrup
100 g (4 oz) treacle
3 eggs
1 large orange
1 teaspoon bicarbonate of soda dissolved in 2
  tablespoons warm water

Grease two oblong pans (approx. 20 × 18 × 6 cm, 8 × 7 × 2½ in) and line them with greaseproof paper. In one bowl cream the butter with the sugar till soft, light and non-gritty. Sift the flour and cream of tartar into a second bowl and add the sultanas. In a third bowl mix together warm milk, sherry, spices, syrup, treacle and beaten eggs. Add the flour mixture alternately with the milk and spice mixture to the basic creamed butter and sugar. Beat thoroughly till well

mixed. Finally beat in the orange juice and rind, plus the dissolved bicarbonate of soda. Pour into pans and bake at 170°C (325°F, Mark 3) for the first 30 minutes then reduce to 150°C (300°F, Mark 2) for another 30 to 40 minutes. Leave to cool before turning out. Sliced thinly and buttered, this gingerbread is delicious.

Sticky chocolate cake with fudge icing

Children and men adore this – ladies on a diet must just look the other way. It makes a splendidly archetypal birthday cake which can be jazzed up with silver balls, piped messages, candles or what you will.

225 g (8 oz) plain household flour
15 g (½ oz) cocoa powder
1 level teaspoon bicarbonate of soda
225 g (8 oz) golden syrup
150 ml (¼ pint) milk
100 g (4 oz) castor sugar
100 g (4 oz) margarine
1 large egg

Sieve the flour, cocoa powder and the bicarbonate of soda into a bowl. Melt the syrup, together with the milk, sugar and margarine over a gentle heat, stirring till blended. Cool a little, then add the beaten egg to this mixture. Now add liquid ingredients gradually to the flour, beating all the time. Pour into a greased paper-lined 17 cm (7 in) square tin, or 1 kg (2 lb) loaf tin. Bake in the centre of a cool oven (150°C, 300°F, Mark 2) till it feels firm to the touch. Ice with fudge mixture while still warm.

Fudge icing

225 g (8 oz) icing sugar
15 g (½ oz) cocoa
75 g (3 oz) whipped up cooking fat (Spry, Trex)
75 g (3 oz) granulated or castor sugar
3 tablespoons milk
1 teaspoon vanilla essence or coffee powder

Sift the icing sugar with cocoa into a bowl. Melt the fat and sugar in a pan, add the milk and flavourings and bring to boil. Tip into the bowl containing icing sugar and beat till fluffy – about 1 minute – with a wooden spoon. Pour quickly over the cake.

Biscuits

Ground rice or cornflour can be added in place of wheat flour to make biscuit textures light and short. If the mixture is too crumbly, add an extra egg yolk. The more substantial biscuits like oatcakes make a stop gap if you run out of bread.

Oatcakes

Useful when you run out of bread as they are quick to make. Oatcakes freeze well.

175 g (6 oz) fine or medium oatmeal (not porridge oats)
50 g (2 oz) plain flour
½ teaspoon salt
¼ teaspoon bicarbonate of soda
35 g (1½ oz) butter, margarine or lard
2 tablespoons boiling water

Mix the dry ingredients (oatmeal, flour, salt, soda) together in a bowl. Melt the fat in boiling water, add to the dry mixture and knead lightly (adding a drop more water if needed to give a firm dough). Then roll out thinly on a surface floured with a handful of oatmeal and cut into triangles with a knife. Bake on a greased baking sheet for 15 minutes till crisp in a hot oven (205°C, 400°F, Mark 6). Leave on a rack in a warm place to dry out till crisp.

Shortbread

A particularly good version of the Scottish classic as the ground rice gives a light, short texture. These keep well in a tin.

100 g (4 oz) plain flour
100 g (4 oz) ground rice
100 g (4 oz) butter or margarine
100 g (4 oz) castor sugar
1 whisked egg yolk
2 tablespoons cream or top of milk

Sieve the flour and ground rice together into a bowl and rub in the butter or margarine quickly as for shortcrust. Mix in the sugar, then stir in the egg yolk and the cream to make a stiff dough. Roll out onto a lightly floured surface until approximately 6 mm (¼ in) thick. Cut out with cutter, glass or cup, lay on greased paper on a baking sheet and bake for 15 minutes in a moderate oven (180°C, 350°F, Mark 4) or till golden brown. Cool on a wire rack.

Grissini

These are the crisp bread-sticks one nibbles in Italian restaurants.

225 g (8 oz) plain flour
¼ teaspoon baking powder
½ teaspoon salt
15 g (½ oz) butter or margarine
2 to 3 tablespoons of boiling water

Sieve the dry ingredients (flour, baking powder, salt) into a bowl, rub the fat in finely and add just enough water to make a stiff dough. Turn onto a floured board, knead till quite smooth and roll small lumps between both palms till just thicker than a pencil and about 22 cm (9 in) long. Lay on a greased baking sheet and bake in a warm oven (150°C, 325°F, Mark 3) for 40 minutes or till hard and lightly tanned. Cool before eating or storing in an airtight tin.

Water-biscuits

These are ridiculously easy to make, cheaper than the bought kind, and delicious with cheese.

225 g (8 oz) plain flour
1 teaspoon baking powder
a pinch of salt
50 g (2 oz) margarine or lard
150 ml (¼ pint) water
ground rock or sea salt

Sift together the flour, baking powder and salt and rub in the fat finely. Add just enough water to mix to a firm dough. Roll out thinly on a lightly floured surface with a floured rolling pin. Stamp out rounds (if you use an old round biscuit tin lid for this you can store them neatly), prick them all over with a fork, sprinkle with ground sea or rock salt and bake on a lightly greased baking sheet for 20 minutes in oven set to 150°C (325°F, Mark 3) or till golden and crisp. Cool on a rack and store in an airtight tin. Crisp up, if necessary, in a warm oven for 3 or 4 minutes.

Brandy snaps

These look impressive with their lacy texture, but they are easy to make. You don't *have* to use brandy, they are tasty without – some people fill them with whipped cream.

50 g (2 oz) butter
50 g (2 oz) castor sugar
50 g (2 oz) golden syrup
50 g (2 oz) plain flour
¼ teaspoon ground ginger
¼ teaspoon grated lemon rind
1 teaspoon brandy (optional)

Melt the sugar, syrup and butter together in a pan, then stir in the flour, ginger, lemon rind and brandy and mix well. Drop the mixture a teaspoon at a time onto a greased baking sheet, leaving a space of 7 cm (3 in) between each. Bake in a cool oven (150°C, 300°F, Mark 2) for about 10 minutes. Leave on the sheet to 'set' for a few minutes, then detach and roll round the handle of a wooden spoon to make the characteristic tube shape. Cool before storing.

Dutch butter cookies

Short, crisp and pretty with their whole almond decoration, these are good cookies to make and store (they will keep excellently in a tin) for all contingencies. For a change add ½ teaspoon of your favourite spice to the mixture.

100 g (4 oz) butter
100 g (4 oz) demerara sugar
225 g (8 oz) plain flour
1 egg
50 g (2 oz) whole blanched almonds

Cream the butter with the sugar till fluffy, then mix in the sieved flour. Bind with beaten egg. Roll out thinly and cut into small (5 cm/2 in) rounds. Brush over with milk, press one whole almond onto each round and bake for 15 minutes in a moderate oven (180°C, 350°F, Mark 4).

Cheese biscuits

Nicest eaten hot and peppery from the oven.

100 g (4 oz) plain flour
¼ teaspoon cayenne pepper
¼ teaspoon salt
50 g (2 oz) butter or margarine
50 g (2 oz) grated cheese (Cheddar or Parmesan)
1 egg yolk mixed with 1 teaspoon of water

Sieve the flour and seasonings, rub in the butter finely, then mix in the grated cheese. Stir in enough of the egg mixture to make a stiff, dryish paste. Knead lightly, roll out on a floured surface until ½ cm (¼ in) thick, prick well with a fork, then stamp into rounds or cut into fingers. Put on a greased baking sheet and bake at 190°C (375°F, Mark 5) for 7 to 10 minutes.

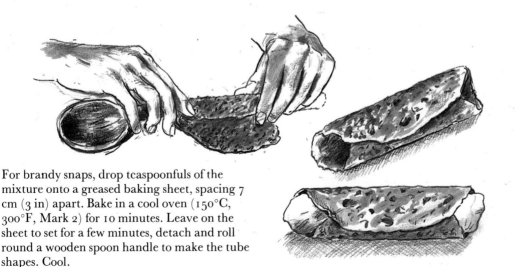

For brandy snaps, drop teaspoonfuls of the mixture onto a greased baking sheet, spacing 7 cm (3 in) apart. Bake in a cool oven (150°C, 300°F, Mark 2) for 10 minutes. Leave on the sheet to set for a few minutes, detach and roll round a wooden spoon handle to make the tube shapes. Cool.

Pasta

'The angels in Paradise eat nothing but vermicelli al pomodoro'
Duke of Bovino, Mayor of Naples 1930

Some say Marco Polo, the 15th century explorer, brought the first pasta back from the Grand Cham's court, others that he introduced it there. Whatever the truth, the fact remains that pasta in some shape or other – Italians have by far the widest and shapeliest – is eaten almost everywhere in the world. Essentially pasta uses strong white flour, with eggs added for richness and sometimes spinach for flavour and colour. Durum wheat is used commercially for its keeping properties. Health buffs will use wholemeal flour but this has the disadvantage of being harder to work.

It ranks alongside mankind's most ancient foods like bread, lentils and rice, sharing their characteristics of extreme simplicity, versatility and convenience. With just a little flour and water, perhaps an egg or two, and a pot on the boil you had the makings of a substantial meal, which could be filled out with cheese, herbs, meat or vegetables, as available. It was first heard of 6,000 years ago in China, reappeared on the menus of Imperial Rome and was carried by Mongol herdsmen in their saddlebags, conveniently frozen by the bitter winter weather. Over the centuries, pasta has undergone all the refinements and elaboration that imaginative chefs could devise. This delightfully plastic substance has lent itself to hundreds of dishes, ranging from the hearty peasant dishes of the Abruzzi, eaten with *pecorino*, a pungent sheep's milk cheese, to a sophisticated *timballo*, or pie filled with richly stuffed pasta and seasoned with fresh truffles. But, of course, all this is mere top dressing for essentially, pasta today retains the sturdy simplicity of its humble origins.

All pasta connoisseurs, Italian, Chinese or whatever, agree that the best pasta, in point of flavour and texture, is fresh, home-made pasta made with eggs. This is known as pasta *al uovo*, or *mien* in China. There are many varieties of commercial dried pasta, or pasta *secca*, on display in good Italian grocers' shops, or delicatessens but, when made well, fresh pasta has a clean delicate flavour and bite which makes commercial pasta taste stodgy and heavy by comparison. A plate of home-made *fettuccine* (narrow noodles) eaten with the simplest of sauces – sour cream, *pesto*, sesame seed sauce, or nothing more than a lump of butter and chopped fresh herbs – is a noble dish. The first step is learning to make good pasta, and for this you need the simplest ingredients and equipment, time, muscle and a little perseverance. Your first batch of tagliatelle may resemble a bunch of rubber snakes, but, with practice, you will be able to produce paper thin noodles in twenty minutes flat.

Fresh ribbons of tagliatelle beside ravioli sheets filled with savoury beef, ready to cook and serve with one of the sauces in jars, either fresh tomato sauce or the green pesto made from fresh basil and, right, aubergine and pasta pie made with tagliatelle.

Pasta making

The rule of thumb every Italian girl learns is an egg and a small pinch of salt to 100 g (4 oz) plain flour. This makes a generous portion for one person, so if you are making pasta for six, 550 g (1¼ lb) flour and five large eggs will be ample. Some recipes advocate using a little oil too, for extra suppleness. Strong white flour, as sold for baking, gives the most flavour. Wholemeal flour is impossibly crumbly. Commercial pasta, or pasta *secca*, uses hard grained wheat milled to finest semolina consistency. If your dough stays too dry to make a nice lump you can use another egg or – cautiously – a little water to make up the moisture content. Purists groan at this, but I do not think it hurts the pasta as long as you do not overdo it. Pasta *verde*, or green pasta, is made by adding a small amount – approximately 75 g (3 oz) per 450 g (1 lb) of flour – of cooked, squeezed, sieved or puréed spinach to the flour at the same time as the eggs, and one egg is usually left out of the above formula because the spinach contributes some moisture of its own.

When rolling by hand, divide your dough into fist sized lumps and begin rolling vigorously from the middle outwards in all directions. At first, unless you are muscled like a gorilla, it will fight back, springing back one inch for every two you stretch it. Patience. Suddenly it starts to give, grows thinner and wider. Roll it as thin as you can – Italians claim you should be able to read the headlines through it, but this takes practice – flouring the pasta, the rolling pin and the work top occasionally to prevent sticking. Do not worry if it tears. Lay the sheet on a floured cloth, or anywhere handy, to dry off while you tackle the next lump of dough. This makes it much easier to cut, otherwise the dough is apt to stick together again.

A machine will do some of the kneading and rolling business for you. The gadget works like a tiny mangle.

To cut the pasta, roll up, or concertina fold, your lightly floured sheet and slice across to the width you want, remembering that the pasta will swell up in the pot. 6 mm (¼ in) slices give a nice slim, but not stringy, noodle. Cut postcard sized pieces for lasagne. When cutting with the gadget, insert rollers grooved to the width you want and turn the handle.

If you can spare the time, leave the cut pasta for fifteen to twenty minutes longer, giving it time to rest and dry a little more. Pile it into little loose heaps, or spread it out for lasagne-type sheets.

To cook, heat the required amount of water to boiling, salt it and drop in the pasta, a handful at a time so as not to take the water off the boil. A dash of oil helps to stop the water from boiling over. Italians estimate 1 litre (2 pints) of water to 100 g (4 oz) uncooked pasta. Stir briefly to separate the pieces. Bear in mind that home-made pasta cooks much faster than the dried sort. For the finest noodles – *fettuccine, mien* – start tasting after three to four minutes, for the others, after five. When it is tender but still firm and tastes not at all of flour, tip the pasta into a colander over the sink and shake off the water. Return it to the pan, or a hot dish, with a knob of butter or drop of oil to put on a nice sheen. Lasagne is usually parboiled before baking although I find it cooks perfectly well when layered raw with a Bolognese and strong white sauce and sprinkled with Parmesan cheese, then baked in a hot oven.

Making fresh pasta

1. Having sifted 550 g ($1\frac{1}{4}$ lb) flour and a pinch of salt onto a floured work surface, make a well in the centre and break into it 5 large eggs or, for pasta *verde* (green pasta), 4 eggs and 75 g (3 oz) of puréed spinach. Using two fingers, draw the flour into the egg mix till it lumps together.

2. Slap the lump down and attack with the heels of both hands with a scrubbing action which stretches the dough away from you. Gather up and repeat the process for not less than 15 minutes. Then divide the dough into lumps.

3. Flatten each lump by rolling vigorously with a floury rolling pin, from the middle outwards in all directions. At first it will spring back but suddenly it will grow thinner, wider. Roll it thinly then lay on a cloth over the back of a chair.

4. A pasta machine can save you this last step. Pass the dough through the mangle and it will stretch it finely, though not to any great width. To make pasta ribbons – or tagliatelle – set the machine with grooved rollers to slice to the width you want: 6 mm ($\frac{1}{4}$ in) gives slim noodles.

5. Pasta comes in all shapes and sizes. For the ravioli below, roll out a rectangle of fresh pasta. Divide one half into lightly marked squares and spoon meat filling into the centre of each square. Moisten the other half of the pasta, fold over the meat-filled squares, press down firmly with your hand and lightly edge with a pastry cutter.

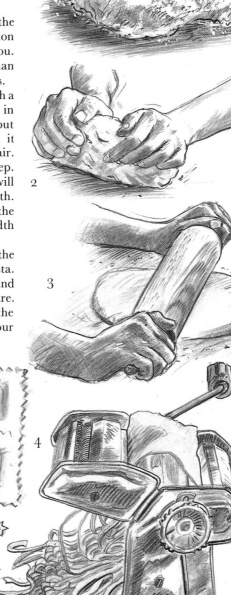

Pasta sauces

Everyone has their own version of the classic Bolognese and Napolitana sauces, but some of the following recipes are less familiar and can be used with home-made noodles of any width you please. Yield: 6 servings.

Onion sauce

Simple, warming and surprisingly good, this recipe provides a winter equivalent to the uncooked sauce. It is traditionally eaten without Parmesan cheese, but suit yourself.

6 medium sized onions
4 tablespoons oil
1 rounded tablespoon tomato purée or concentrate
a pinch of salt, black pepper and sugar

Slice the onions very finely and put them in a heavy pan with the oil (I sometimes add a little butter for flavour). Cover, and cook over a very low heat, till they are reduced to almost a purée. They must not burn, so shake the pan occasionally. After half an hour, mix in the tomato purée, seasonings and a little water and add to the onions. Simmer for another 5 to 10 minutes.

Pesto sauce

A Genoese invention that provides the most delicious way of using fresh – but it must be fresh – basil and Parmesan cheese. If you cannot get fresh Parmesan, to grate yourself, use 75 g (3 oz) of packaged Parmesan and 100 g (4 oz) of freshly grated Gruyère cheese.

6 big handfuls of fresh basil
6 tablespoons olive oil
75 g (3 oz) pine nuts
3 cloves garlic
175 g (6 oz) Parmesan cheese
a pinch of salt and black pepper

Lightly chop the washed, drained basil and place in the blender with all the other ingredients. Blend till smooth. Use a few tablespoons of pasta cooking water to warm and dilute the sauce. When the pasta has been cooked and drained, put it in a large serving dish. Add the sauce, mix well and serve at once.

Any surplus sauce can be stored in the jar in the fridge with a layer of olive oil on top.

Fresh tomato and basil sauce

The simplest of all, a perfect high-summer complement to your own fresh pasta. Both the tomatoes and the basil must be fresh. If basil is out, try chopped chives and a little marjoram.

1 kg (2 lb) tomatoes
1 large handful basil leaves
1 large clove garlic
5 tablespoons olive oil
a pinch of salt, pepper and sugar

Dip the tomatoes in boiling water for one minute then peel. Remove the seeds and chop roughly. Drain off the juice, by standing in a sieve for one minute. Put in a large dish, mix gently with the finely chopped basil, garlic, olive oil and seasonings. Serve with a large mound of hot pasta. Do not add cheese.

Fukien sesame seed sauce

If you like the flavour and breath-taking aroma of toasted sesame seeds, you will find this sauce compulsive eating. Peanut butter may be substituted in which case the sauce resembles Indonesian *sate*.

3 to 4 tablespoons roast and ground sesame seeds
2 tablespoons soya sauce
1 tablespoon sesame oil
1 tablespoon Hoisin sauce
1 tablespoon tomato purée
2 teaspoons sugar
2 tablespoons sherry
150 ml ($\frac{1}{4}$ pint) stock (or half a stock cube plus water)

To make the sesame paste heat four tablespoons of seeds in a heavy pan over a low heat for about three minutes till lightly coloured and fragrant. Put in an electric coffee grinder and whizz to a powder. Mix with all the other ingredients in a small pan and stir over a low heat till smooth and thick. Serve with plain noodles and bowls of chopped spring onions.

Tuna fish and anchovy sauce

This classic sauce is usually served with spaghetti and also makes an invaluable contribution to a variety of baked pasta dishes.

1 small tin of tuna fish
3 anchovies
25 g (1 oz) butter
300 ml ($\frac{1}{2}$ pint) chicken or meat stock
parsley
a pinch of salt and pepper

Chop the tuna and anchovies together, heat in melted butter in a small pan (this can be done while the pasta is cooking), add the stock, the parsley and seasonings. Stir well, simmer for a minute or two. Pour over cooked pasta, mix lightly and serve at once.

Sugo or Bolognese sauce

Just open a couple of cans any time of the year to rustle up this tasty sauce.

1 large onion
1 medium tin of peeled tomatoes
2 cloves garlic
1 carrot
1 stick of celery
225 g (8 oz) minced beef
small glass of wine or wine vinegar
chopped fresh parsley
a pinch of salt and black pepper

Slice the vegetables finely and fry together with the seasoned minced beef. When golden brown, add the liquid, herbs and seasonings and cook for a further fifteen minutes.

Pasta fillings

If you want to spoil your dinner guests, there is a wealth of more elaborate pasta dishes, some stuffed, some baked, which only someone working at home with loving patience can raise to perfection.

Lasagne verde with Bolognese sauce

If you make up the sauces the night before, this dish can be made ready in a few minutes.

575 g (1$\frac{1}{4}$ lb) green pasta
100 g (4 oz) Parmesan cheese
slices of mozzarella (optional)
300 ml ($\frac{1}{2}$ pint) thick béchamel sauce
600 ml (1 pint) rich Bolognese sauce
nutmeg

Roll the green pasta out thinly and cut into half postcard-sized rectangles. Have ready the grated Parmesan and, if possible, slices of mozzarella. Starting with béchamel, well seasoned with nutmeg, layer lasagne alternately with the two sauces, including a layer of mozzarella and sprinkle of Parmesan between every layer. The dish should finish with béchamel thickly sprinkled with Parmesan. Dot with butter, put in a hot oven (205°C, 400°F, Mark 6) for 20 minutes, or until golden on top.

Lasagne with chicken livers and truffles

100 g (4 oz) chicken livers
100 g (4 oz) butter
300 ml ($\frac{1}{2}$ pint) thick meat gravy (or juice from a casserole)
1 tinned black truffle
575 g (1$\frac{1}{4}$ lb) lasagne
150 g (5 oz) grated Parmesan cheese
a pinch of salt and black pepper

Lightly colour the chopped livers in butter, then add the gravy and simmer for half a minute. Keep warm. Cut the truffle into strips. Fill a 23 cm (9 in) ovenproof dish with layers of lasagne, gravy and liver, and cheese, truffle and seasonings. Repeat the layers till the dish is full, ending with a thick layer of cheese. Now leave 12 hours, to allow the truffle aroma to permeate the dish. Dot with butter and bake for 20 minutes in a hot oven (205°C, 400°F, Mark 6).

Ravioli

Envelopes of fine white flour, lukewarm water and egg can be filled with a variety of stuffings for a hearty meal.

450 g (1 lb) flour
5 eggs
1 tablespoon olive oil

Combine the flour, eggs and oil as described in pasta making. When the pasta reaches the proper consistency divide into two roughly equal pieces. Roll these out separately and as thinly as possible into rectangular sheets of roughly equal size. Brush one sheet with a pastry brush dipped in cold water to damp it, then with a knife mark out into 5 cm (2 in) squares. Put one teaspoon of stuffing in the middle of each square. Lay the other pasta sheet carefully on top, press firmly down around stuffing. Cut down and across the sheets to make raviolis 5 cm (2 in) square using a pastry wheel or sharp knife. Lower into lots of boiling water and cook for five minutes.

Piedmontese filling for ravioli

1 medium tin of peeled tomatoes
2 tablespoons oil
1 stick celery
1 clove garlic
1 small onion (finely chopped)
225 g (8 oz) lean minced beef
1 glass white wine
100 g (4 oz) cabbage
a pinch of salt, black pepper and nutmeg
2 eggs
50 g (2 oz) Parmesan cheese

Pour off the liquid from the tinned tomatoes and remove the seeds. Heat two tablespoons of oil in a frying pan and gently fry the chopped vegetables (except the cabbage) till softened. Stir in the minced beef and cook gently till light brown, breaking up any lumps with a fork. Add wine, tomato, chopped cabbage, seasoning and nutmeg. Bring to the boil then cover the pan and simmer for half an hour. The mixture should now be thick and dryish, the right consistency to fill the ravioli envelopes. Cool, add beaten eggs and cheese and mix thoroughly. Stuff the ravioli, cook and serve with melted butter and grated Parmesan.

Pork filling for ravioli

225 g (8 oz) spinach
1 bunch watercress or 150 g (5 oz) spinach beet
225 g (8 oz) pork sausage meat
150 g (5 oz) minced veal
25 g (1 oz) butter
1 clove garlic
75 g (3 oz) Parmesan cheese
a pinch of salt and black pepper
nutmeg

Wash the greens, do not shake off the water, cover and boil for 3 minutes. Squeeze out all moisture, purée and cool. Lightly fry the meats in butter for 5 to 8 minutes with the chopped garlic. Mix with the greens and cheese, add nutmeg and salt and pepper to taste. Stuff the ravioli with the mixture and cook for five minutes.

Vegetarian filling for ravioli

450 g (1 lb) spinach
100 g (4 oz) fresh grated Parmesan cheese
225 g (8 oz) ricotta (or use 100 g (4 oz) cottage cheese
*   and 100 g (4 oz) cream cheese)*
1 tablespoon finely chopped marjoram or basil
3 egg yolks
25 g (1 oz) butter
a pinch of salt and black pepper

Cook the spinach as above, blend with other ingredients. Fill the ravioli envelopes, cook and serve with melted butter and thick cream poured over them and sprinkled generously with Parmesan. Heat under grill till golden on top.

Stuffed Chinese dumplings

These are not *won ton*, but the Northern *giaotze*. They are larger and more garlicky than ravioli. The paste, or dough, is made without eggs.

225 g (8 oz) plain flour
150 ml ($\frac{1}{4}$ pint) cold water
2 pinches of salt
225 g (8 oz) Chinese, or savoy, cabbage
1 leek
450 g (1 lb) finely minced lean pork
2 cloves garlic
1 teaspoon grated fresh ginger root
1 dessertspoon sesame oil
1 tablespoon soy sauce

Make a smooth, stiff dough by working water into the flour and half the salt. Knead it for a few minutes. Leave to rest for 30 minutes covered with a damp towel. The stuffing is not pre-cooked. Finely chop the cabbage and leek (washed well, hard green part removed) and – this is important – wring them in a clean cloth to extract all moisture. Add to the other ingredients and mix together well by hand. Make the dumplings by rolling the dough out into a thin sheet on a lightly floured surface. Keep a damp cloth over the sheet while you work. Using a glass, stamp out circles of dough, put a rounded teaspoon of uncooked stuffing in the centre, moisten and join outer edges of circle, making a little pleat or two to give a crescent-shaped, fat little dumpling. Place on a floured tray, under a floured cloth. Repeat till all the dough is used up. To cook *giaotze*, boil up a large pan of salted water, drop in six or eight dumplings at a time, bring to the boil then add a cup of cold water. Repeat this twice then lift out, drain and serve at once. These are eaten dipped in bowls of soy sauce mixed with a dash of white vinegar.

Aubergine and pasta pie
Aubergines have a rich flavour and this pie can substitute successfully for a meat dish.

450 g (1 lb) tagliatelle
4 small aubergines
a pinch of salt
2 tablespoons olive oil for frying
450 g (1 lb) fresh tomatoes or 1 medium tin of peeled tomatoes
3 cloves garlic
50 g (2 oz) butter
black pepper
1 handful fresh basil (or parsley, thyme or marjoram)
100 g (4 oz) Parmesan cheese
4 tablespoons dried, home-made breadcrumbs

Cook the tagliatelle for 3 to 4 minutes so they are firm. Drain and set aside in a warm place.

Thinly slice unpeeled aubergines, salt lightly and leave for 10 minutes to sweat. Deep fry, a few slices at a time, in olive oil till golden brown, then drain on kitchen paper. Continue till all the aubergine is cooked.

Skin tomatoes, remove seeds, chop roughly and transfer to a colander to drain. Chop garlic and lightly fry in a little oil and butter till golden, then add tomato, salt and pepper and simmer for a few minutes. Chop the basil, minus stalks, or other herbs, quite finely. Mix herbs, tomato mixture and grated cheese together with the cooked tagliatelle. Now butter a deep cake tin generously (it must be big enough to take noodles and aubergines) and coat it evenly all over with breadcrumbs. Fill the dish with one layer of pasta mixture, then one layer of aubergines, and so on till all the ingredients are used up. Top with more cheese, then breadcrumbs, then dot with butter and bake in a pre-heated hot oven (220°C, 425°F, Mark 7) for 30 minutes. Turn onto a dish to serve.

Note: For grand occasions you can substitute a pastry case, with lid, for the crumb case.

Use a shortcrust pastry and cook blind for 15 minutes. Cook a lid of the same pastry, decorated with pastry leaves, on a sheet of foil at the same time. Check after 10 minutes. This is a *timballo*.

Tagliatelle cake
A sweet version of the aubergine pie. An unusual pudding, it tastes delicious as the macaroons, almonds and cocoa give a delicate flavour to the fresh pasta base.

450 g (1 lb) plain flour
4 egg yolks
1 small glass vermouth
250 g (9 oz) granulated sugar
200 g (7 oz) cocoa
150 g (5 oz) almonds
50 g (2 oz) macaroons
drop of vanilla essence
100 g (4 oz) butter

Make a pasta dough using the flour, egg yolks and enough vermouth to stick it together. Knead as usual, roll out, dry and cut into the thin ribbon strips for tagliatelle. Mix together sugar, cocoa, blanched, peeled and chopped almonds, crushed macaroons and vanilla. Flour and butter a deep cake tin. Arrange alternate layers of tagliatelle (uncooked) and the other mixture, ending with the cocoa mixture. Dot with butter and bake in a fairly hot oven (190°C, 375°F, Mark 5) for about 40 minutes. Serve hot with whipped cream.

Malts & Beers

'My two large Piggs, by drinking some Beer grounds
taking out of one of my Barrels today,
got so amazingly drunk by it that they were not able to stand
and appeared like dead things almost . . .
I never saw Piggs so drunk in my life,
I slit their ears for them without feeling.'

Diary of a Country Parson   Rev James Woodforde   1778

Ale and beer are interchangeable words today, but there is a distinction between them. Ale, the forerunner, was a drink made from the fermented liquor extracted from malted grain which could be rye, millet, wheat or barley which soon established itself as the best for the purpose. Around the 15th century ale was flavoured with local herbs and plants: sweet gale, nettles, spruce tassels. When Flemish traders first introduced their own 'bier', a brew flavoured with hop flowers, there was a storm of protest.

Turkeys, Heresies, Hops and Beer
All came to England in one Year

Resistance soon crumbled, however, when the 'hopped' bitterness proved itself on lengthier and thirstier acquaintance to add the very thing the old ales needed, a brisk astringency which perfectly complemented the sweet, rich flavour of malt. So beer came and stayed, ousting the older brews in all but the remotest country districts. The noble title of 'ale' is only used nowadays to describe the finest vintage beer.

During the 19th century beer brewing was a normal part of household routine, a chore housewives undertook along with baking, raising poultry and curing meat for the winter months. They brewed fine ale for special occasions, 'small' or weak beer for harvesters, and strong stouts for expectant and nursing mothers. Indeed, beer was so nourishing that William Cobbett, in 1825, lists it along with bread and meat as essential to a farm labourer's diet.

Home brewing has boomed from a modest hobby to a growth industry with specialist shops, magazines and books devoted to spreading the good news, simply because it is cheap, easy and good. Such a paragon of a drink, in fact, that it can only be deep-seated human laziness which keeps the breweries in business.

Hops stored in a Kentish oast house and malt in barrels, both essential to brewing: grains added to give body and flavour are, centre, golden flaked maize and, right, flaked barley, both for brewing light ale, and background right, roast crystal malt to sweeten nutbrown ale.

51

Brewing

The ingredients
The basic ingredients for beer are simple: malt, hops, water, yeast. As with most simple formulas, little changes make a lot of difference. By using a different colour of malt or more hops, or hard or soft water, a completely different beer is produced. Then there are what brewers call 'adjuncts', flavourings like flaked maize, rice, sugar which enrich, smooth or otherwise modify the basic character of beer.

Malt is available in grain form, or as powdered or liquid malt extract. Grain malt comes in most varieties. Depending on the time and temperature in the kiln, it emerges pale or crystal (used in light and pale ales and bitters), amber or brown (for milds, browns and stouts), or chocolate to black (used to give colour and flavour to some dark beers). These malts, available from specialist shops, are used for all brewing from the grain and in conjunction with malt extract in some recipes to give more strength and flavour. Malt extract is available in only two forms: light and dark. For the home brewer who does not have much time or space it is very convenient.

Use ordinary brewers' yeast, sold as dried granules. Lager, which is a bottom-fermenting beer, uses a special lager yeast.

Water is another essential ingredient in beer making. I have read of fanatics making beer with distilled water, but ordinary tap water is fine for most beers. But try and suit the beer you make to your local water supply: hard water is best for light beers and bitters and soft water areas are famous for their stouts. However you can change the nature of your water supply by adding a little gypsum to soft water to make it more suitable for light beers, and a little common salt to hard water.

Equipment
Start small. A 25 litre (5 gallon) white plastic bucket with a lid is most convenient for fermenting. It is worth investing in a beer hydrometer to measure when the brew has fermented out, i.e. the yeast has converted all the sugar into alcohol. A pressure cooker can be used to extract maximum flavour from the hops. (This is unorthodox

A near relation of the controversial *Cannabis Indica*, the hop plant – or its female flowers – contributes to beer both bitterness and aroma, as well as preservative and other chemical properties. Several varieties are grown: Hallertau is favoured for lager, Fuggles for browns and stouts and Goldings for light ales and bitters. To infuse the hops the green, cone-shaped flowers are boiled for an hour or more in the wort, either loose or tied in a muslin bag. Hops should not be kept too long before use because they lose their potency as they dry out. All these varieties are available from specialist brewing shops.

but it does work.) One extra large (25–45 litre or 5–10 gallon) pan, or several smaller ones, will be needed to bring the water to the boil.

For beers brewed from the grain, a 'mash tun' (a container fitted with a tap or spigot) in which the grain can be mashed or steeped, and the water then drained off, is also required. The mash must be kept at a temperature of 65°C (150°F) so an insulating cabinet, as sold for camping, or, at a pinch, a thick fibreglass blanket is required. There is a special all-purpose plastic boiler fitted with a thermostat and heating element on the market and this does make the whole business much easier though it is fairly expensive. For 'sparging' or spraying the mash, pour over buckets of boiling water, or, more efficiently, siphon hot water from a keg through a simple shower attachment as sold for fitting to bath taps. A long handled wooden spoon, muslin bags and sodium metabisulphite, used in solution with water for sterilizing the equipment, are also essential. Finally, a good thermometer, able to stand immersion in hot water, is vital. A jam thermometer is suitable.

The kit
The last word in convenience, neatly boxed beer kits supply the wherewithal for making a range of beers and ales. They include a suitably flavoured and coloured hopped malt extract which needs only water, sugar and, usually, yeast added. It is the most expensive way to make home brew but the results are very drinkable and quick to mature. A fortnight is sufficient in many cases.

Storage
Bottle or store the finished brew under pressure for carbonated beer, with a foaming head and 'fine bead' (tiny bubbles). Use screwtop beer bottles or standard beer bottles with crown caps which can be tapped into place. *Note:* Beer goes through its secondary fermentation at considerable pressure so make sure all bottles are in perfect condition, free from chips or hairline cracks. A pressure barrel is handy as it holds up to 25 litres (5 gallons) but a special gadget is needed, clamped to the spigot, to re-charge the beer as the barrel empties. Flat or non-fizzy brews can be stored in sealed gallon jars, bottles or wooden kegs. All storage containers must be kept clean and sweet – rinse out with hot water immediately after use, scrub and swill out with a sodium metabisulphite solution. This is the dull part of home brewing but it is necessary if your beer is not to pick up off flavours or the odd unwelcome infection.

Brewing from the grain
Brewing from the grain is the purists' method, beginning with the malted grains (fanatics even malt their own barley) as our great-grandmothers might have done. The advantage is a cleaner flavoured beer with more guts and character. The snag is time: it takes longer, involving many processes spread over several days. It needs more, and larger, equipment but it is still the cheapest and most authentic way to brew. I recommend it to perfectionists in search of a hobby who have lots of space (cellar or outhouses) and plenty of helpers. See the recipe for light ale.

Brewing: the malt extract method for nutbrown ale

1. Wash and rinse a 25 litre (5 gallon) white plastic bucket. Pour in 1 kg (2 lb) malt extract and 2.5 kg (5 lb) granulated sugar, then add a kettleful of boiling water and stir with a long handled spoon till dissolved. Cover with a lid.

2. Gently heat 60 g (2 oz) roast crystal malt in a heavy frying pan till golden brown. The smell is delicious.

All malts are obtainable from specialist shops · and are used to give the beer more strength and flavour.

3. Put the roast crystal malt with 60 g (2 oz) Goldings hops into a muslin bag and cook in a pressure cooker for 20 minutes in a generous litre (2 pints) of water.

If you do not have a pressure cooker or disapprove of shorts cuts, cook for one hour in 5 litres (1 gallon) of water.

4. After removing the muslin bag, add the liquid from the pressure cooker to that in the white bucket and make up the liquid content to 25 litres (5 gallons) using tap water.

5. When tepid, sprinkle one packet of brewers' yeast over the top. Stir thoroughly, cover, but not tightly, so the air can circulate. Leave overnight. By the next morning a vigorous fermentation will be well under way.

6. After two days skim off any 'rocky head' or

discoloured froth, just the top layer. After six or ten days, depending on the weather and room temperature, the fermentation will have stopped and the beer should have fermented out, giving a hydrometer reading of SG 1000.

7/8. For a carbonated, bubbly beer, siphon off the brew into bottles. The bottles must be either screwtop beer bottles or standard beer bottles with crown caps which can be tapped into place with a special gadget once the beer has been 'primed' with sugar to encourage secondary fermentation.

Note: Beer goes through its secondary fermentation at considerable pressure so make sure all the bottles are in perfect condition – no chips or hairline cracks.

Prime the beer by adding sugar at a rate of 1 level teaspoon per generous litre (2 pints) of beer.

9. Screw on the tops or fit crowns and store upright at room temperature for three to four days. Then transfer to a cooler spot till the beer has cleared save for a dark line of yeasty sediment at the bottom. This clearing can take between four and ten days, depending on the temperature.

Note: When pouring out bottled beer take care not to shake up the yeast sediment. Hold the bottle up to the light to gauge this and pour steadily, without shaking, into a jug, stopping just before the dark sludge slides out.

Beers

In these recipes there are examples of malt extract beers and grain mashed beers, with a simple gingerbeer thrown in for those of you too thirsty to wait for the others to mature. These recipes will yield about 25 litres (40 pints) of home-brew.

Mild ale
Crisp, light beer for everyday drinking made by the malt extract method of brewing.

60 g (2 oz) hops (Fuggles or Progress)
185 g (6 oz) crystal malt
60 g (2 oz) roasted barley grain
2 teaspoons brewers' gypsum
1.5 kg (3 lb) sugar
1 kg (2 lb) malt extract
1 packet of brewers' yeast

Bring 5 litres (1 gallon) of water to the boil. Put the hops, crystal malt and roast barley grain (you can roast your own by heating it till golden brown as with crystal malt, see previous page) into a muslin bag, tie up and add to the boiling water with the gypsum. Boil hard for one hour. Tip in the sugar and malt extract and stir till melted. Remove the bag, tip your wort into a clean fermentation bucket, and add cold water to make up to 25 litres (5 gallons) of tepid liquid. Pitch in the yeast granules, stir and cover. Keep at room temperature for about one week, until fermentation stops and the hydrometer registers SG 1000. After 48 hours, skim off the head.

Siphon into bottles, leaving 2.5 cm (1 in) headroom at the top and 'prime' at the rate of 1 teaspoon of sugar per generous litre (2 pints). Screw on tops, secure crown caps and store in a cool place for 2 weeks, till the ale 'falls bright'.

Lager
Light and sparkling but with a marked hop flavour, lager is made by the malt extract method, and uses special lager yeast.

1 kg (2 lb) malt extract
60 g (2 oz) hops (Hallertau or Saaz)
500 g (1 lb) lager malt or 500 g (1 lb) pale malt
 plus 2 teaspoons gypsum
1 kg (2 lb) sugar
lager yeast
water

Note: Lager yeast is best started beforehand by adding it to a little tepid water mixed with 1 teaspoon malt extract in a clean bottle, and leaving it a few hours or till it starts frothing vigorously.

The method is the same as for mild ale except that the liquid should be only just tepid when adding the yeast.

The fermentation bucket should be kept in a cool place (like an unheated room) for a week or so until the fluffy 'head' sinks from the top. Siphon off into bottles, prime with $\frac{1}{2}$ level teaspoon of sugar per 600 ml (1 pint), secure crown caps or screw tops and keep the bottles in a cool place until the lager is bright and clear. Drink well chilled.

Bitter

125 g (4 oz) Goldings hops
500 g (1 lb) crystal malt
25 litres (5 gallons) water
1 kg (2 lb) white sugar
500 g (1 lb) demerara sugar
1 kg (2 lb) malt extract
2 teaspoons brewers' gypsum (if you have soft water)
1 packet brewers' yeast

Boil the hops and crushed malt (either buy it already crushed or crack the grains with a rolling pin) with 5 litres (1 gallon) water for 45 minutes. Then stir in sugars, malt extract and gypsum (if used). Add enough cold water to make 25 litres (5 gallons) of tepid liquid and sprinkle 1 packet brewers' yeast over. Tie a small handful of hops in a muslin bag and drop into the bucket to infuse during fermentation. This is called 'dry hopping' and will sharpen the flavour. Cover and ferment out at room temperature. Siphon off into bottles and prime at the rate of 1 level teaspoon of sugar per generous litre (2 pints). Secure crown caps or screw tops and leave for at least a month to mature in a cool place. This makes good strong beer, with a malty richness.

Light ale

This recipe is brewed from the grain. The addition of flaked barley and maize gives extra flavour and richness. Both can be obtained from specialist home-brew shops.

The answer to mashing the grain is to buy an all-purpose boiler, thermostatically controlled to boil the water and hold the temperature. These boilers have only a 25 litre (5 gallon) capacity which does not give long before the entire long-winded process needs to be gone into again. This is why some purists still prefer a 'mash tun' container fitted with a spigot.

25 litres (5 gallons) water
125 g (4 oz) flaked maize
125 g (4 oz) flaked barley
2 kg (4 lb) crushed pale malt
250 g (8 oz) soft brown sugar
60 g (2 oz) Goldings hops
1 packet brewers' yeast

Either buy ready crushed malt or crush it roughly yourself with a rolling pin. Heat 20 litres (4 gallons) of water to boiling point then cool to around 71°C (160°F). Add flaked maize, crushed malt, flaked barley and soft brown sugar. Stir. Check the temperature. When it has settled at 65°C (150°F) leave to mash (in an insulated container or under a fibreglass blanket, if you don't have an all-purpose boiler) for two hours. Strain off the wort into a 25 litre (5 gallon) fermentation bucket. Use a further 5 to 7 litres (1 to 1½ gallons) of hot water to 'sparge' or spray the sodden mash left behind in the receptacle, collecting this extra liquid in the fermentation bin as it runs through. If the mash is 'set' and the water refuses to run through, stir it up a bit with a spoon. Now boil up the 'wort' plus the hops (added loose for maximum effectiveness). The wort will rise up in the container when boiling so it might be safer to divide the wort and hops between two 20 litre (4 gallon) containers. When the wort has boiled for an hour, strain it off into a plastic fermentation bin. Rinse the hops with a kettleful of cold water to remove the last traces of wort and add this water to the wort. The object now is to cool the wort as fast as possible to the tepid stage yeast likes. You could shift it outside or try standing it in a cold bath. When the temperature is right add the yeast (preferably 'started' in a bottle but straight from the packet will do) and stir well. Leave to ferment for about a week, skimming off the top layer of foam after 48 hours. Now leave covered for 3 days for the sediment to settle. Siphon into bottles, pressure barrel or cask. Add 'priming' sugar at the rate of a scant ½ teaspoon per 600 ml (1 pint) of beer. Leave in a warm place for 4 days to get the secondary ferment going, then transfer to cool place for storage. Drink when clear.

Gingerbeer

Strictly speaking, this is not a beer at all, but a fermented lemon drink hotted up with ginger. Traditionally gingerbeer or 'pop' was relegated to children, but do not knock it back like lemonade – it has quite a kick to it. For hot summer days it makes a delicious, refreshing drink, and it is ready to drink in less than a week!

Note: Use screwtop beer bottles if you are going to drink it fast. Otherwise for safety's sake use bottles with corks as this ensures that if the pressure builds up too much you will only have spilt beer to deal with, not broken glass. Ideally, gingerbeer should be drunk within a week of bottling and under these circumstances I have never had any problems using screwtop bottles. Fresh ginger gives a much fresher flavour as well as a delicious smell.

30 g (1 oz) fresh ginger or 1 level tablespoon ground
  ginger
500 g (1 lb) granulated sugar
5 litres (1 gallon) water
2 lemons
7 g (¼ oz) cream of tartar
1 teaspoon brewers' yeast

Grate fresh ginger (or alternatively pound it in a mortar) and put it in a bucket with the sugar. Pour on boiling water and stir well to dissolve sugar. Squeeze the lemons and add the juice and the rinds to the liquid, plus the cream of tartar, dissolved in the lemon juice. When cooled to a tepid temperature sprinkle the yeast over. Cover with a sheet of polythene and leave for 2 days. Strain the contents into a clean bucket and then siphon off into screwtop bottles. It can be drunk after 3 days.

The Dairy

The fat of the land

Homer meant nothing but praise, I am sure, when he gave to mild-eyed Hera, consort of Zeus, the attributes of a cow. The cow is something of a goddess among domestic animals, gentle, comely, overflowing with milk – that generous stream of life which we skim for cream, churn to butter, curdle and press to make cheese. Silly sheep and pretty shepherdesses decorate the urban poet's Arcadia; the true countryman has always known better.

I know no writing where the poetic and commonplace of country life are more vividly counterpoised than the chapters by Dorset born Thomas Hardy which describe his heroine Tess working in a dairy 'amid the oozing fatness and warm ferments of the Frome Vale, at a season when the rush of juices could almost be heard below the hiss of fertilization.' Milking at dawn in misty fields, scouring pastures for wild garlic which has 'tainted' the butter, skimming and churning in the cool dimness of the dairy – with such details as these Hardy recreates the routine of a Victorian dairy hand's life.

Free milk, cream, butter, cheese are an attractive prospect in an inflationary age, and more and more people are trying their hand at dairying in a small way, keeping a cow or goats on such grazing as is available, which they milk by hand as did Tess and everyone else till about eighty years ago. The price of self-sufficiency, as usual, is loss of freedom. Cows – and goats – need regular milking twice daily, or they dry up – 'go azew' as Tess's master dairyman boss puts it. Buying a cow with calf helps, as a suckling calf drains off enough milk to let the owners take an occasional weekend off. In summer a good cow may give 13 litres (3 gallons) of milk daily, a nanny goat maybe 4 litres (1 gallon). Goat's milk is less rich than cow's, with a faintly chalky taste that one needs to adapt to, but it is very digestible and makes excellent yogurt and cheese. Goats undoubtedly score over cows in that they are hardy, unfussy about grazing and their milk yield just about keeps pace with an average family's needs. Goat and ewe milk cheeses, like the Greek *feta*, have a sharp, salt tang to them.

Almost all the milk sold commercially is pasteurized, that is 'flash' heated momentarily, then cooled – to destroy bacteria, a sound policy where huge quantities of milk from innumerable sources are involved. Untreated milk ('raw' milk straight from the cow) is sold in many parts of the world, subject to stringent checks on the herds for brucellosis, and T.B. Kept clean, it sours naturally and pleasantly in a few days where pasteurized milk and cream usually go bitter and inedible, being more vulnerable to bacterial invasion and 'taints'. Homogenized milk is pasteurized milk processed to redistribute the fat content evenly, making it structurally similar to goat's milk. Like goat's milk, too, it is good for making yogurt and certain cheeses. Sterile, or long-life milk, has been processed a stage further to make it keep longer. Fairly nasty to drink, it remains a useful standby and can also be used to make yogurt. None of these special processed milks can produce cream, or butter, which is solidified cream with the water spun off.

As a glance at any milk bottle reveals, cream rises – fat being lighter than water. The creaminess of commercial milk varies according to how much of the fat, or cream, is removed. If curiosity prompts you to try making cream and butter for yourself, from bought milk, get several litres (4 pints) of full cream milk and gently heat it for several hours to make clotted cream, that thick yellow crust which is the *crème de la crème*. It will not be much, and it will not be cheap, but it might be fun, and instructive. A couple of minutes beating it with a wooden spoon will give you a nut of home-made butter.

Cheesemaking is, and always has been, the most skilled of dairy activities. A whole host of variables go into a cheese; its quality depends on things like the breed of cow, type and abundance of feed, standards of hygiene in the dairy, but above all, it is the long experience of the cheesemaker whose judgment is constantly being tested at every stage of the process which makes the difference between the mass produced rubberized article and a really fine cheese. From the point of view of home cheesemaking this is encouraging – intelligence we may have, judgment and experience we can acquire. Starting with the simple spoon or soft cheeses anyone can make, with ordinary milk and a cloth and bowl, there is no reason, if enough milk is available, why people should not go on to experiment with semi-hard cheeses, of the Brie/Camembert type, and hard cheeses, of the Edam and Cheddar variety. It only needs more confidence, more milk and a bit more equipment.

The fat content determines the cheese; the richer the milk the better the cheese. A hard cheese weighing 1 kg (2 lb) uses about 16 litres (4 gallons) of milk, semi-hard cheeses of the same weight use rather less, as they retain the whey. Using bottled or cartoned milk to make these would be uneconomic.

The next problem with raw milk is whether to pasteurize it or not? The shortest answer seems to be, yes, if you live in a hot climate, have doubts about the cows, the particular dairy or – if it is your own animal – a particular batch of milk. Maybe the teats were dirty, or there is a bug going the rounds of the family. Bugs thrive in milk. On the other hand, pasteurizing at home is tricky, time consuming and creates its own problems – to make cheese with pasteurized milk a 'starter', which you must buy or make and constantly renew, is essential to get the lactic acid forming bacteria going (all bacteria are killed in pasteurizing, remember) in the 'clean' milk. 'Most people cheesemaking at home will tend to use raw milk,' one commercial cheesemaker told me, 'and provided their hygiene is up to the mark, they can get very good cheese that way – but they should expect some variation and some failures.' Commercial manufacturers always use a starter (and pasteurized milk) because they cannot afford to take any chances. Even so, no two cheeses are alike.

Hygiene is the crux of the matter, and here progress is on our side. Today's kitchen, the domestic equivalent to a dairy for most people, already has hygienic, scrubbable worktops, a fridge, stove, surfaces which can be washed down with a mild bleach like the stuff sold to sterilize baby bottles. All equipment used should be washable, and stainless steel in the long run is best value and least bother. The reason for these precautions is that cheeses pick up 'taint' or 'off flavours' and cleanliness is the best safeguard. Our ancestors, making their 'variable' but often excellent cheeses at home, knew this too, from hard experience, but the difference is they had to work much harder, scouring and scalding, to get the same result.

Milk

'Good cows they were and never ailed, and plenty of everything there was in that house, good milk and butter and cheese and buckets and buckets of skim for the pigs.'

Precious Bane   Mary Webb   1924

Not being scientifically trained, I find it odd that milk which is almost 90% water should be the nearest thing to a complete food capable of sustaining life. But drink a glass of good milk slowly, so the fatness of it clings to one's lips, and the statement convinces. When the old writers sought to convey a vision of unimaginable plenty they wrote of a land flowing with milk and honey. Milk *is* the fat of the land made visible, acres of lush herbage churned through the cow's proverbial stomachs and finally transmitted to us through 'large veined udders ponderous as sandbags, the teats sticking out like the legs of a gypsy's crock' to quote Thomas Hardy, always precise about country things.

Cow's milk is only one of many kinds drunk by thirsty humans round the world. All mammals, as we know, ourselves included, secrete milk to feed their young. Of these water buffalo milk is said to be the creamiest of all, and Indians say that *ghee* (clarified butter) and *chenna* (soft cheese) made from it are incomparably rich. Mare's milk is still drunk in Outer Mongolia, camel's and ass's milk in parts of the Middle East, sheep's milk helps support Europe's cheese industry though it is not much drunk, and goat's milk is currently enjoying a revival as more people try their hand at keeping these attractive creatures. Goat's milk, because of its homogenized structure, is easily digested, and makes smooth yogurt and cheeses.

In Europe, however, cow's milk has no rival for versatility, richness and flavour. A cow's udder is a remarkable processing plant – 227 litres (50 gallons) of blood must pass through it to make 450 ml ($\frac{3}{4}$ pint) of milk – which supports a gigantic, complex industry. Milk is high protein food, rich in calcium, and a good source of vitamins A, B and some C and D.

Until the last years of the 19th century when a Glaswegian doctor revolutionized dairying with his Thistle pulsator milking machine, all milking was done by hand. Instead of cows being herded into a milking parlour, milkmaids and men often took pail and stool to where the cows were grazing and milked them on the spot. The early milking might be at 4 a.m. in summer, while the late milking took place some time before dusk, leaving all day for skimming cream, churning butter or cheesemaking in the dairy house itself, a cool and spotless structure, usually of stone, slate roofed and facing north to escape the sun's heat.

White marble and tiles for coolness and cleanliness in the dairy: boned, rolled leg of pork ready to be cooked to a golden crust in milk, flavoured with onions and spices. The lactic acid in milk tenderizes and moistens meat and milk can be used as a marinade.

Cooking with milk

Recipes based on milk are bland, soothing to the stomach, subtle rather than exciting. The 'good for you' tag has left many people with an aversion to milk puddings though they are delicious made with care. Yield: 4 to 6 servings.

Sauce béchamel

Hardly original but *the* basic sauce, not always cooked as well as it might be. The butter and flour mixture should be heated for a minute or two before adding the milk, and the sauce simmered for at least 10 minutes to get rid of the raw flour taste and allow it to reduce and thicken a little. A little béchamel enters into recipes as various as quiches, soufflés, and gratins. A few spoonfuls of this and that added to the basic sauce transform it.

600 ml (1 pint) milk
25 g (1 oz) butter
1 rounded tablespoon plain flour
salt and pepper

Heat the milk to just below boiling point. Meanwhile melt the butter in a heavy small pan, stir in the flour, mix and simmer for a minute over a very low heat as the mixture, known as a white roux, should not brown. Then add the hot milk, bit by bit, stirring vigorously to break up any threatening lumps. Rescue a lumpy sauce by sieving or blending. Season with a little salt and pepper and simmer for 10 minutes or longer over a very low heat. The secret of a good white sauce is to cook it slowly.

For *Sauce soubise*, add an onion purée. Put two onions, boiled till soft and drained, into the blender, and liquidize with a little French mustard. Serve with poached eggs, baked fish, sausages or gammon.

For *Sauce mornay*, add 3 to 4 tablespoons grated cheese (Cheddar, Parmesan, Gruyère) to the mixture and stir till melted. At the last minute, add one egg yolk to thicken. Serve with eggs, spinach, fish, chicken and pasta; it is especially tasty when browned quickly under a hot grill.

For *Sauce à l'Indienne* stir in 1 teaspoon ground turmeric, 1 teaspoon dry mustard and 2 teaspoons curry powder or paste and leave to simmer for 5 to 10 minutes. Not really Indian in origin, this sauce gives a restrained 'devilled' effect to fish, eggs, chicken, pasta and cutlets.

Pork cooked in milk

The lactic acid in milk has a markedly tenderizing, moistening effect on meat. There is an old Swedish recipe for lamb marinated for two days in milk with a little salt and sugar, then roasted plain. The Italians have a tradition of cooking veal and chicken in milk, which makes for succulent eating. I have chosen a recipe for pork *al latte* because the seasonings make it particularly delicious.

1 onion
50 g (2 oz) chopped ham or green (unsmoked) bacon
50 g (2 oz) butter
1 kg (2 lb) boned rolled leg of pork
2 cloves garlic
1 teaspoon coriander seeds
1 sprig fresh (or 1 teaspoon dried) marjoram, fennel or basil
1 litre (2 pints) milk
salt and pepper

Chop the onion and ham or bacon finely and brown for a minute or two over a moderate heat in butter. Cut the skin off the pork joint, tuck the garlic cloves, coriander and herbs inside, roll up and tie into a neat sausage with string. Brown in butter with the onion and bacon. Pour the milk over, add a little salt and pepper and set the pan simmering over a gentle heat, *uncovered*. After about an hour, when the milk has formed a golden skin, stir and scrape back all the delicious gravy stuck to the pan into the bubbling milk, which is by now much thickened. Cook gently for a further 30 to 45 minutes, by which time the milk will have shrunk to a thick gravy. The meat itself should be moist inside its golden crust. Serve sliced hot or cold.

Junkets

Junket is milk curd, set with rennet or, as in Denmark, buttermilk. In Devonshire, famous for its junket, milk was used warm from the cow and then left to set in bowls on the stone flags.

English junket

600 ml (1 pint) milk
1 tablespoon sugar
1 teaspoon rennet

Warm the milk to blood heat, add the sugar, stir till dissolved, then add the rennet, stir and turn into a dish. Leave to set in a cool place, preferably not a fridge. Made in the morning it will be ready the same evening. Pour a thin layer of cream over it before serving, and add a dusting of nutmeg.

Danish junket

1 litre (2 pints) milk
½ teaspoon ground cinnamon
½ teaspoon crushed cardamom
4 tablespoons buttermilk

Make this junket in four individual bowls. Mix the ground cinnamon and crushed cardamom with the milk. Pour 300 ml (½ pint) of milk into each bowl, then stir 1 tablespoon of buttermilk into each one. Put the bowls in a warm place and leave to thicken overnight. Sprinkle with brown sugar. The Scandinavian partiality for cardamom is understandable; the tiny scented seeds add mystery to a simple milk curd.

A cluster of custards

My dictionary defines custard as 'a composition of milk and eggs, flavoured and sweetened'. Custards vary according to how many eggs are used (richer ones use as many as six to 600 ml (1 pint) of milk), whether the whole egg is used, or the yolks only, and whether they are baked in the oven or stirred on top of the stove. Using yolks only gives a creamy, fluid custard – what the French confusingly call *crème* – while adding egg whites and baking sets the mixture. Slow, gentle cooking is the secret of a perfect custard.

Vanilla cream

The texture is creamy, hence the name. It can be used as a sauce with stewed fruit or steamed puddings, but is best eaten on its own, cool and smooth like a sweetened soup.

4 egg yolks
600 ml (1 pint) milk
1 vanilla pod or 1 teaspoon vanilla essence
25 g (1 oz) granulated sugar

This must be cooked in a double boiler or in a pan set in another pan containing simmering water, to prevent overheating and curdling. Whisk the yolks till frothy. Heat the milk slowly with the vanilla pod or essence, and the sugar. When hot, stir a cupful or so into the eggs, then return the egg mixture to the pan and cook for about 10 minutes, stirring constantly, till thickened. Remove the vanilla pod. If in doubt *undercook*, as the mixture thickens as it cools. If you stir constantly till cool you will have the world's smoothest custard. A stir from time to time will prevent a skin forming on top. Eat this delectable dish hot or cold.

Frangipani custard tart

Custard tarts have been popular for centuries and they do make a filling pudding from a simple custard. This one gains elegance from crushed macaroons and orange flower water, a combination I find particularly appealing with a smooth custard. Use 150 g (5 oz) slightly sweetened short crust pastry, or a thin layer of crushed digestive biscuits (add a couple of macaroons to this too) bound with a little softened butter to line the flan case or tin.

1 egg and two additional yolks
25 g (1 oz) plain flour
3 tablespoons sugar
600 ml (1 pint) milk
25 g (1 oz) unsalted, melted butter
2 crushed macaroons
1 tablespoon orange flower water

Beat up the egg with the yolks, then add the flour and sugar and beat till smooth. Add the milk and melted butter and mix, then stir in the crushed macaroons (dry these out for a few minutes in a low oven first) and orange flower water. Pour into the prepared 20 cm (8 in) flan case. Cook in the centre of the oven at 190°C (375°F, Mark 5) for 30 to 40 minutes till the custard filling feels firm and springy. If the top looks like browning, cover with foil for the last few minutes.

Yogurt

'*Mrs Beaver stood with her back to the fire, eating her morning yogurt.
She held the carton close to her chin and gobbled with a spoon. . . .
"Heavens, how nasty this stuff is. I wish you'd take to it, John . . .
I don't know how I should get through my day without it."*'

A Handful of Dust   Evelyn Waugh   1934

There seem to be almost as many countries claiming to have invented yogurt as there are sure-fire ways of making it. Turks, Bulgars, Georgians, Armenians and Indians all have a long tradition of eating, and cooking with, some form of cultured milk. The Bulgars even have an acid forming bacillus named after them. Milk, especially warm milk, is the ideal breeding ground for bacteria of many kinds. If you boil it to kill the noxious variety, cool it to between 38°C (100°F) and 43°C (110°F) and introduce a live culture of fresh, plain, commercial yogurt – the acid forming bacteria contained in this will promptly set about converting the milk sugar into lactic acid. Yogurt is formed by the growth of two different bacterial organisms in fresh milk, *Streptococcus thermophilus* and *Lactobacillus bulgaricus*. Kept at an even warmth for several hours, a soft curd forms which keeps better than milk (one reason for its popularity in torrid climates), is refreshingly uncloying in taste and very easily digested. The health giving properties of yogurt (and the similar *koumiss* and *kefir*) have been long acknowledged. Whether yogurt eating sharpens libido or extends life is unproven as yet; what seems certain is that it encourages the growth of benign intestinal bacteria and these, along with synthesizing vitamins and aiding digestion prey upon less desirable bugs. To keep this internal culture flourishing yogurt should be eaten regularly, especially when one is on a course of antibiotics because these tend towards overkill, destroying the whole of what medicine prettily refers to as our 'intestinal flora'.

It has taken four centuries for yogurt to gain acceptance in the West as a palatable food rather than a vaguely medicinal substance akin to slippery elm and garlic pearls. Now yogurt has zoomed from the health shop shelf to become one of the most widely eaten instant foods of our time.

The smooth, white, commercial yogurt is perfectly good for you. It is made from honest milk with (contrary to popular legend) 'live' bacteria, but I doubt that many Indians, Bulgarians, Turks or Georgians would find much resemblance to the yogurt they have been making for centuries. True yogurt is creamy coloured, with a voluptuous heavy texture and a taste somewhere between rich and sharp.

Fresh plain home-made yogurt ripening in a bowl set on the window ledge. In the Middle East, yogurt gives velvety richness to thick soups: the hot chicken soup (left) simmered with mint and yogurt and the cold tomato soup (right), blended with lemon, chives and parsley.

Yogurt making

Whatever equipment or milk you favour, the procedure for making yogurt is the same, and very simple once you have grasped the principles involved.

Always sterilize the milk first by bringing it to the boil to kill off undesirable bacteria. As soon as it threatens to rise up the pan, turn the heat right down, let it simmer for two minutes, then remove the pan from the heat and leave the milk to cool until it is lukewarm. Between 38°C (100°F) and 43°C (110°F) is correct if you are using a thermometer. Otherwise dip your finger in it – it should feel warm but not hot. (Homogenized milk is already sterilized, of course, and so only needs to be warmed to 43°C (110°F).)

At this point you introduce the culture – usually a spoonful of plain commercial yogurt (any brand will do but it must be plain, not fruit flavoured). Specific yogurt cultures are available from health shops. For yogurt culture, follow the maker's instructions, but for ordinary commercial yogurt add one tablespoon per 600 ml (1 pint) of milk. Stir, breaking up any skin which has formed on the milk, cover and leave undisturbed at a constant temperature for several hours at least. The correct incubating temperature is between 38°C and 43°C (110°F to 110°F), which is, of course, the same temperature at which you added the culture. The longer you leave it, the thicker, stiffer and sharper tasting the curd will be. Yogurt usually sets lightly in about three hours but made at night and left to set overnight it reaches the consistency most people like around breakfast time the next morning. Manufacturers of yogurt making machines, like the one illustrated opposite, that incubate the culture at a low temperature, recommend a minimum of six hours in the machine. Yogurt can be kept in a cool larder or fridge.

What milk to use
You can use almost every available sort of milk to make yogurt – milk from animals as different as sheep, goats, water buffalo and cows, and milk processed in different ways (non-pasteurized, pasteurized, homogenized, sterilized, evaporated, pow-dered, condensed, skimmed milk, fortified with added milk powder or enriched with cream). Some gluttons even make yogurt with thin cream. Everyone insists their way is healthier, tastier and simpler. The truth is they all work, with some variation in flavour, texture and creaminess. Homogenized milk gives the most consistent results. Goat's milk fat is naturally homogenized which makes this the most digestible yogurt of all. The consistency and flavour of half cream milk can be improved by adding some dried milk powder.

Broadly speaking, the richer or stronger tasting the milk, the richer or stronger tasting the yogurt made from it. There is some logic behind the use of evaporated or other concentrated forms of milk because the thicker curd this produces is closer to the old Bulgarian method whereby the milk was simmered till reduced by a third before adding the culture. But of course yogurt made like this works out more expensive. I use non-pasteurized Jersey milk because I find the extra cream it contains makes a particularly delicious yogurt; it is cheaper than evaporated or condensed milk but creamy enough to give delectable, firm curds.

Equipment

There is much controversy about the best way to achieve the ideal environment – steady, mild warmth – for the working bacteria. Solutions range from the basic (bowl, blanket, warm spot), to cosified (tins padded with down pillows), to space age (thermometers and see-through plastic). Once again, they all work, and all have their points, but they are only as infallible as you are. Conscientious cleaning of all equipment (scrub, scald and rinse each time) is most important. The method I use, the thermos flask, is simple. Get a wide-necked flask, and a large bottle brush to clean it out with. The thermos automatically keeps the milk at the right temperature. When the yogurt has set in the flask, transfer it to glass jars for storage in the refrigerator. Traditionally, people used a wide, shallow pottery bowl to set their curd; this is still a simple and attractive method provided you can find a warm corner where the covered bowl can stand undisturbed and out of draughts. Owners of yogurt making gadgets simply fill their containers with prepared milk, add the culture, plug in and switch on.

Things can go wrong

Most people are going to slip up somewhere, sometime. Maybe the milk was insufficiently sterilized, or the culture added when the milk was too hot, or too cool, or not blended in thoroughly, or not left long enough to solidify. Relax, it is not disastrous; buy another carton of commercial yogurt and start again.

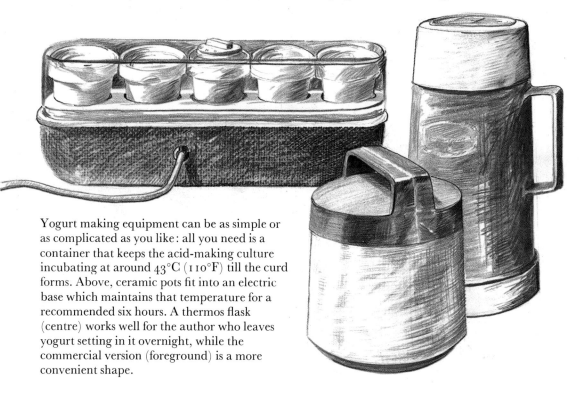

Yogurt making equipment can be as simple or as complicated as you like: all you need is a container that keeps the acid-making culture incubating at around 43°C (110°F) till the curd forms. Above, ceramic pots fit into an electric base which maintains that temperature for a recommended six hours. A thermos flask (centre) works well for the author who leaves yogurt setting in it overnight, while the commercial version (foreground) is a more convenient shape.

Flavouring yogurt

Fresh natural yogurt can be flavoured simply by stirring in honey, jam, fruit, nuts, powdered chocolate, molasses, or maple syrup, after it has set and cooled. After adding the flavouring ingredient, leave the yogurt in a refrigerator for six hours to allow the flavour to develop.

Cooking with yogurt

Home-made yogurt is delicious eaten plain, with a little brown sugar, or added to muesli, or stewed or fresh fruit. It has innumerable other uses in the kitchen: as a low-calorie and economical substitute for thin cream, it becomes an ingredient in soups, cheese dips, cheesecakes and quiches. To borrow an idea sponsored by the cuisine minceur school, you can fold a little whipped egg white and castor sugar into yogurt and use it instead of whipped cream – with fresh fruit, fruit salads, compotes. In hot Mediterranean countries yogurt is diluted to make an odd but refreshing salted drink. Or it is beaten up with mint, garlic and other flavourings to make an instant sauce for cooked vegetables, and grilled fish. Lactic acid has a tenderizing effect on tough meat, so yogurt is used a great deal to make highly spiced marinades for chicken, meat and kebabs. Indians use yogurt to soften fiery curries, either as an ingredient in the curry or more often as a cool *raita* to eat alongside it. A spread of different *raitas*, in little brass or pottery bowls, is one of the pleasures of Indian meals, and they only take minutes to make. The simplest consist of chopped vegetables or fruit mixed with a whipped yogurt base then sharpened with salt, a little garlic, lemon or lime juice, a sprinkling of ground spices, or garam masala, cumin seeds or finely chopped fresh herbs. Chopped raw onion, cooked potato, cucumber, banana, grated coconut – all of these are commonly used. In the Middle East yogurt gives velvety richness to braised meat dishes, slowly simmered casseroles, and thick soups. No meal in Turkey is complete without a bowl of yogurt on the table, and they like it with practically everything.

In some dishes yogurt has to be 'stabilized' first to prevent it curdling and separating, which both looks odd and spoils the texture. If yogurt is added at the last minute, to thicken and enrich a dish – as often happens with curries – the danger does not arise so long as the dish is kept at simmering point only. But where it is a major ingredient, and long cooking is part of the process, it is worth spending a few minutes stabilizing it first.

Stabilizing yogurt

To stabilize 1 litre (2 pints) of yogurt, allow one tablespoon cornflour. Mix the cornflour to a paste with a little milk, stir it into the yogurt and bring the mixture slowly to the boil stirring steadily in one direction, either clockwise or anti-clockwise, but not both. Now leave to simmer *uncovered* till the mixture thickens, which takes between 8 and 10 minutes. It is important not to cover the yogurt during this time as a drop of condensed steam falling back into the pan could undo the good work. Once thickened, however, the stabilized yogurt can be cooked without risk of curdling.

Making plain yogurt

1. Sterilize 1 litre (2 pints) milk by bringing it to the boil and simmering for two minutes to kill off any undesirable bacteria.

2. When the milk has cooled to lukewarm (38–43°C, 100–110°F if you have a thermometer) introduce the culture. This can be a commercial yogurt culture of 1 tablespoonful of plain yogurt. Stir, breaking up any skin which has formed on the milk.

3. Cover with a warmed plate and a small blanket or something similar and leave undisturbed, maintaining the temperature until the curd becomes thick – usually after six to eight hours.

Stabilizing yogurt

1. Mix one tablespoon of cornflour and a little milk to form a paste. Stir it into 1 litre (2 pints) of yogurt, making sure to stir in one direction only, clockwise or anti-clockwise, not both. Stir steadily and bring the mixture slowly to the boil.

2. Reduce the heat and leave the mixture to simmer in an uncovered pan until it thickens. This takes between eight and ten minutes. The pan is left uncovered because a drop of condensed steam falling back into the yogurt could cause it to separate. Once it has thickened, however, the yogurt can be used in cooking without risk of it curdling.

Note: If you are using yogurt made from goat's milk it does not need stabilizing.

Cooking with yogurt

Home-made yogurt has a multitude of culinary uses as you will see from the recipes, both hot and cold, which I have included. It can also be mixed with cream in many other recipes for economy. Yield: 4 to 6 servings.

Cold tomato soup
An interesting recipe because no cooking is involved. It requires a blender. If the tomatoes are fresh, and sweet, the flavour is excellent.

450 g (1 lb) tomatoes
225 g (8 oz) yogurt
1 teaspoon sugar
a pinch of salt
1 tablespoon Worcester sauce
1 tablespoon lemon juice
chives, parsley or basil, finely chopped, to garnish

Drop the tomatoes into boiling water for half a minute, drain and peel. Put them in a blender with the remaining ingredients (herbs apart) and blend till smooth. If the tomatoes are very pippy, a truly conscientious cook will strain the soup, working it through a sieve. If the soup is too thick, add a little cold milk. Chop the herbs finely and sprinkle on top. Serve cold, in bowls.

Hot chicken soup with yogurt
A pleasant change from the Greek *avgolemono*, this recipe uses yogurt and mint to thicken and flavour the chicken soup instead of egg yolk and lemon juice.

1¼ tablespoons rice
1 litre (2 pints) chicken stock
150 g (5 oz) yogurt
1 egg
salt and pepper
1 tablespoon chopped parsley and fresh mint

Simmer the rice in the chicken stock till tender for about 12 minutes. Whisk the yogurt with the egg in a bowl, stir in a little hot stock, then gradually add the contents of the bowl to the rest of the chicken stock which is taken off the heat to prevent curdling. Use plenty of salt and pepper to season the soup and very cautiously bring it to simmering point only, stirring the whole time. Serve in bowls, sprinkled with the fresh herbs.

Tandoori chicken
A classic, irresistible Indian dish of spiced, marinated roast chicken. It is far easier to make than one might suppose and the ideal disguise for dull, frozen birds.

1 good sized chicken (1½ to 2 kg/3 to 4 lb)
2 medium onions
4 cloves garlic
1 small root ginger or 1 teaspoon ground ginger
1 teaspoon cumin seeds
1 teaspoon coriander seeds
2 dried chilies, or ½ teaspoon chili or cayenne powder
sea salt and pepper
300 ml (½ pint) yogurt
1 tablespoon Worcester sauce
2 lemons
50 g (2 oz) melted butter
1 teaspoon garam masala (optional)

If the bird is frozen leave to thaw out overnight at room temperature, removing the giblets inside.

In the morning (to eat that night) cut the chicken into serving pieces (wings, legs and breast into four pieces). Remove the skin with a sharp knife. Grind, chop or blend the onion, garlic and ginger to a mush, adding ground cumin, coriander, chilies and salt. In a large bowl, whisk yogurt smooth, adding Worcester sauce, the juice of one lemon and the spice paste. Rub this fragrant paste all over the chicken pieces, pour over remainder and leave all day to marinate and allow the flavours to penetrate. Preheat the oven to 220°C (425°F, Mark 7) or better still, heat up the rotary barbecue spit. Cook the chicken pieces in a roasting pan, with marinade juices poured over them for 30 to 40 minutes or till the meat is firm and no longer pink in the middle. Baste once or twice if you have time with melted butter. Sprinkle with garam masala, a little sea salt and the juice of the second lemon.

Serve hot, with hot pittas or chapattis and *salat*, which is the Indian name for an onion, tomato and lettuce or green pepper salad.

Spiced fish in yogurt – Dahi Machi

From India, a hot, spicy dish marinated and cooked in yogurt. As different as can be from European fish cookery, and to my mind infinitely kinder to the fish.

675 g (1½ lb) firm fish (cod, halibut, coley, bass, bream or merou)
2 medium onions
1 teaspoon ground ginger or 1 small knob fresh root ginger
2 teaspoons turmeric
4 green or 3 red, dried chilies
450 ml (¾ pint) yogurt
a pinch of salt
2 tablespoons cooking oil
2 tablespoons ghee (p. 92)
1 tablespoon garam masala or juice of 1 lemon

Cut the fish into chunks, removing the bones and skin. Chop one onion finely. Pound the fresh ginger and mix the chopped onion and ginger, the ground turmeric, chopped fresh or powdered chilies, yogurt and salt. Coat the fish chunks with this spiced marinade and leave for at least 30 minutes to absorb the flavours. Now heat the oil and the ghee in a heavy frying pan, slice the second onion and fry gently till golden. Then add the fish and marinade and simmer, covered, very slowly for 10 to 15 minutes, or till the fish is firm, white and cooked through. Sprinkle with garam masala (a ready ground spice mixture usually added at the last minute to refresh the spice flavours) or lemon juice and serve with spicy pan juices on plain boiled rice. A cucumber salad – or *raita* – would complement this dish. For this, peel and slice a cucumber and drain with a sprinkling of salt in a colander for 20 minutes. Rinse and dry. Pour over yogurt beaten with crushed garlic, a squeeze of lemon juice and 1 teaspoon of olive oil, chopped mint and seasonings.

Susbarak or meat dumplings cooked in yogurt

This is the sort of dish I imagine Bedouin tribesmen tucking into, hardy, simple and tasty. The meat need not be tender, but it should be lean and preferably minced twice for smoothness. This dish lends itself to flavouring up with whatever herbs and spices you fancy.

Dumplings

1 onion
225 g (8 oz) minced beef, lamb or pork
a pinch of salt and pepper
½ teaspoon each of ground cumin and cinnamon
350 g (12 oz) plain white flour

Sauce or stock

225 g (8 oz) stabilized yogurt
225 g (8 oz) milk or stock

Chop the onion finely, mix with the minced meat, salt and pepper, and spices and fry in a little oil for five minutes or till the onion is transparent and the meat pale brown.

Mix the flour with enough cold water to make a firm dough. Knead for two or three minutes till smooth. Shape into a sausage sized roll. Roll out the dough to the thickness of a coin, stamp into small circles (5 cm/2 in) and place one teaspoon of meat stuffing on each. Moisten the edges of the dough, fold over and pinch closed. Heat the stabilized yogurt with milk, or stock, in a deep pan till boiling, then drop in the *susbarak* carefully one at a time and simmer gently with the pan lid half on for 30 minutes.

Serve hot with pittas and a salad of chopped tomatoes, raw onions or salad greens, generously dressed and seasoned.

Orange flavoured yogurt sorbet

This is a smashing water ice, with a fine smooth texture and excellent flavour.

300 ml (½ pint) thick plain yogurt
grated rind of 2 oranges
1 can frozen (approx 175 g/6 oz) unsweetened orange juice
2 tablespoons castor sugar
2 egg whites

Blend the yogurt, orange rinds, frozen orange juice and 1 tablespoon of sugar in a liquidizer. Turn into an ice cream maker, or ice tray, and freeze for approximately 30 minutes. Turn into a bowl, whisk, then return. Repeat. When mushy, stir in the egg whites which have been beaten up with the remaining 1 tablespoon of sugar till stiff and thick. Freeze this time without further stirring. Leave to thaw a little before serving.

Cream

'"This will be a country supper, girls" said Polly, bustling about.
"There is real cream, brown bread, home-made cake and honey from my beehives.
Butter the toast, Maud, and put that little cover on it."'

An Old Fashioned Girl   Louisa May Alcott   1870

It is cream, that thick, unctuous, yellowish, clinging, incomparable substance which distils, so to speak, the richness of our milk. If a pan of fresh milk is left to stand overnight, the fat globules it contains rise to the top, as fat is lighter than water, and the yellow skin of fat is cream. In the old days, before separating machines were invented, it was skimmed off with a perforated disc called a 'fleeter'; a wasteful way of doing things since some fat was always left behind in the skimmed milk, but one which produced delicious cream. As much as 63 litres (14 gallons) of milk would go to make 1 litre (2 pints) of cream. Now the process is carried out commercially with separating machines which spin off the heavier skim milk, with such exactitude that creams of precisely gauged fat content are produced with no trouble at all. Thus we can buy half cream (12% fat content), single or thin cream (18%), whipping cream (35%), double or heavy cream (48%) and clotted cream, richest of all at 55%. As with most commercial processes, such gains in efficiency seem to be balanced by a loss not in quality exactly, but things which can only be measured subjectively like flavour, texture, liveliness. One carton of commercial cream tastes just like the next, which is good insofar as it means a consistent standard is maintained, but seems a far cry from the days when a particular farmer's wife in a certain region could become famous for the glorious flavour of the cream her well-fed cows turned out. Today's pedigree dairy herds are superb milking machines, yet a dairy farmer I know speaks wistfully of the days when cows were fed on what one might call the free range principle, because the milk had so much more flavour to it then.

Clotted cream is probably the nearest most of us get to the 'thicke crayme' of old, which one can well believe was eaten 'more for a sensuall appetyte than for any good nouryshment'. But it is expensive. Anyone living near a dairy farm, however, may well be able to buy milk at wholesale prices to make their own clotted cream, and it is not difficult to do provided you can use up all the skimmed milk.

Of all the dairy products, cream contributes most to cooking, or perhaps I should say 'cuisine' since it is the French who have taken this aspect of gastronomy furthest. By this I do not mean that cream is used in greater quantities, but that it contributes a distinctive creaminess to thousands of dishes. There is really no substitute for cream.

Water piped in runnels round a marble slab keeps prepared puddings cool in this old dairy: cremets, thick cream lightened with egg white, in heart moulds; burnt cream layered with brown sugar and junkets in moulds (left); and lemon soufflé topped with rind, and a syllabub (right).

Cream making

To obtain cream from milk

You need a fair supply, say 2 litres ($\frac{1}{2}$ gallon) of fresh, raw milk. Raw milk is untreated, that is non-pasteurized. A wide shallow pan, dish or bowl, preferably with outward sloping sides, and something to use as a skimmer are the only equipment needed. Not so long ago, dairy workers used the flat half of a scallop shell, and it still serves admirably, having a grooved surface for the milk to run off. Otherwise use a slotted frying slice, or thin saucer. Proper (stainless steel) skimmers and bowls are obtainable from specialist shops.

Pour the milk into the pan or dish, put in a cool place for twenty-four hours and you will find a thick, leathery skin of cream has formed on top. If you are making cream from goat's milk you may have to leave it for longer because the fat globules are smaller. Lift this off with your skimmer, turn into a jar and store in the fridge. People with a regular supply of raw milk will probably make cream every other day or so, and this can be added to the jar as it is made. It keeps for about a week in the fridge. To thin down this cream, simply stir in a little milk. This is the old-fashioned, wasteful way of getting cream – wasteful because some fat always remains in the milk – but it has the advantage that the skimmed milk will be all the richer.

Pasteurizing cream

Cream made from raw milk can be pasteurized to ensure that any contaminating bacteria are destroyed. To pasteurize, heat the cream in the top of a double boiler to 71°C (145°F) and hold it at this temperature for 30 minutes. Stir. Transfer the top part of the boiler to a bowl of iced water and bring the temperature of the cream down to 4°C (40°F) as speedily as possible. Store it in clean, sterilized containers in the refrigerator.

Making cream from butter and milk

This Alice-Through-the-Looking-Glass trick can be accomplished easily with the cream making attachment to an electric blender, and is useful when you need some cream urgently for a recipe and the shops are shut. Some people regularly make cream this way; where butter prices are subsidized, it works out somewhat cheaper than buying straight cream. It makes good thick cream, but the butter *must* be unsalted. If you want a thinner cream use less butter. Melt 225 g (8 oz) of unsalted butter in 120 ml (4 fl oz) of milk. Pour into the cream making attachment, whizz away till the butter and milk have combined and leave to cool. Stir before using.

Clotting cream the traditional way

Pour the cream into an earthenware or enamelled bowl, or stainless steel milk pan, then heat gently either on top of an old-fashioned range or in a basin of water (*bain marie*) on a gas or electric cooker turned down very low. Warm for anything up to six hours till the cream has a rich wrinkled crusty look. Never let it boil. Then set the pan to cool and by morning you can lift off a 'clout' to store in jars or lidded pots in the refrigerator.

Clotting cream the quick way

As the cream should not come into direct contact with the hotplate, either use a double boiler or stand a pan in a saucepan of water. You also need a thermometer.

Heat till the cream reaches a temperature around 76°C to 82°C (170°F to 180°F). Check with the thermometer. Keep the cream around this point (not more than 87°C (190°F)) for between 30 minutes and 1 hour, till the cream looks crusty and wrinkled. Early in the proceedings, stir it once, to distribute the heat. Cool the cream pan speedily by standing in a bowl of cold water, then leave in a cool place overnight to set. Pack into jars and store.

To sour cream

A lot of Russian recipes call for 'smetana' or sour cream. The best is made by letting unpasteurized cream sour naturally at room temperature but this takes a few days. You can hurry it up a little by stirring in a spoonful of yogurt or leftover sour cream. On no account use commercial pasteurized cream past the stamped date as it tastes bitter and can contain undesirable bacteria. All equipment must be kept spotlessly clean and sterilized.

To produce a quick sour cream, stir a spoonful of lemon juice or vinegar into bought single pasteurized cream and stand in a warm place for an hour or so. Yogurt or sour raw milk will sour bought cream overnight, while commercial sour cream can be bought in delicatessens and some supermarkets.

To whip cream

Commercial whipping cream produces fluffier whipped cream and costs a bit less than double cream. Dilute double cream with a couple of spoonfuls of top of the milk (or thin cream) before whipping to give a softer, lighter texture. Single or thin cream does not contain enough fat to whip. Cream for whipping should be left in the refrigerator overnight to 'ripen' and become thicker. Chefs use wire balloon whisks for whipping cream because they beat in more air which makes a lighter cream. Scandinavians swear by whisks made from birch twigs but most of us use a plain old egg whisk. Whichever type you prefer, do not overwhip as the cream should be soft and fluffy, not stiff lest it gives a stodgy taste to dishes which should be light and airy.

In some dishes like fruit fools, or mousses, whipped cream can be bulked by folding in beaten egg whites.

To cook with cream

Top of the milk, half cream, and single cream are the best grades to use for most cooking purposes; double or thick cream is unnecessarily lavish. Some ice creams and cream sweets are in effect a sort of cream custard; with egg yolks, single cream is adequate since the yolks provide the thickening. When using cream with wine in a sauce for meat, fish, poultry, reduce the wine by boiling hard before adding the cream. This gives more flavour and helps prevent the cream separating. Always draw the pan off the heat before adding cream to a hot sauce, lest it curdles.

Skimming cream

1. For this you need about 2 litres (4 pints) of fresh raw milk. Pour the milk into a pan or dish with wide sloping sides and leave it in a cool place for a day. You will find a thick leathery skin of cream forms on top. Lift this off with a skimmer – a saucer will do. In South Devon, famous for its cream, half a scallop shell was used as the milk ran down the grooves of the shell. Store the cream for up to a week in a lidded jar in the refrigerator. The quantity of cream taken from the milk will depend entirely on the fat content of the cream.

Clotting cream

This quick method automatically pasteurizes cream skimmed from fresh milk. Clotted cream can be made from bought double cream but it would be ludicrously expensive.

1. Warm the skimmed cream in a double boiler on the oven, very gently. Use a thermometer and heat till the cream reaches a temperature of around $87°C$ ($190°F$). Hold it at this temperature for about one hour till the cream looks crusty and wrinkled. Never let it boil. Stir it once to distribute the heat.

2. Cool the cream pan speedily by standing in a bowl of cold water and leave overnight to set.

3. By morning you can lift off the great clout of clotted cream that has formed. Store in screw-top jars or lidded pots in the refrigerator. Serve clotted cream loaded on scones, already spread with fresh farm butter, and topped with black-currant jam.

Cooking with cream: savouries

The point to remember when adding cream to soups, sauces, pan juices is that it should not boil, because this tends to curdle it, especially if sharply flavoured. The taste is not affected but it does not look so good. Yield: 4 to 6 servings.

Likky soup

Likky is Cornish for leek, and their version of leek and potato soup naturally features Cornish clotted cream.

2 rashers streaky bacon
1 large potato
2 large leeks
25 g (1 oz) butter
salt, pepper, chopped parsley
600 ml (1 pint) beef or chicken stock
50 g (2 oz) clotted cream

Cut the bacon into strips, peel and slice the potato, wash the leeks and slice across. Fry all these gently in butter for a few minutes, season with salt, pepper and chopped parsley. Then add stock and simmer for 20 to 30 minutes. Add the cream just before serving.

Eliza Acton's salmon pudding

In her cookbook of 1845 this doyen of Victorian cookery writers notes tersely, 'A Scotch Receipt – Good'. Not as extravagant as it sounds since it can be made with leftovers or the cheap tail cuts, and the other ingredients make the fish go further.

450 g (1 lb) cooked salmon
4 eggs
150 g (5 oz) fine white breadcrumbs
150 ml (¼ pint) single cream
salt and cayenne pepper
25 g (1 oz) butter

Skin and bone the salmon, and pound, mash or blend till smooth. Make the crumbs by trimming the crusts off stale white bread and grating, or whizzing in the blender. Whisk the eggs till frothy. Mix the fish, eggs, crumbs, single cream and seasonings well together then press down into a well buttered soufflé dish, about 1 litre (2 pints) in size. Dot with butter and bake at 180°C (350°F, Mark 4) for one hour or till firm.

Serve with the following simple but excellent sauce which is also good with fried fish fillets.

150 ml (¼ pint) whipping cream
1 teaspoon anchovy essence

Whip the cream till fluffy, adding the essence gradually. Pour over the fish and serve at once.

Pork or veal cooked with apple and cream

Apples, Calvados, and cream are characteristic ingredients of cooking in Normandy. Here they turn a simple meat dish into something grander. I make it with pork loin and whisky and it is just as good. The ideal dish to rustle up at short notice. This amount serves four.

350 g (12 oz) pork loin or veal escallops
salt, pepper and lemon juice
1 large or two small sweet apples
50 g (2 oz) butter
1 small glass Calvados or whisky
300 ml (½ pint) thick cream

The pork loin should be sliced across into miniature steaks, and beaten flat with a cleaver. (Escallops should also be flanttened.) Rub salt and pepper into the meat and sprinkle with lemon juice. Peel, core and finely dice the apple. Melt the butter in a heavy frying pan. Add the meat and sizzle over a moderate heat till lightly browned on both sides. Add the apple cubes, stir about and cook for a moment longer. Heat the Calvados or whisky in a little pan, set light to it and pour it over the contents of the pan, shaking them cautiously till the flames subside. Add the cream, reduce the heat and simmer gently for a few minutes, stirring the sauce and scraping the meat juices into it. When thickened, arrange the apple on top of the meat and serve immediately with the sauce poured round. Serve this with just one simply cooked vegetable, like steamed green beans, *petits pois* or broccoli.

Cooking with cream: puddings

Memories of childhood are evoked by delectable puddings made with cream: fools, ices, mousses, trifles, syllabubs, soufflés hot and cold. A cream pudding should be smooth, cool and rich without being oversweetened. Yield: 4 to 6 servings.

Cremets

Starting with the most artless of all cream sweets, and one of the best – thick cream lightened with egg white and left to drain overnight. The result is neither cloying nor sickly. Use double, not whipping, cream for cremets, to provide the necessary texture.

300 ml ($\frac{1}{2}$ pint) double cream
2 tablespoons top of the milk
2 egg whites

Some sort of perforated mould is necessary to let the mixture drain. Use a little basket lined with muslin or commercial moulds.

To make the cremets, whip the cream with a spoonful of the top of the milk till thick, beat the egg whites till fluffy and fold in the cream. Turn into the muslin lined mould and set to drain on a wire rack over a pan or dish. Leave the pudding in a cool place. (If you are using the refrigerator make sure no aromatic food is nearby, as cream absorbs smells.) The next day, turn out onto a plate, pour over enough unsweetened single cream to cover and serve with castor sugar and any fresh soft fruit in season, or alone.

Syllabub

Another uncooked cream, sweetened and flavoured with lemon and marsala.

1 lemon
1 small glass (approx 120 ml, 4 fl oz) Marsala,
  Madeira or sweet sherry
2 tablespoons castor sugar
300 ml ($\frac{1}{2}$ pint) double cream
pinch of ground nutmeg

Grate the lemon rind, squeeze the juice and combine both with the sherry and sugar. Leave to stand for a few hours, or overnight. Strain (to remove rind) and add to the cream. Then whisk till thick, fluffy but not too stiff. Spoon into little glasses and serve cold with biscuits.

Sack cream

Sack is a corruption of *vin sec*, which in Elizabethan England was imported from Spain, and seems to have been closer to sherry than wine. Wines were drunk sweeter then; a sweetish sherry gives a better flavour than the white wine usually called for. Sack creams are as old as the syllabub but this cooked version is Victorian.

1 egg yolk
600 ml (1 pint) single cream
3 tablespoons castor sugar
small glass sherry or Madeira
grated lemon peel

Put all the ingredients together, having beaten the egg yolk well first, in the top of a double boiler. Heat gently, stirring, till the mixture is as thick as double cream. Remove from the heat and stir till cold. Pour into glasses and serve, traditionally, with bread oven-dried till brittle.

Cold lemon soufflé

Always an acceptable pudding, neither too rich nor too sweet.

1 tablespoon powdered gelatine
1 tablespoon milk
3 eggs
3 lemons
150 g (5 oz) castor sugar
300 ml ($\frac{1}{2}$ pint) whipping cream
ratafia biscuits (optional)

Stir the gelatine in the warmed milk till dissolved. Separate the eggs, combine the egg yolks, the juice of three lemons and rind of two, the sugar and the gelatine in the top of a double boiler. Heat, stirring, till thick. Allow to cool. Whip the cream till fluffy. Whip the egg white and then fold both into the lemon custard mixture. Turn into a soufflé dish, serve cold, with ratafia biscuits.

Baked potato pudding

From Italy, a thoroughly unusual hot pudding made from sweetened mashed potatoes baked with raisins and pine nuts. The eggs give it a cake-like consistency.

450 g (1 lb) hot boiled potatoes
75 g (3 oz) butter
150 ml (¼ pint) single cream
a pinch of salt
1 tablespoon flour
3 eggs
3 tablespoons sugar
100 g (4 oz) sultanas or raisins
cinnamon and nutmeg
25 g (1 oz) pine nuts

Mash the boiled, peeled potatoes till smooth, then stir in the butter, cream, a tiny pinch of salt, the flour and heat, stirring to mix. Separate the eggs. Stir in the three egg yolks, the sugar, ground spices, raisins (soaked for a few minutes in warm water to soften) and the pine nuts. Fold in the stiffly whisked egg whites and turn into a buttered floured 20 cm (8 in) cake tin. Bake in a hot oven, 220°C (425°F, Mark 7) for 45 minutes. Serve hot with thin cream.

Vanilla mousse with butterscotch sauce

The combination of hot butterscotch sauce with cold mousse, demurely flavoured with vanilla, is the point of this dish.

3 egg yolks
4 tablespoons castor sugar
1 teaspoon vanilla essence or 1 vanilla pod
1 tablespoon gelatine
150 ml (¼ pint) milk
300 ml (½ pint) whipping cream

Butterscotch sauce

50 g (2 oz) butter
100 g (4 oz) soft brown sugar
2 tablespoons golden syrup
½ teaspoon vanilla essence

To make the mousse, combine the egg yolks, sugar and vanilla essence or pod in the top of a double boiler and heat, stirring, till thick. Take

care it does not boil. Take off the heat. Remove the vanilla pod. Stir in the gelatine dissolved in a little milk. Whisk or stir till cold – this takes less time if you stand the pan in a bowl of cold water.

When it shows signs of setting, fold in the whipped cream. Pour into an attractive bowl and leave to set.

For the sauce, merely combine all the ingredients in the top of a double boiler and heat gently, stirring, till smooth. Serve hot in a jug.

Burnt cream

Cambridge University claims to have invented this elegant dish, and it can still be ordered from college butteries (kitchens) for May Ball suppers.

The 'burnt' refers not to the cream but to a sugar layer on top, caramelized to a hard transparent amber disc. This is not the easiest thing to achieve with an ordinary grill (a salamander – metal disc heated red hot – was used) but it is spectacular if you succeed.

4 egg yolks
600 ml (1 pint) single cream
2 tablespoons castor sugar
small piece grated orange rind
small piece stick cinnamon
1 teaspoon cornflour mixed with milk
100 g (4 oz) soft light brown sugar

Whisk the egg yolks, combine with the cream, castor sugar, orange rind, and cinnamon in the top of a double boiler. Mix the cornflour with 1 teaspoonful of milk as a precaution against curdling, and add to the mixture. Heat slowly stirring, till thick. Remove the cinnamon and the rind and leave to cool, stirring now and then. Pour into a dish, and chill till firm. Now sift the brown sugar evenly over the top, making sure the sugar continues right up to the rim. Heat the grill and set the dish on a baking sheet under the grill till the sugar turns to caramel – you may have to turn the dish carefully to reach every bit but do not cook too long or the caramel will blacken. Remove and cool. Serve cold.

Note: use a tough soufflé dish, like Pyrex. Cambridge chefs set the cream dish inside another bowl of crushed ice while browning the top. This helps prevent curdling.

Ice-Cream

It is quite amazing how resourceful and clever people can be when it comes to gratifying an appetite. How those egregious gluttons, the patricians of old Rome, managed to transport ice from the nearest glacier to make ice-caves where frozen creams and other dainties could be made and stored in the Roman summer heat, is a mystery. Italy seems to have held the lead in the ice-cream department, for the frozen confections Marie de Médicis introduced via her Italian chef to the French court were so elaborate they put to shame the childish mess of sweetened snow which Chaucer mentions.

Making ices today is no problem, as every house has its own ice-cave in the shape of the freezing compartment of the refrigerator. Some own freezers too. A perfectly good ice-cream can be made in a fridge or freezer provided you remember to take it out from time to time and beat it well, to inhibit the formation of crystals. Some people, however, prefer the crunchy texture of crystals, in which case do not beat the mixture when it is partly frozen. To produce an ice-cream of velvety smoothness, the ingredients need to be kept moving as they are cooling. The old fashioned hand-cranked ice-cream churns fulfilled this requirement by churning a little metal tub of ice-cream round and round in a bed of cracked ice and salt. These are still the best ice-cream makers around but it is difficult to get enough cracked ice (fishmongers no longer use it) and people are reluctant to sit turning handles for twenty minutes at a time. Technology has come up with the solution – an electrical ice-cream making gadget which you pop into the ice compartment of the freezer, switch on and leave paddling away quietly like an Arctic troll. Various models are obtainable. The ice compartment must be defrosted first and you need to make sure the gadget's flex has not been pinched too tight in the fridge or freezer door. To remove the ice-cream from the moulds, dip them in hot water for a moment. Prizing out the ice with a knife would wreck the mould. The pan and paddles can be immersed in hot water to clean, but the casing should only be wiped over with a damp cloth as it is electrical. Some brands stop paddling automatically once the ice-cream has reached the proper consistency, and the paddles lift out of the ice. With others you need to keep an eye on proceedings otherwise the ice-cream simply sets round the paddles.

Icy cold ices, creamy smooth, served on a summer's day: raspberry-flavoured frozen fruit mousse, then sack cream served in a giant goblet, an orange-flavoured yogurt sorbet in a tall sundae glass and simple vanilla ice-cream topped with crunchy almond praline.

Ice-cream making

Points about ice-cream making

Use the ice tray or a plastic box in the freezing compartment of a refrigerator. Stir the mix at 30 minute intervals, then when it is beginning to set firm all the way through, turn into a chilled bowl and beat hard with a rotary whisk to stop any crystals forming. This is also the best time to add liqueurs, nuts, bits of chocolate or fruit. If you are using a machine, add these extras when the paddles stop. Allow four hours in all for the making, freezing and a period of mellowing.

Ice-cream can be too cold: this annuls the flavour and it is agony to eat. Take an ice out of the freezing compartment or freezer and let it ripen, or mellow, in the centre of the fridge for between 15 minutes and 1 hour depending on how hard it is. Ice-cream keeps well for about a month in the freezer but needs considerable thawing before use.

Ingredients

Ice-cream can be made from various mixtures, ranging from pure cream flavoured and frozen solid, to custards of varying degrees of richness according to the ratio of cream to eggs. Rich ice-cream results from richer, more expensive mixtures but a thinner mix, using twice as much milk as cream, gives excellent results in an electric ice maker. Long-life cream, bought in cartons from the supermarket, is a good substitute for the richer, fresh cream.

The right amount of sugar is important – too little gives too solid an ice, too much prevents it freezing properly. All the ingredients must be chilled before use. If you make the custard base and leave it to chill overnight before adding the cream, it takes only one hour to finish in the gadget and a little longer in the ice compartment.

Ices are cruel to filled teeth unless they are smooth enough to swallow without chewing. So if you are adding nuts, it might be kinder to add them only on top – chewing frozen nuts has been known to make guests scream aloud.

Budget ice-creams

For cheaper ice-cream, popular with children though not perhaps with gourmets, you can substitute evaporated or condensed milk for fresh single or double cream. Both these milk concentrates have a powerful flavour of their own, quite different from that of the fresh products, which the purist might object to, so the usual advice is to use these only when making strongly flavoured ices, such as coffee, chocolate or strawberry. In both cases look for the unsweetened variety, otherwise you will upset the sugar balance in the recipe concerned. A useful rule of thumb when making a basic vanilla ice is that three to four tablespoons of sugar per 600 ml (1 pint) of cream or custard ice-cream base, is the maximum quantity needed. When making fruit ices, the proportion of sugar to base mixture is increased. The evaporated milk is usually scalded, chilled, then whipped before the remaining ingredients are added. The cheapest ices are the water ices, usually a frozen fruit purée into which some whipped egg white is incorporated for lightness. See the yogurt section for a refreshing orange ice with a smooth texture based on plain yogurt.

Ice-creams

Ice-cream can be made from various mixtures, ranging from pure cream flavoured and frozen solid to custard mixes. I have included both simple and rich recipes for you to experiment with. Yield: 6 servings.

Simple vanilla ice

2 eggs and 2 additional yolks
75 g (3 oz) sugar
450 ml (¾ pint) milk
1 teaspoon vanilla essence
200 ml (7 fl oz) double cream

Beat the eggs and extra yolks with the sugar till smooth and thick. Heat the milk to scalding point, then pour it into the eggs, beating all the time. Strain into the top of a double boiler and stir over a gentle heat till thickened. Chill. Add the vanilla essence and fold in the lightly whipped cream. Turn into an ice-cream paddler or ice trays – in the latter case, beat three times at 30 minute intervals during freezing. The ice-cream will set in two hours.

Use this plain vanilla ice-cream as the base for the following three recipes:

Ginger ice-cream
Add 50 g (2 oz) chopped preserved ginger and one tablespoon syrup to vanilla ice-cream.

Caramel ice-cream
Spread 175 g (6 oz) sugar in a thick bottomed pan and stand over a medium heat to caramelize, watching it all the time. Boil for a short time, stirring with a metal spoon, till evenly golden brown. Quickly pour a thin layer onto a greased baking sheet. When cold, pound to a powder in a liquidizer or mortar. Follow the vanilla ice recipe using 75 g (3 oz) of the caramel powder instead of sugar. The remainder can be folded into the ice at the final beating, or sprinkled on top.

Praline ice-cream
Praline is a candy made with chopped almonds and sugar, ground finely as for caramel.

Put 50 g (2 oz) unblanched almonds and 65 g (2½ oz) castor sugar into a heavy pan and heat gently, stirring with a metal spoon, till the sugar melts. Raise the heat a little and cook till nut-brown. Pour quickly into a well greased tin.

When cold, pulverize coarsely.

Add the praline powder to the basic vanilla ice after final beating.

Brown bread ice
An arresting and delicious combination of slightly crunchy crumbs and smooth ice-cream.

300 ml (½ pint) whipping cream
1 tablespoon vanilla sugar or sugar plus vanilla essence
2 tablespoons top of milk or thin cream
75 g (3 oz) brown breadcrumbs
75 g (3 oz) soft brown sugar

Whip the cream lightly with the vanilla sugar, add the milk and freeze, beating three times once every 30 minutes – or churn in an ice-cream maker. Meanwhile combine the breadcrumbs with the brown sugar, spread on a baking sheet and cook in a hot oven (200°C, 400°F, Mark 6) till the sugar is just caramelized. Cool quickly, crush then chill. Fold the crumbs into the frozen mixture. Freeze for a further 30 minutes and serve.

Frozen fruit mousse
Any fruit can be used for this – from tinned guavas to fresh mulberries. A mousse base is a little different from a custard base, rather easier and quicker to make. A good family ice.

300 ml (½ pint) chilled double cream
450 ml (¾ pint) fruit purée made from fresh, tinned or
* cooked dried fruit, sweetened to taste and chilled*
2 large or 3 small egg whites

In a large bowl, fold the lightly whipped cream into the fruit purée, then fold in the softly whipped egg whites. Pour into containers and freeze without stirring. For an elegant touch, put a paper collar round the inside of a soufflé dish and overfill so that on removing the paper, before serving, the mousse appears to have 'risen'.

Butter

'Ellen put in the dasher and the cover and began to churn.
It was tiresome work : the cream was rich and cold,
and at the end of half an hour grew very stiff.
It splattered up on Ellen's face and hand and apron,
and over the floor; legs and arms were both weary;
but still the dasher must go up and down; she must not stop.'

The Wide, Wide World   Elizabeth Wetherall   *1893*

If milk is largely water with a little fat in it, butter, conversely, is largely fat with a little water in it. It is made by agitating (rocking, spinning, shaking) fresh or sour cream steadily until the fat globules in the cream clump together and separate from the cloudy, slightly acid liquid called buttermilk. The butter, churned from good rich cream, and eaten fresh, or very lightly salted, has a purity of flavour which beats anything commercial.

Making butter is neither complicated nor difficult. It is most economic for those people who keep cows or can buy suitable milk at wholesale prices. In earliest times it was made by simply shaking cream vigorously in a skin pouch. Today scientific know-how and mechanization has the whole process firmly under control, but traditionally butter making was reckoned to be a temperamental business. Some days, for no apparent reason, the butter 'went to sleep' and refused to 'come'. Women, who did so much of the dairy work, came in for some of the blame, and fairies were thought likely culprits, as Shakespeare acknowledges when he earmarks Robin Goodfellow as the saboteur who 'bootless makes the breathless housewife churn'. Pastures were regularly inspected for weeds (ivy, wild garlic, buttercups were all suspect) which might 'taint' the milk, and thus the butter.

In the days before refrigeration, much trouble went into keeping the dairy, or wherever the milk and its by-products were stored, cool and airy. Roofs were thatch or stone-tiled to keep out the summer sun's heat, surfaces inside were of smooth slate or stone and windows faced north. All equipment was scalded to keep it sweet, and left to bleach in the sun and wind. A dairymaid's hands were supposed to be as white as milk, smooth as butter and cool as spring water, though it was a matter for pride (and hygiene) that the butter was handled as little as possible between churn and table. A skilled worker used wooden butter 'hands' to press out whey and shape the pats, which might then be further embellished with the farm's individual butter stamp formed in a hand carved wooden mould.

Butter is churned, then worked with butter 'hands' on the cool slate table beneath the dairy window; three savoury butters in pots: black olive butter (left), anchovy butter (centre) and mint butter. Carved moulds add an individual touch to the plain butters. So do butter curls.

Butter making

Equipment
A standard electric mixer with adjustable speed settings may not be as aesthetically rewarding as the old fashioned plunge or rocker churns which still turn up occasionally in country junk shops and sales, but it efficiently turns cream into butter. Small glass jar churns, with hand turned wooden paddles, can still be bought, though an electrically operated churn seems the obvious choice for regular butter making. Wooden spoons or butter making 'hands' are required for squeezing and shaping the finished butter, while there is a revival of the wooden butter moulds to print out the pattern on commercial rounds of butter.

Cream
Fresh or sour cream may be used for butter making but do not use any pasteurized cream which has been allowed to go 'off'. Pasteurized cream does not sour naturally like the non-pasteurized variety, and the bitter taste it develops would spoil your butter. Fresh cream may be used pasteurized or non-pasteurized, according to whatever is at hand and your preferences in the matter – non-pasteurized cream from a reputable tuberculin tested herd is quite safe. The thicker the cream the more fat it contains and thus the more butter it will make. So it is false economy to buy more of a cheaper, thinner cream. Butter made from fresh cream tastes delicately sweet, and ineffably 'buttery', best eaten straight away unsalted. Butter made from sour cream has a richer, stronger flavour – it does *not* taste 'sour' by the way – and is best for salting and storing. Also sour cream takes about a third of the time to churn.

Churning
Churning adequately describes the whole range of ways of keeping cream on the move; hand or electric whisk, electric mixer, hand cranked churn, power churn. Everything for butter making (*vide* the old dairies) should be cool, between 10°C and 18°C (50°F and 65°F) is ideal. Keep the ripened cream in the fridge for an hour or so beforehand to harden the fat and help it turn to butter. If you are whisking in a bowl use a big one as the cream will splatter. A guideline is that 1 litre (2 pints) of heavy cream makes approximately 450 g (1 lb) butter, but it depends entirely on the fat content of the cream.

The method for making butter is the same whether you use fresh or sour cream. Tip the cream into a bowl, mixer or churn. If you are using the mixer, set it at a slow speed and keep your eye on it. Otherwise just start slowly and steadily churning away. The cream will get thicker, and thicker, and suddenly 'break', the vivid term for the moment when the stuff separates out into solids and liquid. At this point a splash of *cold* water – 'breaking water' – helps, but do not overdo it, no more than a quarter of the total amount of cream. Churn on till the butter granules are about the size of barley grains, then pour off the buttermilk into a bowl – it is excellent for mixing bread, scones, soda bread. Add a cup full of *cold* water to the churn (or the mixer) and churn on for a few seconds. This is to wash out the traces of buttermilk (if left in they can turn butter rancid) and should be repeated till the rinsing water runs off clear. Now turn the butter into a fine sieve or muslin and leave in a cool place to firm and drain.

If you are in a hurry, the butter can be eaten but ideally, it should be worked further to expel the last dregs of water. To do this turn it onto a wet board, and with a pair of wet wooden spoons, spatulas, or butter 'hands' pat it out flat, squeezing it at the same time and tilting the board to help the water to run off. When you think you have worked out all the water, you can salt the butter. Use one or two teaspoons per 450 g (1 lb) of sea salt for the keenest flavour. Simply sprinkle salt over the butter and pat it in, pressing and squeezing with your wooden implement.

For storing, shape into pats (carved moulds are not expensive and add an appropriately individual touch), wrap in greaseproof or foil and store in a refrigerator or a cool larder. Alternatively store butter in the deep freeze, where it will keep for months.

To wash salt out

I frequently find some of the cheaper commercial butters are oversalted. By reversing the above procedure it is quite simple to remove excess salt. Chop up the butter, pat into smallish chunks, turn them into a bowl of cold water, squeeze with the hands for a moment or two, then run it under a cold tap to rinse. Press out most of the water as described above, shape and chill.

Carved moulds for shaping butter pats add a decorative and individual touch to butters. Traditionally, dairy farms had their own wooden butter stamp – a carved swan indicated the farm stood among watermeadows, a myrtle spray that it was a hill farm with richer milk, a cornsheaf that it was a mixed arable and dairy farm. Butter curlers come in a variety of shapes and materials: the elegant Parisien butter curler is made of boxwood and the modern butter curler of stainless steel and wood has a distinctive spade shape. Use them to enliven bought or home-made butters.

The dairy

Making salted butter

1. To make 450 g (1 lb) of butter, leave 1 litre (2 pints) thick cream in an earthenware bowl or panshon to 'ripen' at room temperature for anything up to 48 hours.

2. Tip the cream into a bowl, mixer or churn. If you are using a mixer, do not fill it more than half-full as the mixture will splatter, and set it at a low speed. Otherwise, churn slowly and steadily until the cream separates into butterfat and buttermilk.

3. Add a splash of cold water – no more than 300 ml ($\frac{1}{2}$ pint) at the point when the mixture separates into solids and liquid. Then churn on until the butter granules are about the size of barley grains.

4. Pour off the buttermilk into a bowl. It is excellent for making bread, scones and soda bread.

5. Add a cupful of cold water to the butter and churn on for a few seconds, to wash out any traces of buttermilk that can turn butter rancid if left.

6. Turn the butter into a fine sieve or muslin and leave in a cool place to firm and drain. The butter could be eaten now but ideally it should be

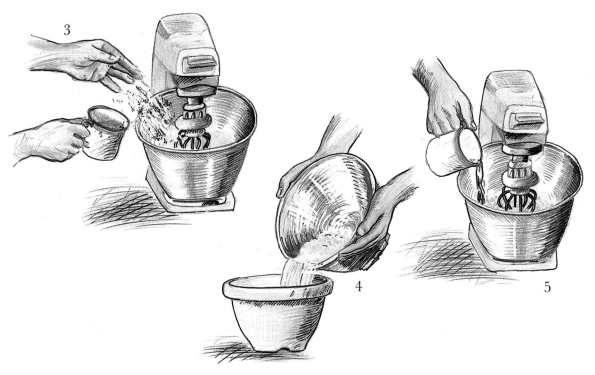

worked further to expel the last dregs of water.

7. Turn the drained butter onto a wet board and, using a wet, wooden spoon, spatula or wooden hands, pat it flat, squeezing it at the same time and tilting the board to help the water drain off.

8. Sprinkle 1 or 2 teaspoons of sea salt over the butter and pat it in, pressing and squeezing with your wooden implement.

9. Shape into pats, wrap in greaseproof paper or foil and store in a fridge or cool larder. Before freezing, I usually make up a few interesting flavoured butters to be used as spreads on grilled meats and fish as a substitute for a sauce. Butter will keep for months in a deep freeze.

When moulding butter, first place the softened butter in the carved wooden mould, making sure that the corners of the mould, spikes of the thistle, or whatever are filled, then freeze overnight. Leave the butter to thaw the next morning for about half an hour, then quickly run it under warm water, and ease it out of the mould with a round edged knife blade. Freeze the butter immediately, before the edges begin to soften, to keep the imprint of the mould sharp.

9

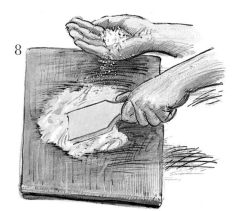

8

6

7

Butters

Here are a few interesting, flavoured butters which can be used as spreads on toast and crackers, or on grilled meat and fish where they substitute for a more elaborate sauce, and the recipe for clarified butter to seal cooked dishes.

Clarified butter or ghee

Ghee, or clarified butter, is a mainstay of Indian cooking and deserves to be more widely used in the West; it tastes rich and nutty, keeps up to a year in a cool place without going rancid, and can be heated to a higher temperature than any other frying medium (oil, lard, margarine) without catching and burning. One snag though – it is a butter concentrate and therefore expensive. I make a large jar and reserve it for frying rice for risotto or pulao, frying fritters and doughnuts. The classic Western use for clarified butter is as an edible airtight seal for the more elegant potted shellfish. Do not use it to cover a large pâté, or terrine, where melted lard is cheaper and as effective a seal. In India, tiny bowls of *ghee* and salt accompany every meal.

One kg (2 lb) of butter, preferably unsalted, yields a medium sized jar of *ghee*. A heavy, thick bottomed pan is essential to prevent the melted butter sticking during the long cooking. What happens during the cooking is that any moisture left in the butter evaporates, and any of the impurities that cause butter to burn, sink to the bottom of the pan.

To make *ghee*, put the butter in a heavy pan and melt it over a gentle heat. Keep it just below the simmering point for between forty minutes and an hour, or until you can see the sediment settling on the bottom. The *ghee* should be crystal clear. Line a conical sieve with clean muslin and pour off the *ghee* into a warmed jar (I use a bottling jar with a screwtop) leaving the sediment behind. *Ghee* is quite soft so you can scoop out what you need with a spoon. For a clarified butter seal, melt one or two tablespoons of *ghee* over a low heat and pour over your shrimps or whatever. Cover completely, excluding any air. Cool, then cover with a lid or foil and store in the fridge.

Green or Snail butter

Do not keep this garlic delight for the rare snail, but use it on grills, or steamed carrots and broad beans, or field mushrooms on toast.

3 to 4 cloves garlic
2¼ tablespoons finely chopped parsley
2 tablespoons finely chopped chives, chervil or tarragon
100 g (4 oz) butter
2½ teaspoons olive oil
salt and pepper to taste

Pound the garlic and herbs to a paste, or chop to a mush. Work into softened butter (not melted, but with the chill off), adding olive oil, herbs, seasonings to taste. Roll in foil and chill.

Anchovy butter

A basic fish and butter paste.

a handful fresh parsley
6 anchovy fillets
¼ clove garlic or 1 shallot
100 g (4 oz) unsalted butter
salt and black pepper
juice of ¼ a lemon

Simmer the parsley in a little water until limp, squeeze out the water. Pound to a paste with the anchovy fillets (wipe these first) and the finely chopped garlic or shallot. Mix the paste into the softened butter. Season to taste with salt, black pepper and lemon juice and chill before using.

Excellent with meat, potatoes, or as a spread.

Mushroom butter

A sumptuous and unusual sandwich spread.

100 g (4 oz) mushrooms
100 g (4 oz) butter
lemon juice, salt, pepper or cayenne

Cut off the dusty ends of the mushroom stalks but do not peel. Chop the mushrooms roughly, simmer in a little butter till just tender, about three or four minutes. Blend till smooth in a mixer or mortar with butter and seasonings to taste. Chill till just workable before use.

Tarragon butter
A way of storing fresh herbs throughout the winter to use with meat, fish and to glaze vegetables.

2 tablespoons fresh tarragon leaves
225 g (8 oz) butter
1 lemon
salt, and cayenne pepper

Chop the tarragon leaves very finely, and work them into the softened butter with the juice of a lemon, salt, pepper and a little cayenne. Either roll in foil or pack into jars, and freeze.

Mint butter
Mint butter is good with lamb, white fish, kippers, peas, carrots, new potatoes and small boiled beetroots.

100 g (4 oz) butter
2 tablespoons finely chopped mint
a pinch of salt, pepper and sugar

Work the chopped mint into the butter, mix well with sugar and seasonings, wrap and freeze.

Black olive butter
Black olives are best bought loose from a Greek grocer or delicatessen. If you have to use the sort packed in brine, wash them in a couple of changes of cold water to get rid of excess salt. Anyone who likes black olives will find this butter delicious with roast lamb, steak, plain pasta, toast or runner beans past their prime. I use olives and butter in roughly half and half proportions but this can be altered to suit your preferences and purse.

100 g (4 oz) black olives
a little finely chopped onion, garlic or shallot (optional)
100 g (4 oz) butter (unsalted if possible)
black pepper
juice of ½ a lemon

Stone the olives. Chop them coarsely with the onion, then either put them through the blender with the butter till smooth, or pound the mixture in a mortar. Add seasonings and the lemon juice.

Curry butter
Add an instant touch of exoticism to grills, sausages, fried fish, cheese biscuits and ham sandwiches with this butter.

2 teaspoons curry powder or paste
100 g (4 oz) butter
juice of ½ a lemon
a pinch of salt

Mix the powder or paste into the softened butter, add the lemon juice (a little more may be needed) and salt, to taste. Chill or freeze.

Cinnamon butter
The best and classic use for this is to make hot cinnamon toast. Nothing is easier, or more welcome on a cold winter afternoon. If you *can* use the whole stick ground, do, because cinnamon is a subtle spice and loses strength quickly when exposed to air.

75 g (3 oz) unsalted butter
3 teaspoons soft brown sugar
3 teaspoons ground cinnamon

Soften the butter and work in the sugar and spice – spread on hot toast, remove the crusts and stack in a pile to keep warm (this lets the spicy butter drip through). Cut into fingers just before serving.

Rum butter
This needs no introduction to British readers as it is the traditional accessory to Christmas pudding. Others might like to try it, less conventionally, with steamed puddings, mince and apple pies. The pudding should be hot, the butter cool but not rock hard.

225 g (8 oz) unsalted butter
450 g (1 lb) soft pale brown sugar
1 small glass rum
¼ teaspoon each powdered nutmeg and cinnamon

Blend or beat the butter till soft, then add the sugar and blend or beat till non-gritty. Add the rum and spices, mix well, spoon into small dishes and smooth the top. Chill slightly.

Cheese

'Half the white milk he curdled, and gathered it with speed
In baskets of woven wicker; and half in pails he stood,
Leaving it waiting ready to be his evening's food.'

The Odyssey   Homer

A noble cheese, like a fine wine, is an aristocrat and an individual. Both are made from the simplest ingredients, elaborated upon by man, time and nature, and the result is unique. A good cheese may be pungent, yet subtle, substantial but melting, rich but cleansing to the palate. Commercial ingenuity, backed up by technology, has reduced most of the mysteries of cheesemaking to a set of formulae, yet even now one element in the process – the effect of time – escapes analysis. Even cheese made according to a time tested recipe, salted, pressed and cured exactly as before, will, after a certain period of time, take on a character all its own.

Cheese is the best way to store perishable milk for any length of time; indeed, until refrigeration, the only way. In the days when most families kept a 'milch cow' cheesemaking was a regular part of the household routine and an excellent way of turning surplus milk into a compact, nourishing food which not only lasted through the winter months but actually improved with keeping. Working from instinct and commonsense, our ancestors came up with a concentrated food which contains more protein than meat, twice as much calcium as milk and vitamins A and B.

Cheesemaking is, and always was, by far the most challenging aspect of dairying. Women handed on family recipes to their daughters and the best regional cheeses became classic: Caerphilly, Gorgonzola, Gruyère, Roquefort. An outstandingly successful cheese could make your name and fortune. The celebrated Stilton, for example, is said to have been first made by a farmer's wife for her brother-in-law to serve to travellers stopping at his inn in the small market town of Stilton.

Cheese can be roughly classified as soft (Americans call these spoon cheeses, which is usefully vivid), semi-hard and hard. Cheesemaking is based on the principle that certain enzymes and acids can cause milk to coagulate, forming solid curds and liquid whey. The natural lactic acid producing bacteria in milk work on the protein 'casein' causing the milk to clot. Broadly, curds (clotted casein) provide the body of a cheese while acidity gives it flavour and helps to preserve it. The other element is moisture, or whey. Most soft cheeses should be eaten within a few days, semi-hard ones after a couple of months, while a really hard cheese – Parmesan leads the field – is matured for two years and more.

In the dairy, fresh raw milk in pails ready to be stirred with rennet and allowed to drip through a muslin bag for curd cheese, the small, shallow bowl of 'crowdie' or cottage cheese, and, foreground, four cream cheeses, including a herb cheese flavoured with parsley, chives and tarragon.

Soft cheese making

Making soft cheese is the process most likely to interest people who live miles from the nearest dairy farm. Master the terminology and it is childishly simple. It can be made from a range of commercial dairy products in a matter of hours and costs rather less home-made than the commercial equivalent. It is the obvious way to use up sour (but it must be non-pasteurized) milk or skimmed milk, from cream making. Eat it straight, or flavoured with herbs and spices to make 'dips' (popular with children), or use as a basis for lots of interesting and tasty dishes.

I am using the term 'soft cheese' to include all the quickly made, perishable mushy sort of cheeses made from drained curds: curd cheese, cottage cheese, cream cheese, lactic cheese, acid or immature cheese and so on and so forth. To a purist these distinctions are important but apart from slight variations in the making (dealt with in the recipes) and slight differences in flavour and texture, most of these soft cheeses are virtually interchangeable. The real criterion is expense and convenience, and few people would go to the extra trouble and expense of buying buttermilk or yogurt to make curd cheese, when ordinary milk will do just as well. If you must have cream cheese for cheesecake, and can afford the cream to make it, well and good. I have made cheesecake for years using cottage or sour milk cheese, and it is as tasty and cheaper though less rich.

Equipment
Most kitchens already have the necessary equipment except possibly for cheesecloth or muslin squares to drain the curds in (a clean napkin will do instead, or squares of well boiled old sheets) and junket rennet to set the milk with. You also need a sieve or colander to turn the curds into, somewhere to hang the bundle up while draining and something in the way of a small mould, perforated in most cases, to shape the cheese in if you are not eating it with a spoon. These can be bought from the classier sort of kitchenware shop, or improvised from little baskets, cartons with holes punched, or even made up at home from wheat or rye straw, or rushes roughly woven together as for the traditional 'rush cheese'. Straw mats are required for some of the recipes. All cheesemaking equipment must be kept scrupulously clean and sterilized lest the milk becomes tainted.

Ingredients
Soft cheese can be made from fresh or sour raw milk, fresh pasteurized milk, single or double cream, yogurt, buttermilk and skimmed milk. Raw milk and its by-products will sour and separate naturally, but slowly, to make curds. Pasteurized milk and its pasteurized products need help, from rennet or acid (lemon juice) and sometimes a 'starter' too. Pasteurized milk which is on the point of souring can be used – tasting will soon tell if it has reached the bitter stage and should be tipped down the sink. The Indian method of producing a firm curd cheese, using lemon juice to curdle the milk is used in many vegetarian Indian dishes which are among the best in the world. Panir, as it is called, has no special taste of its own but it absorbs spices and seasonings wonderfully, like all soft cheeses.

Making a sour raw milk soft cheese

1. For 225 g (8 oz) soft cheese, allow 1 litre (2 pints) fresh full cream milk to stand in a shallow earthenware pan or saucepan until a thick clout forms on top. To speed this process you can add a starter, such as commercial rennet or a tablespoon of yogurt, or buttermilk or sour milk.

2. Heat the soured milk gently in the top of a double boiler to separate the curds from the whey.

3. Turn the curds into a muslin-lined sieve or colander and hang the bundle up over a sink or bowl to allow the whey to drain off. Curds made by souring the milk naturally without heating it take longer to drain.

4. When the curd reaches the consistency you want, it can be turned out and eaten straight or mixed with a little cream or butter to make it richer. It can be salted and blended with chopped herbs to make a soft spreading cheese, and eaten within a few days.

To 'ripen' and flavour a soft cheese like crowdie that keeps in the fridge for 3 or 4 days wrap it in various leaves – dock or vine leaves, or spring's early nettle leaves before they become bitter and prickly.

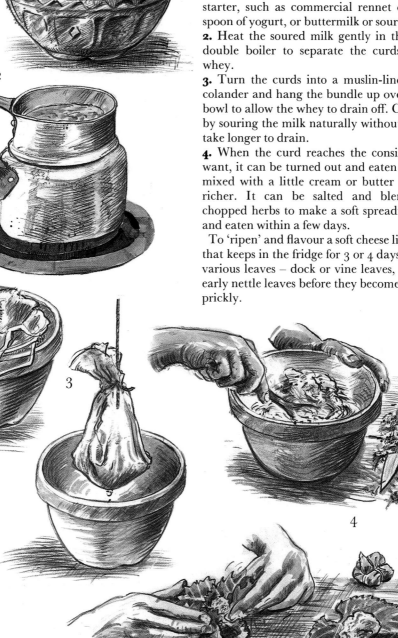

Soft cheeses

There are quickly made but perishable cheeses made from drained curds that should be eaten within a few days of making. Both 'raw' milk and pasteurized milk will make a perfect curded cheese without inconvenience or expense.

Crowdie
Crowdie is the Scottish term for cottage cheese. Still the best way of using up skimmed milk, but pasteurized whole milk can be used.

1 litre (2 pints) milk
1 junket (rennet) tablet

Heat the milk till tepid and add 1 junket tablet dissolved in water. Stir well, then leave in a warm place till set to a firm curd. This takes about two hours. With a long bladed knife, slice the curd across one way, then the other to make 2 cm/1 in cubes, spoon the cut curd over and cut the long pieces up into more cubes. Now heat the curd in its whey gently till warm, stirring. Leave to settle for a few minutes, then turn into a muslin bag and drain for a few hours. (The curd cutting is routine in hard cheesemaking and enables whey to drain freely off the curd.) Salt the crowdie lightly and mix in a little top of the milk to make it spread better. It will keep for several days in the fridge.
Note : if crowdie is mixed with butter in a ratio of 2 : 1, you have Cruddy butter which my old Scots cookbook tells me will keep for months in wooden moulds 'when it becomes very highly flavoured though mellow'.

Panir
An Indian firm curd cheese using lemon juice to curdle the milk.

1 litre (2 pints) whole milk, preferably Jersey milk
2 lemons (or 1 teaspoon powdered alum)

Bring the milk to the boil, remove from heat, stir in the lemon juice or alum, then return to the heat and stir till the curd separates cleanly from the whey. Turn into a muslin bag and drain for an hour or two. It can be cooked up in its crumbly state, with spices, or for some dishes, made firm enough to cut and fry, by pressing, in its muslin, under a weighted board overnight.

Cream cheese
Two recipes for cream cheese, one old and one modern. It is amusing to compare the casual authority of the old 'receipt' with the fussy detail of the modern one. Both work – but the old one needs non-pasteurized cream which has been left to ripen.

Old receipt
'Put a wet damask napkin on a marble or stone slab and pour on a mutchkin (600 ml/1 pint) of thick cream. Spread it out and leave to dry till next morning. Now put it into a small form in which a wet cloth has been laid and place a weight above – it will be ready by dinner time.'

Modern recipe
600 ml (1 pint) double cream
1 rennet tablet (or 1 teaspoon of liquid rennet)

Heat the cream in the top of a double boiler till warm, then add liquid rennet or a rennet tablet dissolved in cold milk. Stir, set aside in a warm place to curdle. Drain for 24 hours. Open the bag a few times to scrape the curd off the muslin and mix into the softer stuff inside. Changing the cloth once or twice will drain the cheese quicker. Add a little salt, mix and shape into a pat. This cream cheese will taste sweeter and last a little longer than the old recipe because it uses rennet.

Labna
A Middle Eastern soft cheese made with yogurt, inexpensive if you make your own. This is very simple to make, with a light, soft, creamy texture.

600 ml (1 pint) plain yogurt
½ teaspoon salt
paprika

Mix the yogurt with the salt, turn into muslin and drain overnight. Shape into little balls and roll in paprika.

Soft cheese dishes

Recipes that make use of the soft curd cheeses which, delicious though they are, cannot mature. Flavoured with herbs and spices, roasted with seeds, sweetened with honey, soft cheeses are the basis for many tasty dishes. Yield: 4 to 6 servings.

Herb cheese in sesame seeds
Easy to make, impressive to serve at a party.

225 g (8 oz) soft cheese
2 tablespoons top of milk
1 clove garlic
2 tablespoons chives
2 tablespoons parsley
1 tablespoon tarragon or fresh basil or mint
salt and pepper
4 tablespoons toasted sesame seeds

Blend or pound the cheese with the top of the milk till smooth. Add crushed garlic, very finely chopped herbs and salt and pepper to taste. Shape into a little cushion and chill till firm. Then roll in sesame seeds, toasted till aromatic over a gentle heat.

Cheese flan with eggs and mint
A surprising combination of cheese, cucumber, baked eggs and mint, to be eaten cold. Refreshing, but substantial enough to make a main lunch course with a tomato salad.

175 g (6 oz) shortcrust pastry
225 g (8 oz) crowdie
5 eggs
salt and pepper
a bunch of fresh mint
½ cucumber

Line a 20 cm (8 in) flan tin with shortcrust pastry, pricking it here and there. Beat the cheese till smooth with one whole egg. Season with salt, pepper and a little finely chopped mint. Pour this into the prepared flan tin. Cover with overlapping rings of very finely sliced cucumber. On top of this, gently break four eggs, one in each quarter. Dot with butter, sprinkle with more chopped mint and cover with a piece of buttered paper. Bake in a moderate oven (190°C, 375°F, Mark 5) for 30 to 40 minutes till the eggs are set and the pastry is golden.

Cheese dip
Make a large bowl for children's parties and give them crisps, carrot and celery sticks to dip.

450 g (1 lb) crowdie or cottage cheese
100 g (4 oz) plain yogurt
100 g (4 oz) single cream
a small bunch of spring onions
parsley and chives
½ cucumber
2 tablespoons horseradish sauce
salt and pepper

Blend the crowdie, the yogurt and the cream till smooth. Clean the spring onions, removing only the tough green tip, then chop finely with the herbs. Peel and dice the cucumber small. Stir the onion, horseradish sauce, herbs and cucumber into the cheese dip and season to taste. Serve cold.

Soft cheese quiche with bacon
A richer version of the standard bacon quiche and rather quicker to make.

100 g (4 oz) streaky bacon
175 g (6 oz) shortcrust pastry
2 eggs and one additional yolk
225 g (8 oz) crowdie, curd or cream cheese
4 tablespoons cream or yogurt
salt and pepper

Cut off bacon rind and fry till just crisp, cut into small pieces. Line a 20 cm (8 in) flan tin with shortcrust pastry, prick all over, dot with the bacon. Break the eggs into a bowl, reserving one white, and beat till smooth with the cheese and the cream. Salt and pepper well. Whisk the remaining egg white till fluffy, fold into cheese mixture, and pour into the prepared flan tin. Bake in a hot oven (204°C, 400°F, Mark 6) for 15 minutes then lower to 177°C (350°F, Mark 4) for a further 15 to 20 minutes, or till the top is puffed and golden brown.

The dairy

Spiced cheese loaf
A quite different approach from cheesecake, though using similar ingredients, the spiced sweetened soft cheese mixture is bulked out with breadcrumbs and has no pastry base.

225 g (8 oz) crowdie or curd cheese
3 egg yolks
25 g (1 oz) butter
4 tablespoons sugar
tiny pinch each ground cloves, nutmeg, cinnamon
¼ teaspoon vanilla essence
1 thick slice of stale white bread

Sieve or blend the cheese till smooth, and mix with beaten egg yolks, softened butter, sugar, spices and vanilla. Grate or grind the bread (minus crust) in an electric grinder into fine crumbs, then mix well with the cheese mixture. Pour into a well buttered glass or pottery oven or soufflé dish. Grate a little nutmeg over the top and bake for 45 minutes at 190°C (375°F, Mark 5). The loaf should be well risen and browned on top. Eat hot from the dish, or turn out when warm.

Peas and panir with tomatoes
Typical of the brilliant Indian vegetarian dishes, so spicy, tasty and colourful that one never regrets the absence of meat.

225 g (8 oz) fresh panir
4 tablespoons ghee or margarine
1 medium onion
1 teaspoon each ground turmeric and cumin
½ teaspoon ground dry chilies
225 g (8 oz) frozen peas
5 fresh tomatoes
a pinch of salt
chopped fresh coriander or basil

Make panir from 1 litre (2 pints) of full cream milk, drain but do not press. It should be crumbly, like dry scrambled egg. Melt the *ghee* or the margarine (less apt to burn than butter) in a heavy pan, fry the chopped onion till soft, then add the spices and fry till the spice smell is warm and rich – three minutes. Stir in the panir and cook gently, stirring for another two minutes. Add the peas (thawed and heated till tender,

then drained) and chopped, peeled tomatoes. Salt to taste. Cover the pan and simmer till the juice from the tomatoes is absorbed – this is a 'dry' dish. Sprinkle with chopped herbs and serve with rice or chapattis.

Moroccan egg and cheese pasties
Imjibinah, as these are called, are savoury egg and cheese stuffed pasties, fried or baked, then – for the daring – dipped into a spiced syrup. These savoury-sweet mixtures are typically Middle Eastern and very good.
   Use the Indian panir cheese as a base.

Cheese filling
1 onion
a small bunch of parsley
175 g (6 oz) panir cheese
4 hardboiled eggs
salt and pepper
2 teaspoons ground cinnamon

Pastry
100 g (4 oz) butter or margarine
225 g (8 oz) plain flour
a pinch of salt

For the filling, finely chop the onion and parsley together. Cut the panir (pressed overnight till firm) into small cubes. Chop the eggs roughly, then mix the cheese cubes, egg, chopped onion and parsley together with salt, pepper and ground cinnamon.
   For the pastry, work the chilled fat into the flour and salt, adding enough water to make a firm paste, roll out to make a thin – but not paper thin – sheet. Stamp out rounds approximately 12 cm (5 in) across (or cut into roughly equivalent squares) put a dollop of stuffing on each half, then fold over the other half and pinch shut. The *imjibinah* can either be fried in hot oil till golden brown (not all Moroccan households have ovens) or baked at 200°C (400°F, Mark 6) till the pastry is firm and golden brown.
   Make a syrup by heating together 225 g (8 oz) sugar, 150 ml (¼ pint) water and 1 stick of cinnamon, and simmering for a few minutes. Use tongs to dip the pasties into the boiling syrup for just long enough to soak them, then set aside on a plate. Eat hot, warm or cold.

Pashka

The traditional centrepiece to a Russian Easter-time celebration, this is a rich, sweetened cream cheese mixture – like an uncooked cheesecake filling. Uncooked pashka is finer and more delicate than cooked.

450 g (1 lb) home-made unsalted cream cheese
225 g (8 oz) unsalted butter
225 g (8 oz) castor sugar
4 egg yolks
1 teaspoon vanilla essence
100 g (4 oz) chopped lightly toasted almonds
100 g (4 oz) sultanas soaked in sherry

Sieve the cream cheese into a bowl. Cream the butter, sugar and egg yolks together till smooth, adding the vanilla essence. Now mix carefully and lightly with the cream cheese, fold in nuts and fruit. Pashka should be pyramid shaped – line a scalded flowerpot with muslin – pour in the cheese mixture, top with a small plate or saucer and a 1 kg (2 lb) weight. Leave for 24 hours to drain. Turn out and surround with garlands of tiny spring flowers.

Cheesecake with honey and biscuit-crumb base

A scented honey flavours soft cheese most delicately. This is a richer, creamier filling than the classic mixture, with a closer texture. The base is quicker and easier to make than pastry, and it does combine particularly well with cheesecake. Serve it unadorned – covering a cheesecake with cream cannot improve on a perfect formula.

Crumb base

225 g (8 oz) digestive biscuits
½ teaspoon cinnamon
50 g (2 oz) butter or margarine

Filling

225 g (8 oz) cream cheese
2 eggs
4 tablespoons thin cream, yogurt or top of milk
2 tablespoons sugar
1 teaspoon grated lemon rind
50 g (2 oz) sultanas and raisins
2 tablespoons honey

Crush the biscuits finely, add powdered cinnamon and melted butter, stir well, then press out to cover the base of a flan tin about 20 cm (8 in) in diameter. To make the filling, sieve cream cheese into a bowl and beat in eggs, yogurt (or cream), sugar, grated lemon rind, sultanas, raisins and honey. Bake in a moderate oven (190°C, 375°F, Mark 5) for 40 minutes. Leave to stand for 10 minutes in the oven with the heat off. The flavours improve with time – eat it 24 hours later if you can wait that long.

Classic sweet cheesecake

There are countless minor variations on the theme of sweetened, soft cheese bound with egg and studded with dried fruit, baked in a flan case. Some recipes call for a richer mix – cream cheese with added cream. It is all according to taste and your pocket. This is an old English recipe laced with a little optional liqueur.

225 g (8 oz) soft cream cheese or crowdie
2 eggs
175 g (6 oz) shortcrust pastry
50 g (2 oz) butter
100 g (4 oz) sugar
50 g (2 oz) ground almonds
1 lemon
50 g (2 oz) sultanas, currants or raisins
2 tablespoons brandy, rum or whisky
grated nutmeg

The soft cheese should be well drained, squeezed to remove as much moisture as possible then sieved, or blended, till smooth. Line a 20 cm (8 in) flan tin or case with the shortcrust pastry, pricking it here and there. Separate the eggs. Cream the butter with the sugar, till soft, then beat in egg yolks, ground almonds and the cheese. Add grated rind and juice of the lemon, and the dried fruit, soaked for a few minutes in the brandy, if you have time, to soften it. Whip the egg whites till fluffy, fold in the cheese mixture, then pour the lot into the flan case. Bake in a moderate oven (190°C, 375°F, Mark 5) for 40 minutes, or till well risen and firm to the touch. Look at it after 20 minutes – if it already looks golden brown, turn the heat down a notch for the rest of the cooking time. Sprinkle with grated nutmeg before serving.

Hard cheese

The making of semi-hard and hard cheese, once undertaken routinely in every household which kept a cow or goat, is obviously not beyond the capabilities of any sensible person. A sensible person, however, is not going to seriously consider investing time and money making something, however interesting and delicious, if it is cheaper to go out and buy a good commercial product. It takes 9 litres (2 gallons) of milk to make a small semi-hard cheese (750 g/1½ lb) and proportionately more to make a hard cheese. If you are buying your milk through the usual commercial channels that works out rather expensive. I should hate to discourage enthusiasm and enterprise, but I am sure cheesemaking on any serious scale only makes economic sense if you keep cows or goats, and must use up the surplus milk, or know a dairy farmer who will let you have milk at wholesale prices. If you burn to try your hand at cheesemaking, and have to use commercial milk, experiment modestly with simple curd cheeses like Mozzarella. These give more cheese per 600 ml (1 pint) of milk, are not complicated to make (no expensive equipment is needed) and make a mild cheese of delicate flavour if kept for a few days. Making a true hard cheese, of the calibre of Cheddar, Double Gloucester or Parmcsan, is probably beyond the scope of most non-specialists, even those with a dairy herd, because it really requires expensive equipment and a lot of attention.

Cheesemaking is a pleasant, sensuous process, right through from the cutting of the curd, white, shiny and sweet smelling, to the rather proud moment when the enticingly bouncy little cushion of cheese is brushed with a coat of melted lard and set on a cool shelf to cure. Having tried my hand at making a few cheeses for the purposes of this book I am now addicted, and making cheese regularly is going to become a part of my life. I hope readers will follow suit, because there is a great deal of forgotten expertise waiting to be rediscovered, and the more people are involved in sampling and experimenting, the more information will sift back, and the better cheeses we shall all be making.

The instructions may appear complicated, but once you have made your first cheese the unfamiliar terms will soon make good sense. If in doubt at any point, trust your instinct – people once made superb cheese without the help of thermometers, special 'starter' cultures, or stainless steel presses, and I am sure instinct, which I will define as intuition plus commonsense, was their most useful piece of equipment.

All cheesemaking equipment should be clean, not hospital sterile maybe but super clean. The wrong bacteria, traces of detergent, smell of bleach can all taint a young cheese as ripening curd is extraordinarily absorbent. Wash all equipment first in cool water, then scald, then rinse in hot and set it in the sun or wind if you can to dry off. This applies to shelves where cheeses sit, as well as the things you make them with. Do not make bread, beer or wine in the same room simultaneously. Having said that, relax – cheesemaking should not be intimidating.

Two of the author's cheeses made at home: a Coulommier semi-hard cheese moulded till firm, rubbed with salt and ripened for two weeks in a cool dark room (left) and a mild simple cheese wrapped in muslin, pressed till smooth and solid, then sealed with melted lard (right).

Hard cheese making

Equipment

For the simpler, semi-hard cheeses equipment can be improvised. The most important item is some sort of arrangement for pressing the cheese. Pressure on the moist curds needs to be steady, all around, and adjustable, so it can be increased to force out more and more whey. I use a meat press, a simple kitchen gadget. A home-made press can be improvised with a couple of thick boards (non-resinous hardwood is best) and 2 lengths of dowel. The upper board slides down the dowel uprights, securely bedded down in holes drilled through the base. Pressure is supplied by bricks, or kitchen weights, piled on the top board.

The next requirement is moulds to contain the curd during pressing. A cake tin with detachable bottom is a good improvised mould but a coffee tin with the bottom cut out can make a mould for a smaller cheese. Each mould needs a 'follower' i.e. a rigid disc of wood, metal, even stout plastic, cut to the inside diameter of the mould and deep enough to be driven down inside the mould onto the curds by whatever type of pressure you are using. The cake tin base illustrates the principle perfectly. Also needed is a spare tin or other cylindrical object to stand on top of the follower and supply necessary pressure.

Other equipment needed: a large enough container to hold the milk, and an even bigger one to put the milk container in for scalding. A 9 to 11 litre (2 to $2\frac{1}{2}$ gallon) plastic bucket and big preserving pan or old fashioned boiler will serve. A thermometer. Muslin or cheesecloth squares, for draining, wrapping and storing. A long, sharp, stainless steel knife for cutting the curd, a slotted frying slice or thin saucer for skimming, a wooden spoon for stirring and a ladle for ladling.
Note: All cheesemaking equipment should be kept as clean as possible. The wrong bacteria, traces of detergent or the smell of bleach can all taint a young cheese.

Rennet and starter cultures

Diluted cheese rennet is added to the milk to coagulate the curd. Cheese rennet is available from specialist shops in liquid or tablet form. Buy the smallest size bottles as liquid rennet loses strength gradually. Junket rennet is not strong enough for hard cheese-making.

For some recipes a 'starter' (available by post from specialist shops in frozen or dried form) is required. A starter is not essential in cheese made from raw milk, and can make it too acid, but it is essential with cheese made from pasteurized milk. Briefly, what it does is encourage lactic acid production in the milk – this compares with using a yeast nutrient to get a healthy ferment started in wine or beer. Or substitute a home-made starter of a spoonful of yogurt, sour raw milk, or buttermilk. Add it to the fresh milk a few hours before cheesemaking or as stated in the recipe. Raw milk is unpasteurized. If you are in any doubt about the cleanliness of your milk, pasteurize it. To do this, stand the milk bucket in a bath of boiling water. Raise the temperature of the milk as quickly as possible to 73°C (163°F) stirring constantly. Maintain this temperature for fifteen seconds then cool the milk as quickly as possible to 4°C (40°F) by standing the milk bucket in iced water.

Ripening

The milk, bought fresh from a farm, or brought in straight from the evening milking needs ripening first. This means warming the milk slightly, and leaving it to sit for a while to encourage lactic acid bacteria. Before doing this, however, skim off any cream which may have risen to the top, warm it to around 29°C (85°F) and stir it back into the milk. This is important otherwise it may not set with the rest of the milk and the cheese will lack valuable fat. Leave for an hour. Now set the milk bucket in a large pan of hot water, set that on the cooker, and gently raise the temperature to 32°C (90°F) (or 29°C/85°F for goat's milk). If you are adding a starter, put it in now. Remove the bucket from the hot water and leave the milk covered for an hour.

Renneting

Use cheese rennet in a ratio of 1 teaspoon to 9 litres (2 gallons) of milk. Dilute it in three or four parts cold, boiled water, add to the milk and stir with a long handled spoon which reaches the bottom of the bucket, for 1 minute. Then top-stir (stir just the top 12 mm ($\frac{1}{2}$ in) or so) until the milk begins to form a curd. Top stirring stops the cream from rising to the top which makes a 'thin' cheese. Or stir the milk around with your hand, keeping the milk moving till it begins to set and cling to your fingers. Then 'top stir' or stroke the emerging curd gently for a few minutes to send the cream down. As the renneted curd turns the milk stiffens dramatically.

Now leave the curd to set solid in ten minutes or less. If it takes much longer you may have to scald longer so note the time taken. Cover the curd and leave. When the back of a finger pressed into it causes a clean split, with no curd sticking to the finger, it is ready – after 45 minutes. Do not hurry this part – too short a time means the rennet has not coagulated all the solids in the milk which means a smaller cheese.

How to cut the curd

When you do this you will find it by no means easy – the curd spins round in its curd bath while you cut. Remember, however, that you are simply trying to reduce the curd to small even fragments, and relax. Spoon the curd over gently when you have done your best with the old slashing technique, and cut any large lumps.

Scalding

To scald means simply warming (not usually to much beyond 38°C/100°F) the cut curd very gradually, meanwhile stirring it by hand or with a spoon. Keeping the bucket in a pan of hot water on the stove is one method, but difficult to control. Otherwise stand the bucket in the sink filled with hot water. The third method is to ladle out whey into a pan, heat that, tip it back and stir. Check repeatedly with the thermometer. The effect of this scalding is to firm and separate the curds. Instead of the voluptuously yielding texture of renneted curd the milk has become rubbery.

Pitching

Pitching means that the scalded curd is left to settle and soak. The time for this varies.

Milling

Break up the sturdy fragments of curd into little bits by hand. This is not difficult, indeed rather delightful, but it takes longer than you might expect. Ladle the morsels with a slotted spoon or slice (to let the whey drip off) into the muslin lined mould which is standing ready. Now salt it.

Salting

Use natural flake or sea salt if possible. Add salt at the specified rate, mix in thoroughly with both hands. Now wrap the bundle of curds tenderly in its muslin square, squeezing a little with both hands to help any excess whey drain off, and smoothing the muslin as much as is feasible. Put the cheese into the press.

Pressing

For the first press tighten the screw, or pile on bricks, till a good bit of whey can be seen oozing up round the sides of the mould. The mould should stand on something which helps the whey drain freely: a clean, scalded straw mat, or grooved bread board. Stand the whole press over something to catch the overflowing whey. Do not squeeze so hard the soft curd starts being forced up round the rim of the follower. Leave to stand under this pressure for the prescribed time. Then remove the cheese – by now firm enough to handle – change the cloth, replace and increase the pressure. This process can be repeated many times, but for the average semi-hard cheese, two or three turns of the screw, plus changes of the wrapper should be enough. Scald your mat or board as often as you can, to prevent them smelling 'off'. When sufficiently pressed for your purposes, unwrap the cheese and seal it for storing.

Sealing or covering

The simplest method of sealing is to dip the cheese in hot whey or water for just long enough to cool the outer skin and form an airtight rind, about one minute is usual. Alternatively brush it over with melted lard or paraffin wax. Some cheeses do not need to be sealed, but if they are to be matured for any length of time it is a useful protection. In country districts, leaves (nettle, dock, vine, nut tree) were tied on with string and changed regularly. Alternatively, cover the cheese with a muslin or cheesecloth wrapper and paint over this with melted lard.

Storing or maturing

A young cheese fresh from the press tastes of nothing much, though it has a pleasant clean texture. After a few days you will begin to notice a faintly cheesy odour. The longer this goes on, the more powerful and yet richly complex your cheese will taste. Store cheeses in cool dry places. Turn them frequently to begin with, two or three times a day in summer, once a day in winter – not to air them so much as to prevent the fat content settling to one side. Brush off any mould that forms. After some time the cheese wrapping will feel dry and taut, and the cheese will have a distinct though delicate 'bouquet'. Eat it when you cannot wait any longer.

Making a simple semi-hard cheese

1. Take 13 litres (3 gallons) of raw, fresh milk. First skim off the cream and warm this to 29°C (85°F), then stir it into the milk in a bucket. Leave for 1 hour.

2. Set the milk bucket in a large pan of hot water on a cooker and gently raise the heat to 38°C (100°F). Then add 4 tablespoons of plain yogurt.

3. Remove the bucket from the hot water and leave the milk, covered, for 1 hour.

4. Stir in 2 teaspoons of rennet diluted in 8 teaspoons of boiled water. Stir thoroughly for 2 minutes. Leave for 1 hour till the curd forms a solid mass from top to bottom.

5. Top stir the mix (just the top 1 cm/$\frac{1}{2}$ in) till the milk forms a curd. Cover and leave for 45 minutes until a finger pressed into it causes a clean split, with no curd sticking to the finger.

6. Cut the mass from left to right, top to bottom then diagonally both ways into small even fragments. Spoon the curd over, cutting any long piece into dice.

7. Warm the curd to 38°C (100°F) – check with a thermometer – by standing in a sink of hot water. This drives out more whey.

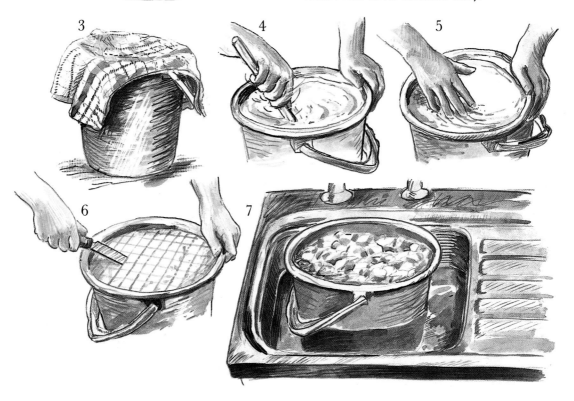

8. After the scalded curd has pitched (settled and soaked) for 30 minutes, break up the sturdy curds by hand into small pieces.

9. Ladle the morsels with a slotted spoon into a muslin lined mould to let the whey drip.

10. Mix in 1 tablespoon sea salt.

11. Wrap up the bundle of curds in the muslin square, squeezing out the whey a little. Smooth the muslin and stand the mould on a scalded straw mat to allow the whey to drain freely.

12. Press the cheese under a weight, not so hard that the soft curd is forced up round the follower rim. Turn the cheese, changing the cloths 2 or 3 times. Gradually increase the pressure every day till the cheese looks smooth and feels solid. Then lower the cheese in its muslin bag into water heated to 71°C (160°F) for 1 minute to form a skin.

13. Cut two rounds of muslin to fit top and bottom and bandage the side. Stitch round to hold the shape, brush with melted lard and turn daily till the cover is dry. Store in a cool place and turn twice daily. It can be eaten after 1 month but gains flavour if kept longer.

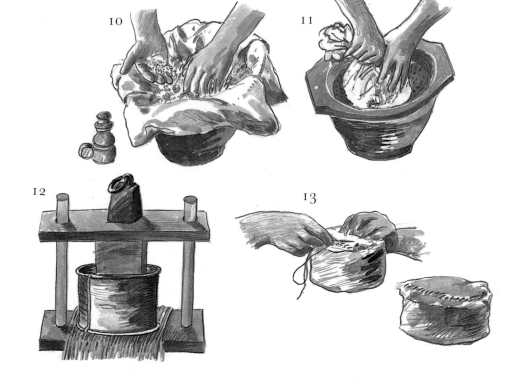

Semi-hard and hard cheeses

Now that you have familiarized yourself with the technical terms, try your hand at one or all of the following semi-hard cheeses. Basically, the more whey that is pressed out, the harder the cheese and the longer it keeps.

Pressed and cured crowdie

This is a good cheese to try first as it is the next step on from cottage cheese or crowdie. Make a large batch from skimmed milk if you are taking the cream off your own milk.

1½ kg (3 lb) crowdie or cottage cheese
3 tablespoons sea salt

Mix the salt with the cottage cheese, turn into muslin and fit into a small mould. Put the follower in place on top and press till the whey oozes out visibly. Leave under pressure till the next day, then replace the cloth, and increase the pressure slightly. Repeat daily till the cheese coheres, and feels solid, with a smooth outer surface. Then lower the cheese, in its muslin bag, into water heated to 71°C (160°F) for one minute. This forms a thin skin, the basis for a healthy protective rind. Cut two rounds of muslin to fit top and bottom and bandage the side. Now brush the whole cheese with melted lard or paraffin wax. Store on a cool shelf, and turn daily till the outer cover feels quite dry. Then turn once a week, and eat after a month.

Coulommier

The most interesting thing about Coulommier – a semi-hard cheese – is that the renneted or 'set' curd is not heated but ladled straight into the special two part mould. Make your mould with two identical sized tins – about 15 cm (6 in) across and 10 cm (4 in) deep. Cut out bottoms, put together and sellotape.

4 litres (1 gallon) milk
½ teaspoon cheese starter
1 teaspoon rennet

Heat the milk to 32°C (90°F). Add the starter and leave for 10 minutes, covered. Add the rennet (diluted in eight teaspoons of boiled water) to the mixture and stir well. Top stir the mixture for ten minutes to prevent the cream

from rising. As soon as the milk starts to clot you should cover it and keep it in a warm place for one to two and a half hours or until the curd breaks evenly over your knife.

When the curd has sunk to the lower half of the mould (in a few hours) remove the top. Place a mat and board on top of the mould and carefully invert. Gently take away the straw mat, which may stick a little. Scrub the board and mat. Turn the cheese twice a day for the next two days. Keep the cheese in a room with a constant temperature, preferably 18°–21°C (65°–70°F).

When the cheese is firm, rub the surface with salt. Keep in the refrigerator until the next day when it will be ready to eat.

If you wish to ripen the cheese, keep it in an airy, dry room for a few days. Then leave it to ripen in a cool, dark room for two to three weeks, turning it daily. If any light mould develops, wipe it off with a cloth.

A stronger, mellow cheese will result.

Cantal

A hard, sharp-flavoured cheese.

13 litres (3 gallons) fresh, raw milk
4 tablespoons plain yogurt as a starter
2 teaspoons rennet
3 tablespoons sea salt

Make the cheese exactly as for the semi-hard cheese on pages 107 and 109 until you have pressed the curd under 13 kg (30 lb) of pressure till firm. Now remove it, unwrap and leave at room temperature for a day. Break it into small pieces by hand and work in two tablespoons of sea salt. Knead well, put back into muslin and press for another two days. Now unwrap, wipe with a clean cloth and wash in hot water for a firm rind. Keep in a dry place, turn and wipe daily till a rind starts to form. Cure for at least three months, washing every four days by dipping into salt water – four tablespoons of salt to 900 ml (1½ pints) water.

Mozzarella

Easy to make, it can be eaten at once or used as a layer on pizzas because it melts well.

9 litres (2 gallons) fresh raw milk
4 tablespoons plain yogurt as a starter
1 teaspoon rennet
1 tablespoon sea salt

Heat the milk to 30°C (86°F), add a cupful of yogurt or 'starter' and leave in a warm place overnight. Add the rennet (already diluted in four teaspoons of cooled, boiled water) and stir hard for 2 minutes. Cover the bucket and leave for 45 minutes till the curds are well set. Now, instead of cutting the curd, break it up into small pieces by hand. Heat slowly till the mixture is as hot as you can bear, then stir continuously, crumbling the curds till they 'squeak'. Tip the curds and all into a muslin lined colander over a bowl and drain till fairly dry. Keep the whey. Now whip away the muslin and shake and tilt to remove dry excess whey. Work with butter hands (wooden paddles) till cool – about 32°C (90°F) then add 1 tablespoon of sea salt and mix it in thoroughly. Cool further then ladle into a muslin lined mould and press. Increase the pressure over the next hour or two to 13 kg (30 lb) starting with a 5 kg (10 lb) weight. It should now be solid enough to handle. Put the cheese into whey pre-heated to 82°C (180°F). Remove from the heat and leave the mozzarella in the whey till cool. Then drain, on a straw mat, for 24 hours.

Feta

Feta is a slightly salty, fresh tasting, crumbly, Greek goat's milk cheese.

9 litres (2 gallons) goat's milk
4 tablespoons plain yogurt as a starter
2 teaspoons rennet
2 tablespoons salt

Warm the milk to 30°C (86°F), add the yogurt and stir well. Cover and set in a warm place for several hours or overnight. Now add 2 teaspoons of rennet (already diluted in 8 teaspoons of cooled, boiled water). Stir for 2 minutes to mix in the rennet. Let it stand undisturbed for 30 to 45 minutes, till the milk has coagulated. If the curd splits evenly over the finger it is ready to be cut. Make 3 cm (1 in) sized cubes by slicing the curd every way with a long bladed knife. Break up any oversized lumps by hand. Heat the curd, in the whey, slowly and gradually bringing the temperature up to 35°C (95°F) (this will take about 30 minutes). Hold at this temperature and stir gently till the curd firms. Pour the curds and whey into a cheesecloth bag and hang for 48 hours to drip till the cheese is firm. Feta is not pressed. Remove the cheesecloth, slice the curd, sprinkle with 2 tablespoons of salt and work in well by hand. Return the curd to the remaining whey. Leave for 24 hours. Pat the cheese with a clean cloth and put it on a scrubbed board to form a rind. It is ready to eat in 3 or 4 days.

Caerphilly

A fine sharp-but-mild cheese.

13 litres (3 gallons) fresh milk
180 ml (6 fl oz) cheese starter
1¼ teaspoons rennet
sea salt

Heat the milk to lukewarm, add the starter then cover and leave to ripen for an hour. Add the rennet (already diluted in six teaspoons of water), stir hard for one minute then top stir till the curds start to form. Cut the curd as before. Heat quickly to 33°C (92°F) and keep the curd at this heat for 40 minutes, stirring constantly. To test if the curd is firm enough, press your hand onto the top – the impression should linger. If not stir on. Leave the curd to 'pitch' in the whey for five minutes, then tip the bucket and pour off as much whey as you can. Leave the bucket on its side, and after five minutes pour off any more whey if possible. Cut the curd into cubes and again tilt off any free whey. Keep turning the curd. After ten minutes break it up small and add 25 g (1 oz) of sea salt per 2 kg (4 lb) curd. Pack the curd into a mould lined with a damp cloth and press lightly with a 2 kg (4 lb) weight. Remove after ten minutes, turn and double the weight. Repeat twice more, stepping up the pressure each time, then leave under 9 kg (20 lb) pressure for a day. Take out, unwrap, dry with a clean cloth, bandage and brush with melted lard. Ripen for two weeks or more, turning daily.

Cooking with hard cheese

Hard cheese is so concentrated in flavour that a little goes a long way. Cheese is best cooked either with a little starch – mustard, flour, potato – to stop the fat separating and hardening, or with something acid to cut the richness, like wine or shallots.

Gougère

Cooked cheese dishes seem to be either tricky or absurdly easy. This is a tricky one, a great golden puffy ring of choux paste studded with cheese, which is a smashing accompaniment to red wine and so no surprise that it should be a Burgundian speciality. The choux paste is no problem but the oven heat must be just right. However, the combination is so delicious that I am happy to eat a gougère which has gone flat.

300 ml (½ pint) water
50 g (2 oz) butter
salt and pepper
100 g (4 oz) sifted, plain flour
4 eggs
100 g (4 oz) Gruyère or home-made semi-hard cheese
1 tablespoon milk

Do not be alarmed at the prospect of making a choux paste; it requires chiefly a strong right arm.

In a heavy pan bring water, butter and salt to the boil and stir to disperse the butter. Remove from heat, and beat the sifted flour in all at once, to make a sticky yellow lump. Return to a very gentle heat and beat your paste hard for as long as you can bear – 5 to 15 minutes. Remove from heat. Beat in the eggs one at a time, incorporating each one thoroughly before adding the next. By now the paste should be smooth, shiny and fluid enough to stir. Cut the cheese into tiny dice, reserving one spoonful, and stir the remainder into the paste. Grease a baking sheet. Set the oven to 200°C (400°F, Mark 6). Spoon the paste onto your sheet to make a ring shape, building it as high as need be to use up the paste. Brush with milk, sprinkle remaining spoonful of cheese on top and cook in the middle of the oven for 45 minutes. Resist peering in during that time or the gougère – sensitive to temperature changes – may collapse. A very gentle and cautious look after 40 minutes is allowable – it is ready when firm to the touch. Rush to the table, shielded from draughts and eat immediately.

Aligot

An interesting, easily made regional French dish, combining mashed potatoes, cheese, cream and butter, scented with a little garlic. The French use a local semi-soft white cheese which melts easily but I use a home-made Caerphilly or a pressed crowdie cheese. This is very filling.

1 kg (2 lb) floury white potatoes
50 g (2 oz) butter
1 large clove garlic
225 g (8 oz) Caerphilly or crowdie
150 ml (¼ pint) single cream
salt and pepper

Boil the potatoes in their skins, peel and sieve to make a dry purée or mash. Melt the butter in a large heavy pan, heat the crushed garlic in it for 1 minute (uncooked garlic spoils these dishes) then add purée, cream and stir till mixed. Chop or grate the cheese small, then add. Stir till the cheese melts and the mixture becomes thick and smooth, season to taste, and serve at once.

Courgettes au gratin

A vegetable gratin is a mixture of lightly pre-cooked vegetables, usually chopped fairly small and baked in a cheesy custard mixture till firm.

225 g (8 oz) small courgettes
75 g (3 oz) grated cheese
salt, pepper and grated nutmeg
300 ml (½ pint) béchamel sauce
2 eggs

Steam the courgettes till just tender, then chop them up finely, skins as well. Mix the grated cheese and seasonings into the hot béchamel sauce, stir for a minute or two, then add the well-beaten eggs and chopped courgettes. Mix, turn into a buttered dish, strew the top with grated cheese and bake in a moderate oven (180°C, 350°F, Mark 4) standing in a pan with a little water for 45 minutes, or till set.

Fondue

One of the best cooked cheese dishes, and best kept simple. The most superior fondue is nothing but plenty of Gruyère melted with Riesling, Kirsch and bound with a pinch of cornflour (note: acid plus starch) and maybe a nut of butter.

Classic Swiss fondue

Allow approximately 100 g (4 oz) Gruyère, half a glass of Riesling and 2 tablespoons of Kirsch per person. One tablespoon cornflour and 25 g (1 oz) butter are stirred in to thicken. Fondue should be cooked in a special dish – shallow earthenware – over a small spirit lamp stove at the table, and everyone dips their French bread or squares of toast into the communal dish, washing it down with more Riesling.

Rub the dish round with a cut garlic clove. Set grated cheese and wine to heat slowly over a spirit lamp, stirring till they combine to make a thick mixture. Mix the cornflour separately with the Kirsch, stir it in, and continue stirring till it thickens. Add the butter, stir till melted and eat at once.

Note: Add more wine if too thick.

Poor man's fondue

A tasty, if coarser, fondue can be concocted with various odds and ends of cheese, soft as well as hard, stretched with a few eggs. Use any dryish white wine and a little mustard and skip the Kirsch.

1 clove garlic
1 glass white wine
100 g (4 oz) grated cheese
1 teaspoon dry mustard or German mustard
salt and pepper
4 eggs
50 g (2 oz) butter

This is best made in a double boiler, so the eggs do not set, but it must be stirred constantly. Crush the garlic and place with the wine in the top half of the pan. Heat, add grated cheese, mustard, salt and pepper and stir till thick. Add well beaten eggs, and butter and go on stirring for 7 or 8 minutes, till smooth and thick. Eat at once.

Potted cheese

A delicious spread for crackers, sandwiches and savoury toasts (that nice Edwardian bachelor indulgence) which can be made from stale odds and ends of cheese. Use a pungent cheese for preference. It will keep for ages, sealed with clarified butter or lard.

450 g (1 lb) cheese
100 g (4 oz) butter
1 small glass sherry, port or brandy
½ teaspoon of grated nutmeg
a pinch of mustard powder or curry powder (optional)

Pound the cheese (remove hard rinds), butter, sherry and seasonings in a mortar, or blend in a mixer. When smooth pack down into little jars or pots, seal the top with melted clarified butter or lard and cover with waxed paper and string. Store in a cool place.

Cheese soufflé

A well made cheese soufflé manages to be light and firm yet slightly creamy all at once. With garlic bread and a good salad you have a quick, cheap and attractive lunch.

25 g (1 oz) butter
1 level tablespoon flour
150 ml (¼ pint) milk
3 eggs plus one additional egg white
salt, pepper, mustard and cayenne
100 g (4 oz) grated cheese (Cheddar will do)

Butter the soufflé dish or ramekins. Melt the butter in a pan, stir in the flour, add hot milk and stir till smooth and thick. Separate the eggs. Stir in the well whisked egg yolks, mustard, grated cheese, salt and pepper and keep stirring over a gentle heat till smooth. Whip the whites till fluffy and firm, but not 'rocky', and fold into the soufflé base. Turn into a dish or dishes and bake in a hot oven (200°C, 400°F, Mark 6) till well risen, firm and golden brown on top. This will take 8 minutes for small, individual soufflés and 20 minutes for a large one. Reassure yourself with a squint into the oven towards the end of cooking time, but open and close the door as stealthily as a burglar. Eat at once, with a dusting of cayenne pepper on top.

Fish

Keeping the catch

The sea is generally held to be the cradle of life on this planet. Covering as it does three-quarters of the earth's surface, it offers by far the largest reservoir of wild food at our disposal, though as the declining whales sadly illustrate, its riches are not inexhaustible. While overfishing is a real danger, other and stranger phenomena can affect fish distribution – submarine waves, shifting currents, climatic changes – and these can redirect marine traffic with disastrous consequences, as was the case with the Baltic herring fisheries in the Middle Ages. However, give or take the odd tidal wave or cod war, the source has always been pretty reliable.

Fish is an excellent food for man, rich in high grade protein, vitamins (A, D, and E especially) and in minerals, as one would expect in sea creatures. Fatty fish – like herring, or mackerel – are also rich in polyunsaturates which inhibit cholesterol formation. Pound for pound, fish offers more meat and less waste than animal meat. Easily digested, it is a classic item in an invalid diet. Best of all, from the cook's point of view, fish in prime condition is delicious eating, as good quickly grilled and served with a knob of herb butter as treated with all the pomp and ceremony of *haute cuisine*.

The bulk of fish eaten throughout the world comes from three main groups: the herring group, including pilchards, anchovies, sprats, sardines and whitebait; the cod fishes, pollack, hake, haddock, whiting and coley, as well as Atlantic cod (four million tons of cod are taken annually); and the mackerel and tuna family. Thanks to advanced equipment which allows fish to be kept frozen, or chilled on ice, from capture to point of sale, more fresh fish is eaten today than ever before – in some parts of the world fish accounts for a fifth of people's annual animal protein intake. To replace this with land animal protein would require half as much land again as is now under cultivation, an impossibility which gives some idea of the importance of fish as a food.

Early man looked to the sea for some of his first instant meals, finding molluscs on the shore and, it seems, even venturing out to sea to fish, as he has continued to do, at some risk and much profit, throughout history. In the days before refrigeration and rapid transport, fresh fish must have been a rare item of diet unless you lived on or near the coast, or had access to inland waters. Big houses and monasteries went to the lengths of creating fish ponds, stocked with freshwater fish, which were netted periodically and the fish transferred to 'stews' – similar to the tanks used in some European fish restaurants – where they were kept alive until required. However most people would have eaten their Friday and fast-day fish preserved by one or other of the traditional methods – dried, dried and salted, pickle-cured (in brine, not vinegar by the way) in barrels, or pickle-cured and then smoked for as long as three weeks. Pickle-cured and smoked red herrings, mahogany coloured and dry as a chip, would be far too salty for modern tastes but they kept safely for years.

All these methods seem to have been in use since earliest times. The method chosen would probably have been determined by the type of fish – lean fish, such as cod and whiting, were most efficiently and cheaply preserved simply by drying, or salting and drying. Salt cod or stockfish (dried cod) was a staple food for centuries, despite the fact that it needed lengthy soaking and careful cooking to make it palatable. Since harmful micro-organisms require moisture to multiply, thoroughly drying fish – or anything else – is a sure way of preserving it. Salt, by extracting the natural fluid in the fish, helps speed up the process, as well as acting as a powerful preservative in itself. Fatty fish such as herrings, however, are turned rancid by drying, unless the fish are heavily smoked as well. Traditionally the way to preserve oily fish such as herring was to pack them in brine in airtight barrels; they kept well enough this way to be exported overseas.

Smoking, unless prolonged and intense, as it was with the red herrings where it acted as an anti-oxidant to prevent the herring going rancid, is a mild preservative, allowing fish to be kept for only a few days. If you own a deep freeze, the most practical proposition is to store the bulk of your fish in the freezer, smoking only for immediate use. And remember that all cool smoked fish must be cooked before eating, since cool smoking itself is not enough to kill harmful bacteria.

However, the success then, as now, of the final preserved product stemmed to an enormous extent from the freshness of the original articles, for freshness with fish is everything. Perfectly fresh fish, as any fisherman knows, is sweet tasting with a firm, flaky texture, and no 'fishy' smell. Though eating fish straight from the water is a rare treat for most people, there is no good reason – given today's refrigeration techniques – why we should not all be able to buy the next best thing, which is fish held at temperatures low enough to prevent deterioration throughout its journey from fishing ground to fishmonger's slab.

Where fish have been rapidly and conscientiously 'processed' (chilled or frozen immediately, gutted in some cases, packed and transported in cold storage), the results, say the experts, are virtually indistinguishable from the fish which leapt straight from the water into your frying pan – a point you might like to raise with your fishmonger next time you are offered the flaccid, bleary-eyed specimens too often displayed for sale.

If everyone knew exactly how to tell fresh fish from stale, fishmongers would be prevented from offering the latter up for sale. Look fish in the eyes: these should be clear, bright and bulging – sunken, bloodshot eyes are a giveaway. Gills should be bright red – bleached or brownish gills denote staleness. The flesh should be firm, tight-skinned and springy – a fresh mackerel, as one authority vividly puts it, should be 'cool and firm as a cucumber'.

Stale fish tend to be limp, the skin loose and slimy. Stale fillets – usually cod or haddock – can be spotted by brownish red discoloration along the fillet in line with the backbone; in steaks this radiates out from the centre bone. Really fresh fish has no unpleasant smell.

Fish caught in local waters, however unfamiliar, are often more rewarding than those which may have spent days *en route* to your shop. Conger eel for instance has dense, sweet white meat. Spider crab legs are a nuisance to prepare but tastier than the ordinary crab meat. Bream, grey mullet and John Dory are all excellent eating when fresh.

Preparing fish

Fishmongers will of course clean and fillet fish for you, but it is sensible to know how to go about it yourself. Provided you have sharp knives and plenty of newspaper, cleaning and filleting is not the gory ordeal pictured by squeamish souls. I suggest you wear rubber gloves, not just to make you feel braver, but because fish scales can be surprisingly sharp.

Equipment
A short, sharp, pointed knife for gutting, removing the gills and head, and a bluntish blade for scaling are both essential. A small stiff brush is useful for cleaning out the gut cavity thoroughly. Professionals, dealing with masses of fish, keep a trough of clean water handy to rinse fish and knife as they proceed. For domestic purposes a bowl of cold water should be adequate, or the sink, but make sure you do not block up the outlet with scales. Kitchen paper is handy for a final wipe over, and newspaper for wrapping up the guts (burn these where possible).

Scaling
1. This is the first step in preparing a fish. Holding the fish firmly by the tail and using your blunt blade, scrape vigorously up towards the head – against the grain as it were – trying not to break the skin. With most fish this dislodges the scales quite easily. Some, like grey mullet, have tougher scales which need really energetic scraping. Wipe and rinse both the knife and fish as needed. When the skin is sleek, the fish is done. Don't ever be tempted to skimp scaling. Loose scales will get inextricably mingled with the fish or sauce in cooking, and they are not nice to eat.

Gutting and cleaning
2. Leave the head on, to use as a handhold. Grip the fish by the head, insert the knife point just below the gills and slit down to the vent before the tail.
3. Then stick the blade into the cavity and scoop out the gut on to your newspaper. Rinse the cavity under cold running water. This should not, in fresh fish, smell too unpleasant, except in the case of the grey mullet, which being vegetarian, has a particularly large and offensive gut. Be careful to brush out all the gut, including the kidney which is situated just below the backbone. Cod, and similar species, have a thick white swimbladder which must be removed to

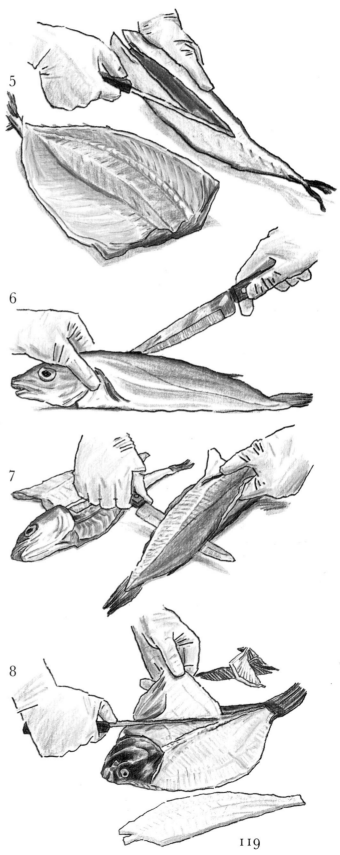

expose the kidney. Where the fish head is to be left on, the gills should be cut out cleanly with a sharp blade. To remove the head, slice off with a slanting cut to avoid wasting good edible fish meat. Cut along the line of the gills, then diagonally out of the top of the head.

Skinning
4. Where recipes allow it, leave the skin on during cooking and remove before serving. Otherwise for round fish, split the skin down the back and across the tail (the belly is already open), hold the tail firmly and cut the flesh away from the skin underneath in one movement, keeping the knife blade at a slant. To skin flat fish run the point of your knife round the fins, make an incision at the tail, dip thumb and finger in salt and strip off dark skin (the white skin is usually left on) in one sweep. The tension between skin and blade makes this easier than it sounds, but the knife must be sharp.

Splitting
5. To split fish for grilling, simply extend the ventral cut as far as the head or gills one way and the tail in the other. Open the fish out flat like a book. Head and tail may be left on or not, according to what you want to do with the fish. For kippering, split the herring (or mackerel) down the *back*, leaving the belly wall intact. Cut off the head and remove the gut from the dorsal rather than the ventral side. The backbone remains, lying to one side and lending strength while smoking (see page 127).

Filleting
Most round and small flat fish are best separated into two fillets, one each side. For round fish, first slit the stomach from head to tail and scoop out the gut as shown for gutting, left.
6. Cut cleanly along the spine.
7. Keeping the knife flat, prise and loosen the fish from the backbone and cut away in one piece as cleanly as possible, while gripping the fish firmly with your free hand. Turn over and repeat.
8. The method is similar for flat fish. Cut off the side fins which surround the body with a sharp pair of kitchen scissors. Make an incision by the head and begin filleting. In the case of a large flat fish, slit it down the backbone and separate into four fillets, in smaller fish take off in two.

Preserving fish

All the traditional methods of preserving and preparing fish – drying, salting, pickle curing, smoking and potting – can successfully be applied, in some cases in a somewhat modified form, by people today, faced with a sudden glut of fish to dispose of, or make the best of. While the bulk of a catch is probably best stored in the freezer, if you want to keep it for long, there comes a time when choosy eaters rebel at plain unvarnished fish, and then it is a great asset to be able to choose from a variety of techniques which give results as different as, say, a kipper and a rollmop.

For straight preservation purposes, where keeping qualities count for more than sheer deliciousness, drying or drying and salting, suggest themselves as first choice for lean white fish. A fair bit of space is needed, and the process is fairly lengthy and needs watching, but provided you get your fish bone dry you can rest assured that it will keep perfectly for months, even years.

In the case of fatty fish, like mackerel or herring, a modified form of the old pickled-in-the-barrel treatment is quite a neat and compact solution, and if you add spices to the brine the fish will emerge tastier as well. The same applies to the various vinegar and/or brine pickles and souses of which the Dutch and Scandinavians make such a feature in their cold spreads.

For short term keeping, fish pâtés and potted fish dishes generally are an easily made delicacy accompanied by toast, or salads. These have a long history in the English kitchen, probably because housewives found them useful for 'putting by' leftover fish for later in the week. However it would be unwise to lean too heavily on the preservative aspects of these methods. Soused, pickled or marinated fish dishes, however, have a longer safe life expectancy, since the acidity of the marinade is a more effective safeguard.

I am quite certain that smoking, particularly cool smoking, is the technique which will come as a revelation to most people. Once upon a time the notion of producing kippers, smoked haddock and so forth in one's own back yard would have seemed far fetched, but today there is a growing number of home smoking enthusiasts who have cut their teeth on miniature smoke boxes of the type sold in most large stores and are raring to try something bigger and better, which gives greater control over the end results. A light, cool smoke gives fish a rich but subtle smoky flavour, without appreciably drying it, so the texture – especially with prime fat fish – remains succulent.

Flat dwellers, or people who simply want to give an intriguing smoky taste to a few fish for supper without too much hassle, will find the small Scandinavian-type smoke box the best choice, as the whole operation takes hardly longer than putting the fish under the grill and they emerge cooked as well as smoked – this is the technique known as hot-smoked. Most people are probably familiar with commercial hot-smoked products such as smoked trout, mackerel, eel, with their wrinkled amber skin. All these, like the fish (or sausages) cooked in your smoke box, are cooked and should be eaten within a few days, as for any cooked meat or fish.

With the cool smoker, which any reasonably handy person with enough space can knock up out of scrap materials, the possibilities are greatly increased. Provided you can get 1. prime fat fish and 2. suitable hardwood sawdust, it is not difficult to cool smoke your own kippers, haddock, mackerel, or any other suitable fish (oily or fatty ones seem to smoke most successfully), not to mention much larger items such as turkey and goose (p. 176), with results which compare very well with anything you could buy and which will certainly be vastly cheaper.

It takes a little practice to get a cool smoker working smoothly unless you are one of those lucky people with a natural flair for building and controlling fires, but it really is worth persevering because there can be few cheaper ways of raising simple materials into the luxury food class. Even if your home-made kippers look a bit rougher than the commercial ones, they will have a far superior freshness of flavour.

One last word, about food poisoning. Various types of bacteria can grow in foods, causing illness ranging from minor stomach upsets to the dreaded, though fortunately rare, botulism. Fish in its raw state is one of the safest protein foods, but cooking kills the numerous and competing harmless bacteria and, if conditions are right, allows food poisoning bacteria, which may accidentally be introduced, to grow unchecked.

There are certain simple rules that should be observed, and if carefully followed will prevent the risk of illness from this cause. All equipment must be kept scrupulously clean, to reduce the risk of infection. Bacteria grow more rapidly as temperature rises, and many grow most rapidly at about blood heat. As soon as food is cooked, and this includes hot smoked fish from the kiln, allow it to cool and put it in the fridge. Do not leave it sitting in a warm kitchen. Remember also that cool larders may not be as cool as they feel and a marble slab is no cooler than the air surrounding it. Food poisoning bacteria will not grow at temperatures around 0°C (32°F) and even if your fridge is a bit warmer than this, the growth will be very slow.

Where cool smoked products are concerned, fish are safe so long as you cook them before eating them after only a day or two in the fridge (they may also be frozen). This is common practice, except in the case of smoked salmon. The makers of commercially smoked salmon naturally impose the most rigorous checks and precautions but since it would be difficult to follow their safety code at home, on balance I think home smokers might be better off avoiding smoked salmon.

Where a product is hot-smoked, the risk of poisoning is eliminated provided you eat the food within a day or two, as you would normally do with cooked food in any case. Any leftovers should be kept in the fridge, and if in any doubt, you can always cook them up again before eating them, in kedgeree, or fish pie.

Finally, pâtés and potted fish. These present a special problem, since bacteria may breed more rapidly in airless – that is sealed – conditions, especially where the basic materials have been previously cooked, thus destroying all competing organisms. Here the rule is store the product in the fridge and eat within 48 hours. Or, for longer keeping, store in the deep freeze and eat as soon as thawed.

Provided you observe these precautions, and maintain scrupulous hygiene as a matter of routine when you are preparing all these foods, then you should not have anything to worry about.

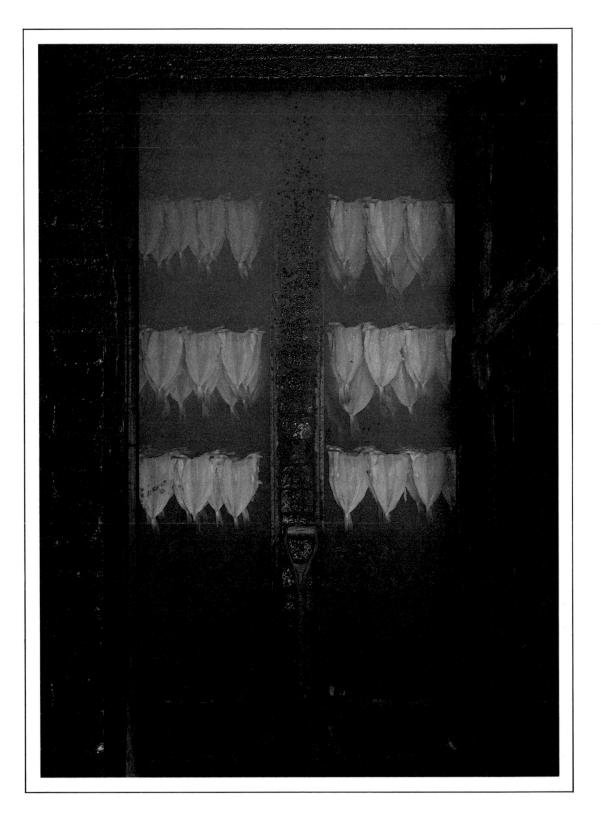

Smoked Fish

'A Finnan haddock dried over the smoke of the seaweed
and sprinkled with salt water during the process
acquires a relish of a very peculiar and delicate flavour.'
Notes to Boswell's 'Tour of the Hebrides'   Sir Walter Scott

Smoke plus fish is one of those ideally harmonious blends, like Earl Grey tea, producing a substance of suave texture and mellow flavour which really can claim to be a whole new food, quite different from the untreated fish.

Originally, back in the Middle Ages, smoking seems to have been used chiefly for its preservative effect, which increased the longer the fish hung smoking and drying in the old brick smoke towers – three whole weeks for red herring. The results would have been hard, bone dry and indescribably pungent – a little like Bombay Duck. Today, with cold storage taking care of the preservative side of things, smoking is used to enhance fish flavour and texture. A short spell in the smoke kiln produces fish which has a distinctively smoked taste without being unpleasantly dried out.

You will not need me to tell you that fish smoking, essentially, involves suspending raw fish in a continuous stream of smoke for a prescribed length of time. But not everyone realizes that there are two types of smoking which produce rather different results. Cold, or cool smoking, which gives you smoked salmon, kippers and smoked haddock for instance, is done at a temperature of around 26°C (80°F), well below blood heat, so the product is saturated with smoke but remains raw. Cool-smoked fish (except for salmon) are invariably cooked before eating. In hot smoking, which produces smoked trout and buckling for instance, the fish are usually cool-smoked to begin with to give the desired flavour but the kiln temperature is raised gradually towards the end of the smoking time. The product emerges cooked, and ready to eat.

I have found with our own home-made smoker (p. 125) that cool smoking gives the best results for the time and effort involved, and if you want a hot-smoked effect you can simply pop the cool smoked product into your domestic oven, wrapped in foil, for five or ten minutes till cooked. Or, alternatively, buy one of the small tin smoke boxes (or make one out of biscuit tins for a fraction of the cost, p. 129), which will hot smoke anything fairly small – half a dozen small herrings, a pound of sprats, a fillet of coley (making it into poor man's Finnan haddie) – in a few minutes.

Curing in the silvery haze of an oak sawdust fire, split haddocks skewered on rods. The fish are split, brined in a salt solution, then hung on rods to drain and put into the smoke hole. Haddock are cured high, buckling, sprats and mackerel brought closer to the heat.

Building a smoke house

The home-made smoker

There are various possibilities to consider, from an *ad hoc* arrangement of ground sheets propped on sticks over a small camp fire of green twigs (the angler's or camper's version) to a permanent bricks and mortar job like my own back yard smoker, which looks for all the world like a surrealist brick fridge with a small stovepipe chimney. If you are planning to smoke food regularly, it is worth building a permanent structure, in my experience. It need not be any bigger than a fridge, but site it far enough away from house windows, patio and washing line to prevent everything reeking of hardwood smoke – delicious in the right place, but overpowering to live with.

Basically what is required is some sort of airtight, or potentially airtight, container, through which you can channel your smoke stream from a separate firebox via an inlet pipe and out through a chimney. A galvanized water tank, old cooker or office safe are all possibilities but although these have the charm of all *objets trouvés*, I would plump for the bricks – or breeze blocks – and mortar structure as being more attractive, more efficient and purpose built.

Points to observe when building your smoker: the separate firebox should be set at least a foot below the level of the smoker floor, to encourage the smoke to rise up through the pipe and thence through the smoker and out through the chimney. You can achieve this either by raising the smoker up on a brick platform with the firebox at ground level (the advantage of this is that you could fix it so a second fire can be lit directly below the smoker itself, for hot smoking), or by siting the smoker on the ground but digging a pit below ground level for the firebox. A slope facilitates the second system. Either way the smoker and its satellite firebox should be linked by a clay drainage pipe of about 15 cm (6 in) diameter, both ends of which need to be cemented in. One hundred per cent smoke-tightness is not vital to success, but nor do you want precious smoke rushing out all over the place.

Roof the smoker with overlapping roofing slates and then spread a 2·5 cm (1 in) layer of mortar over the top. Leave to harden. A small chimney pipe should be set into the roof too, roughly diagonally opposite the clay pipe funnelling the smoke in from below, plus a tile as damper to adjust the amount of smoke coming out of the smoker chimney. Once put into use, more roof slates, or a metal sheet, or something similar, will be needed to cover the firebox. The firebox cover needs to be easily removable as you may have to inspect your fire fairly often, until you gain experience.

As far as furnishing the smoker goes, provide it with a door, even if it's only a sheet of ply, and some way of suspending your 'tenters' (poles with hooks for hanging the fish) while smoking. Look out for the grooved bricks used inside old storage heaters. Incorporated in the smoker walls these provide good supports for tenters or mesh trays. Alternatively use shelf bracketing cemented in, or screwed in place, or soldered if the smoker is metal. But do not make the positioning of your tenters and fish too awkward. In a smoky atmosphere you will not enjoy groping about for a minuscule bracket on which to rest your load of fish.

The fire

No smoke without fire, and getting the right sort of fire – basically hardwood sawdust brought to a pitch where it gently and constantly smoulders and smokes – is the secret of successful cool smoking. The professionals are up to all sorts of dodges – some keep the sawdust in a tin with a small open fire burning below, others stick glowing logs or coals into the tin of sawdust itself. The way we find works best (my husband is the fire maker in our home) is to get a hearty blaze going in the firebox with a heap of dry kindling wood (greengrocers' boxes work well for this) before you load the fish into the smoker. When this has burned down to a hot red heap, rake a mound of *dry* sawdust over and leave until the smoke is flowing well. It takes about quarter of an hour to get a constant stream of smoke billowing through the smoker. When you see it spiralling through the chimney, block the chimney off partially with a tile, and the smoker is ready to use.

Then it is in with the fish, all prepared, brined, dried and impaled or netted and apart from periodic checks, every 30 minutes or so, to see if more sawdust is needed or an occasional booster of kindling, that is it. To rescue a burnt out heap, try shoving in a hot coal or glowing red log with fire tongs. If necessary – it may be at first – to get the fire started over again, clear a little pit in the middle of the extinct ashes. It is not disastrous if the fire goes out for a short period during smoking, interrupting the smoke flow, but it is better not to make a practice of it.

Sawdust

Commercial fish smokers sometimes use softwood sawdust only when smoking white fish, or perhaps a blend of softwood and hardwood sawdusts to give their products a resinous flavour, but hardwood sawdust used alone gives fish the most delicate and appealing taste. Almost any hardwood sawdust may be used – elm, beech, oak, juniper, apple or hickory – depending what sort of trees grow where you live. But it is important that the sawdust comes from trees which have not been sprayed and treated with fungicides or insecticides as these could leave harmful deposits on the smoked food.

People who saw up their own firewood will be well placed for sawdust – if you do not, however, you may have a friend or neighbour who would help out in return for a sample of your smoked products. Otherwise contact timber merchants, large estates who supply firewood, jobbing builders, carpenters or joiners. However, you must be confident in your source, not only with regard to fungicides, but also alert to the possible infiltration of plastics into your sawdust supply. Few joiners nowadays can entirely avoid laminated and plastic faced materials, and to use sawdust containing anything but untreated wood could be a little risky. If you live in the country, or near it, and you ask around, it is surprising how many people may be able to help, or think of someone who could. For city folks, a kind friend living in the country is the best bet. It is impossible to give accurate estimates of how much sawdust it takes to operate a given smoker, but roughly speaking, half a sackful seems to provide enough for six hours' smoking.

Preparing fish for the smoker

1. Split the fish head to tail along the spine.

2. Cleanly slice off the head, spread the fish open like a book, and scrape the gut out from the back, leaving the belly wall intact.

3. Brining fish prior to smoking firms the flesh, improves the flavour and adds an attractive salt-gloss to the finished product. Use a large white plastic bin, glazed sink or wooden cask, well scalded and aired, as the brining vessel. For a strong solution, add 1.25 kg (2 lb 9 oz) of coarse salt to 4 litres (1 gallon) of cold water. Don't overcrowd fish in the brine bath, and stir now and again to make sure the ones on top get a good soak. Small fish should be well enough salted in ten to fifteen minutes, larger ones take up to half an hour. On removing the fish from the bath, hang them immediately for an hour or two to drip and dry, before going into the kiln.

4. When preparing fish for the kiln, remember that the entire surface should be exposed to the smoke throughout the process. The simplest way to achieve this is to impale fish on sharpened nails studded along wooden poles or tenters made from a 25 mm × 25 mm (1 in × 1 in) section cut to fit across the smoker. If the nails are slightly curved upwards with pliers, there is little risk of the fish becoming dislodged. Alternatively, two fish may be tied by their tails back to back, and looped over sticks, but care must be taken not to knock them off when loading and unloading the smoker. Threading fish on wire passed through their eye sockets, as well as being a grisly business, can also result in unevenly smoked fish as they tend to hang folded like clothes on hangers.

Smoking techniques

Cool smoking

The fish should be prepared as described on the previous page and loaded onto the tenters – a rather laborious process – while you start the fire going in your firebox. Commercially, a thermometer would be used to check that the temperature inside the smoker is around the 26°C (80°F) mark, but in practice – using the separate firebox type of smoker – there is little likelihood of overheating, since it is only smoke, and not heat that you are channelling through.

You might find wearing goggles or a skin diving mask is a help when loading the fish, as the smoke makes one's eyes water copiously. Fix the fish with sufficient space between each fish and between tenters to let smoke circulate freely, then shut off or block the smoker door. Incidentally, if you want to smoke small fry such as sprats or sardines, which are delicious treated this way, you will have to contrive some sort of mesh tray on which to spread them out so the smoke envelops each fish. This should be positioned near the top of the smoker.

In commercial smoke kilns it is usual to shift the fish round once or twice during the smoking process, since the intensity of smoke in the kiln varies somewhat with the position of the fish, but it is rarely necessary to do this if one is only smoking a dozen or so fish.

The length of time needed for thorough smoking varies with the size and type of fish, but again, for domestic purposes, I do not think this is critical. Three or four hours will give small fish, such as herring, a distinct kippered flavour, though six to twelve is the professionals' allowance. Between six and ten hours might be needed for a large fat haddock or cod fillet, but this is really a matter of personal taste. A little experience will confirm your preference as to degree of smokiness. Keep a log in which to note briefly times of brining, drying and smoking, and the results, to guide you. Do not expect your cool-smoked fish to have the deep tan of the commercial variety – this is achieved by dyeing. If the fire peters out during the smoking period, re-light it at once. Do not aim for billowing clouds of smoke, a light haze will soon build up in the smoker.

When smoking is complete, leave the fish in a cool place for an hour or two. Fish you do not want to eat immediately can be stored in the fridge or a cool place, protected by flycovers. I find flies avoid smoked fish on the whole, but there is always a risk with amateur smoking that one or two fish are not evenly smoked and the flies will go for any untreated flesh. Smoked fish can be frozen, if you want to keep them longer than a couple of days, but the flavour and texture are not so fine.

Recipes using smoked fish are given overleaf but first, one tip from the experts – the best way to cook kippers made from spent (ie spawned and lean) herring is the simple old way of steeping them for three minutes in a jug of boiling water. Any other way dries them out too much.

Note: There is a vogue for treating uncooked kipper as poor man's smoked salmon, and eating it raw, thinly sliced or made into pâté. I have done so in the past. Alas, expert advice recommends we drop this practice since cooking is necessary to destroy any harmful organisms naturally present in the fish.

Hot smoking

Your cool smoking kiln can be converted into a hot smoker if it is designed so that you can introduce an added source of heat. If built up on stilts, a second fire may be lit directly below the kiln, or you could insert into the smoker itself an electric hot plate or butane gas flame.

The fish are prepared in exactly the same way as for cool smoking, and indeed start life in the smoker just as they would for a cool smoke. However, to achieve the cooked, wrinkled characteristics of hot-smoked fish (smoked trout or buckling for example) the temperature inside the smoker will need to be raised gradually to about 94–110°C (200–300°F) for the last hour or two of the smoking time. The time necessary will vary, depending on the size and fatness of the fish. A thermometer is essential, and you must take frequent temperature readings, since there is the risk of the fish disintegrating as they cook and dropping off their tenters. Too much heat and the fish may become dried out, 'case-hardened' as they say in the trade, too little and they are undercooked, less pleasant to eat, and a possible health risk. Undercooked fish can of course be rescued by a short spell in the domestic oven or a minute under the grill.

Alternatively you can improvise a 'one off' hot smoker, perhaps not as efficient or tidy as the commercial smokebox, but *free*. This can produce some delicious results, if a little crude in comparison with the kiln-smoked variety. One example is illustrated and described below, using a pair of biscuit tins. If you can get hold of one, a large, sturdy, solidly made can of approximately 4 litre (1 gallon) capacity will also make a good home smoker following the same principles. Don't waste hours measuring and perfecting such equipment – the idea is to knock it up quickly, use it and chuck it out. And don't forget always to use oven gloves when handling this type of smoker – at its best used out of doors.

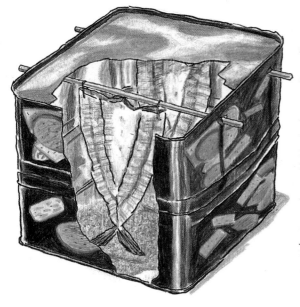

The fisherman's answer to the hot smoker (left) can easily be copied by even the least practical among us. All you need is two identical biscuit tins, two canes or straight sticks and a handful of sawdust.

Puncture holes on opposite sides of one biscuit tin near the base, and suspend canes to which your fish are secured. This tin is to be placed upside down on top of its twin (which is the right way up) and the sawdust is heaped on the floor of the lower tin.

To raise the necessary smoke, place the tins on either a camp fire out in the open or a small camping butane gas ring or over a domestic gas ring, adjusting the flame so the sawdust just smoulders without catching fire. Leave for eight to ten minutes until the sawdust is consumed and the fish cooked.

Cooking with smoked fish

Home smoked fish is an inspiring food to experiment with. It has endless versatility –
delicious plain; hot or cold; it can also be dressed up for parties or down for economy,
pounded into pâtés, whizzed into a mousse or baked in a flan. Yield: 4–6 servings.

Ways of cooking whole smoked fish
Three recipe suggestions for smoked fish, such as
mackerel, herring, small haddock, whiting,
buckling, bloaters:

Grilled with cream
Cook the fish under a hot grill till done, rubbing
them with a little butter if necessary. Serve with a
large blob of clotted cream melting on top.

Flamed in whisky à la Rob Roy
Buckling or bloaters are best for this dashing
19th-century dish.
   Split the fish and remove the heads and as many
bones as possible. Lay them in a frying pan and
heat a ladleful of whisky over a low flame for a
moment. Pour over the fish, tilting the pan, set
light to the whisky and when it stops blazing the
fish will be done.

Fried with bacon and mushrooms
The smoked fish should be divided into fillets. To
make the dish fry two or three rashers of bacon
per person, until the fat runs, then add the fish
fillets and fry for a further three or four minutes.
Lastly add the mushrooms, and cook till just
tender. Serve at once on hot plates.

Smoked fish mousse
Urbane food for summer lunch parties,
especially when served with cucumber and
cream sauce. The swankiest version uses smoked
salmon, but hot-smoked mackerel, trout or
buckling or cooked kippers may be substituted.

225 g (8 oz) smoked fish
4 tablespoons homemade mayonnaise
½ lemon
salt, pepper
tabasco sauce or anchovy essence
a pinch of cayenne
15 g (½ oz) powdered gelatine and water to mix
3 egg whites
150 ml (¼ pint) double cream

Put the smoked fish and mayonnaise into a
blender, and whizz smooth. Add the juice of half
a lemon, salt, pepper, a dash of tabasco and a
small pinch of cayenne. Dissolve the gelatine in a
few tablespoons of warm water, then blend with
the fish mixture. Put in a bowl in the fridge till it
just begins to set, then fold in the egg whites,
whisked till fluffy and the cream, whipped till
thick. Return to the fridge for three hours, till
firmly set. To turn out, dip the bowl or dish very
briefly into hot water (just the bowl, not the
contents), then reverse carefully onto a dish.

Smoked fish bolster
Flaky pastry makes the bolster cover, and the
stuffing consists of smoked fish, hardboiled eggs
in a creamy béchamel sauce speckled with
parsley. Using frozen commercial pastry,
this is a quick dish to make, and attractive
enough for a supper party.

450 ml (¾ pint) béchamel sauce
flavoured with 1 tablespoon grated cheese, nutmeg and
*   parsley*
1 packet frozen flaky or puff pastry
250 g (8 oz) cooked smoked fish
2 hardboiled eggs

Make béchamel sauce and leave to cool. To
make the bolster roll the pastry into a rectangle
roughly 30 cm × 20 cm (12 in × 8 in). Flake the
fish, removing any skin or bones and mix gently
with the sauce. Slice the hardboiled eggs and
spread them over the middle of the pastry. Spoon
the fish mixture on top – it should be thick
enough to stay put. Moisten the edges of the
pastry rectangle, fold the side flaps up over the
fish to meet in the middle and pinch all the seams
shut. Lift the bolster tenderly onto a baking
sheet, and put into a preheated oven at 220°C
(425°F, Mark 7) for ten minutes, then lower heat
to 190°C (375°F, Mark 5) and cook for another
twenty-five minutes, or until the pastry is crisp,
risen and golden.

Kedgeree

Khichri, the Indian ancestor of this dish, is a spicy mixture of rice and lentils. The only thing Indian about our kedgeree is the light seasoning of curry powder.

350 g (12 oz) patna or long grain rice
salt
4 large onions
100 g (4 oz) butter
1 tablespoon oil
250 g (8 oz) cooked smoked fish
1 sliced hard boiled egg
1 teaspoon curry powder or garam masala
black pepper
4 tablespoons thin cream (optional)
½ lemon

Boil up a large pan of water, and when boiling throw in the rice and a little salt. Cook for twelve minutes, drain through a sieve, run hot water through the rice then put it into a large shallow dish and into a low oven to dry off. Meanwhile peel and roughly chop the onions and fry gently in a little of the butter and a spoonful of oil. When the onions are softening add the smoked fish, which has been flaked and the skin and bones removed. Cook for a minute. Turn the hot rice into the pan with the fish and mix lightly with a fork. Add the sliced hardboiled egg, curry powder or garam masala, salt and pepper to taste. When hot put in the rest of the butter and fork it about till the rice is buttery. Spoon the cream over, add a squeeze of lemon and serve on hot plates.

Zapekanka

Russians make this with salt herring, but smoked fish is just as good.

1 onion
chopped fresh dill (optional)
750 g (1½ lb) hot mashed potatoes
3 eggs
1 thick slice white bread soaked in milk
225 g (8 oz) smoked fish, flaked
100 g (4 oz) butter
dry breadcrumbs
salt, pepper
100 g (4 oz) sour cream

Finely chop the onion and the dill, and mix into the mashed potato, which should be smooth and rather thick. Separate two of the eggs, beat the yolks and add to the potato, then stir in the bread, soaked in milk and squeezed out. Mix well, then add the fish. Beat the egg whites until firm, and fold into the mixture. Season. Butter an ovenproof dish, sprinkle with crumbs, then fill with the fish mixture. Beat up the third egg with the sour cream and spread over the top. Bake in a moderately hot oven 190°C (375°F, Mark 5) for half an hour, or till golden. Serve cut in squares with a sauce made of sour cream, chopped dill (or parsley) and a little lemon juice.

Quiche surprise

Smoked fish quiches or flans are deservedly popular, the smoky fish taste contrasting nicely with the bland custard filling. This is a grand and partified version.

175 g (6 oz) shortcrust pastry
75 g (3 oz) choux paste for topping

Filling
150 g (5–6 oz) smoked fish – buckling, mackerel,
  kipper
4 teaspoonfuls tinned lumpfish roe (optional)
3 egg yolks and 2 egg whites
100 g (4 oz) single cream
50 g (2 oz) grated cheese
salt, pepper, nutmeg

First make the shortcrust and choux paste. Grease a 20 cm (8 in) flat tin. Roll out the shortcrust and line the tin, pricking here and there with a fork. Arrange the flaked fish (skin, bones removed) evenly over the pastry, with blobs of roe in between. Whisk up two whole eggs and one yolk, plus the cream and grated cheese. Season with salt, pepper, nutmeg. Pour this over the fish. With a large spoon cover the flan filling with large blobs of choux paste, leaving no filling showing. Then slide onto the baking sheet and bake for 30 minutes at 200°C (400°F, Mark 6). *Do not* open the oven door before the time is up, as choux paste hates draughts. On the half hour mark open it a crack, to check the choux cover is firm and golden, if not cook a further 5 minutes. Serve at once.

Drying and salting

The pungent flavour of dried and salted fish is the making of certain traditional and hearty peasant dishes, and has a particular charm for those who enjoy it – by no means everyone – so it might be best to buy a bit and try it on your family first.

To follow these efficient traditional methods of preserving fish you will need quantities of suitable lean white fish like cod (stockfish). Herrings are never salted and dried because the salt encourages oxidation of the fat. So oily fish are pickle cured in brine. The best time to dry fish is when the weather is blowy and cold, and after a week or two of hanging in the breeze, they should be dry as a bone and stiff as a board and ready to keep for a year.

Equipment

You will need knives for scaling and gutting (p. 118), and a large clean container. White (not coloured) plastic bins as sold for wine making are suitable, as are earthenware crocks and glazed sinks, but scour, bleach and scald them carefully. For drying and draining the fish, a washing line or wooden clothes rack will serve to support small fish tied together by the tails in pairs. For large fish, like cod, slatted racks or plastic netting trays are needed for stacking and eventually drying the fish, spread out. Salt, if you are using it, should be the coarsest available since fine salt can cause the outer layers of fish to become altered too quickly thus preventing the salt from 'striking through', and the fish would then be liable to go off.

Method

In the right weather conditions the fish may simply be dried outdoors after cleaning and splitting, leaving on heads and tails and pegging or stringing them up on a line, or impaling them on nails or hooks driven into a long piece of 25×25 mm (1 in $\times$ 1 in) section. Protect all drying and salted fish against cats and birds and at night take them into a cool shed or cellar. After a week or so most of the fluid will have drained out and the fish will be acquiring the proper hard dryness of texture. Leave them till they are stiff and no moisture can be felt when you pinch them. These may be fried or grilled and served with butter and parsley.

To speed the process of drying by encouraging the fluids to drain out (as well as giving a stronger flavour) fish may first be salted. A brine is the easiest method with small fish. Make a brine by mixing salt with really cold water in proportions of 500 g (1 lb) salt to 3 litres (5 pints) water – there should be enough to cover all the fish. Clean, scale, remove the heads and split open, then pack them – not too tightly – into the brine and leave for one hour if small, two if large. Remove and hang up to dry.

Large fish such as cod are generally dry salted. Use approximately 500 g (1 lb) salt to three times that weight of fish. Rub the salt in well all over both sides of the cleaned, split fish, then stack the salted fish in piles on your slatted racks, fleshy side up (with an extra sprinkle of salt between) till you have a stack ten deep. Now put the top one on skin side up and salt the top. After a couple of weeks of dry salting, spread the fish out so the air can get at them and leave to dry out completely, which is when they are hard, stiff and resist an enquiring pinch. Store in a cool dry place.

Dried and salted fish

Countries all over the world relish their own particular dried and salted fish recipe, some plain, some offset with sweet root vegetables, some hotted up with garlic and herbs, and some simply 'wind dried'. Yield: 4–6 servings.

Salt cod, parsnips and egg sauce
A favourite medieval dish, which nicely balances sweet mashed parsnips with salty fish. The sauce is a classic English one, simple but good with all fish.

1 kg (2 lb) salt cod
450 ml (¾ pint) milk
1 kg (2 lb) parsnips
150 g (5 oz) butter
salt, pepper
coriander (optional)
1 tablespoon flour
3 egg yolks

Soak the cod in several changes of cold water (they used to peg it down in a stream bed) to extract most of the salt. Put it into a pan with cold water, bring to the boil, then throw this water away. Repeat two or three times (depending how salty the fish is) then cover the fish with milk and water (50–50) to cover. Add the peeled parsnips cut in strips. Simmer, covered for 45 minutes or until the fish and parsnips are tender. Lift the fish out carefully, and set in a low oven to dry off. Pour off the stock into a jug. Mash the parsnips well, with butter, salt, pepper (possibly a little crushed coriander) and a little of the stock, until creamy. Make the sauce by melting the rest of the butter, stirring in the flour, and adding about ½ litre (1 pint) of the stock slowly, stirring until smooth. Dish the cod surrounded by the mashed parsnips. Just before serving, remove the sauce from the fire and stir in the well beaten egg yolks. Stir until thick and golden and serve in a hot jug.

Bacalao
In the classic Basque recipe which is much more long drawn out, the fish and sauce are cooked separately, and only combined at the end. This is a simpler, rustic and tasty fish stew.

If the tomatoes are not very juicy, add a little juice from tinned tomatoes.

450 g (1 lb) salt cod
3 onions
4 potatoes
1 large green pepper
6 large tomatoes (or tinned tomatoes)
parsley
cooking oil (preferably olive oil)

Prepare the salt cod for cooking as in the recipe above, but without boiling. Pick off the skin and bones, and break into small pieces. Peel the onions and potatoes, remove the seeds from the pepper and slice all thinly into separate heaps. Slice the tomatoes, and chop the parsley. Put a layer of oil in the bottom of a deep thick saucepan, then make alternate layers of vegetables, parsley and fish, starting with tomatoes (for their juice) and ending with a potato lid. Cook very gently covered on the lowest flame (use asbestos mat over gas) or heat, for about one hour, or until the potatoes are tender. Shake the pan now and then to prevent sticking.

Salt cod with scrambled eggs
An unexpected, sophisticated mixture of flaked salt cod and scrambled eggs.

450 g (1 lb) salt cod
300 ml (½ pint) milk
100 g (4 oz) butter
6 eggs
salt, black pepper
½ lemon
4 slices bread

Soak the cod for 8 hours, changing the water twice. Cover with equal quantities of milk and water and simmer for about half an hour until tender. Drain, flake and dry off in a warm oven. Melt the butter in a heavy frying pan, stir in the beaten eggs, add salt and pepper, and cook slowly stirring until thick egg flakes are formed. Add the fish flakes, mix gently, squeeze the half lemon over and serve with fried bread triangles.

Pickled & Potted Fish

'*The breakfast is the prosopon of the great work of the day.*
Chocolate, coffee, tea, cream, eggs, ham, tongue, cold fowl – all these are good
and bespeak good knowledge in him who sets them forth : but the touchstone is fish :
anchovy is the first step, prawns and shrimps the second ;
and I laud him who reaches even these : potted char and lampreys are the third . . .
but lobster is, indeed, matter for a May morning and demands
a rare combination of knowledge and virtue in him who sets it forth.'

Crotchet Castle   Thomas Love Peacock   *1831*

These succulent ways of preparing fish, formerly (erroneously) favoured for their preservative qualities, are now enjoyed on their own highly individual, often spicy, merit alone.

Traditionally herring, mackerel and salmon are the fish used for pickling and sousing, probably because their oiliness consorts well with the sharp spicy pickle. Use ovenproof casseroles of any shape and size, preferably with lids. The finer the vinegar the more subtle the pickle. I add a little sugar which I think improves all fish dishes. The fish are cleaned and filleted, but the skin – with herrings anyway – is often left on. The fish are packed into a suitable dish, the pickle poured over and the dish then baked in a low oven, for an hour or so. Cooked like this the bones are softened enough to be eaten – you do not have to, but they are rich in calcium. Despite the long cooking, the vinegar keeps the fish surprisingly firm in its texture. Alternatively, the fish may just be left for longer to marinate to obviate the need for cooking.

Most fish can be potted, including smoked fish, shellfish, and leftovers, but fish of strong flavours – shrimp, bloater, mackerel, herring, crab – give the most interesting results. Small pottery dishes make the most attractive containers. An electric blender is useful for making fish pastes. Unsalted, or lightly salted butter is the best for the purpose, and the spices, as usual, are more aromatic bought whole and ground in a mortar or mouli grinder. Nutmeg, mace, allspice, pepper are traditional. Usually the fish are gently baked in the oven, with spices and seasoning until tender, then mashed, flaked or blended – depending on how smooth a consistency you want – pressed into pots, and covered with clarified butter (see ghee). Shrimps are left whole. Eat within 48 hours if kept in the fridge, or freeze for longer and eat as soon as thawed.

Fresh fish for filleting in barrels, freshly cooked fish dishes on the barrow: potted shrimps sealed with butter, rollmop herrings soused in brine, Arabic *Shtoon Fufarran* with sardines marinated in a spice paste and Chinese crispy red mullet flavoured with garlic and ginger.

135

Pickled and potted fish dishes

The common link between pickled and potted fish is that they have both been previously cooked. From there on, they differ entirely – potted fish offering a delicious convenience, pickled, an unexpected piquancy. Yield: 4–6 servings.

Rollmops
The classic soused herring dish.

8 herrings
600 ml (1 pint) water
50 g (2 oz) salt
900 ml (1½ pints) white wine vinegar
2 shallots or one onion
2 bay leaves
4 pickled gherkins
1 tablespoon pickling spices

Clean the fish, split down the back and remove the backbones. Fillet if large. Mix the salt in the water, and soak the fish in this brine for about three hours, then dip them in vinegar. Roll each fish or fillet round a little chopped shallot or onion, pack into a jar with the broken bay leaves and gherkins. Boil up the vinegar with the pickling spices; when cold pour over the herring. Store in a cool place and eat after 48 hours. Will keep three weeks, or longer.

Chinese crispy red fish
The Chinese are marvellously skilful at bringing out the best in fish, using a combination of flavourings – especially the garlic/ginger/sherry mixture as here – which makes the flesh sweet and tasty, or as the Chinese say 'de-fished'. The redness comes from a drop of cochineal or other red food colouring. The distinctive feature of this recipe is that while the fish bones are soft and edible, the skin becomes delectably crisp.

1 kg (2 lb) herring or fresh sardines or red mullet
3 medium onions
3 cloves garlic
25 mm (1 in) knob of root ginger
4 tablespoons sugar
4 tablespoons soy sauce
6 tablespoons wine or cider vinegar
6 tablespoons sherry
900 ml (1½ pints) fish or chicken stock
½ teaspoon red colouring

Scale, gut and clean fish. The Chinese leave heads and tails on for elegance, but to economize you could remove these and simmer them with a little soy sauce, sherry and chopped onion to make stock. To cook fish slice the onions, crush the garlic and finely chop the ginger and spread over the bottom of a large shallow casserole or cast iron dish which can go on top of the stove. Then arrange the fish on top, head to tail, in layers if necessary. Mix sugar, soy sauce, vinegar, sherry with stock and pour over fish. Bring to the boil, add the food colouring and simmer gently uncovered until the liquid has completely evaporated – about an hour. Or transfer to a low oven 160°C (325°F, Mark 3) and cook until the liquid is gone, but check after half an hour to see that it is not drying up too fast and scorching the fish.

Arabic pickled pilchards (Shtoon Fufarran)
Make this dish with any small fish – sprats, sardines, etc. It is splendid for a drinks party.

1½ kg (3 lb) small fish
1 head garlic
2 large handfuls parsley
½ teaspoon cayenne
1 tablespoon cumin
juice of 3 lemons
6 tablespoons olive oil
4 tablespoons water
1 tablespoon salt

Soak fish in cool salty water for a few minutes. Snap or cut off the heads, pulling out the guts. Pour boiling water over the fish, let stand two minutes till they have split open. Then remove the backbones, so you have 2 tiny fillets. Pound the garlic, parsley, cayenne and cumin together to a paste. Mix the liquid ingredients together with the salt and spicy paste. Arrange the fish and spice mixture in layers in a shallow dish, ending with the paste. Cover and refrigerate. Eat after 24 hours. It will keep for one week.

Marinated anchovies

Anchovies – sardines, sprats, even whitebait
would be good for this. The quantities given
here would be enough to fuel a small party – for
domestic purposes half is enough.

6 small onions
7 tablespoons olive oil
1 glass dry white wine
chopped fresh herbs – fennel, parsley, 1 bay leaf, pinch
  of thyme (about 2 tablespoons in all)
1 clove garlic
1 teaspoon coriander
1 lemon
salt and pepper
1 kg (2 lb) fresh anchovies or other small fry

Make the marinade by frying sliced onions in half
the oil, and when golden adding wine, herbs,
garlic, coriander and lemon juice. Season with
salt and pepper and simmer for 10 minutes.
Clean and fillet the fish as described for Arabic
pickled pilchards. Spread the fillets in a large flat
dish, sprinkle with the remaining oil, plus a little
salt and pepper and bake in hot oven – 220°C
(425°F, Mark 7) for 12 minutes or till golden and
crisp. Cool, pour over the cooled marinade and
keep in the fridge for 48 hours to develop flavour
before serving.

Scandinavian pickled herring (Inlagd sill)

1 kg (2 lb) fat fresh herring
2 medium sized onions or shallots
3 rounded tablespoons sugar
3 teaspoons allspice
½ litre (1 pint) white wine or cider vinegar

Use a large sterilized glass jar to pack the fish in.
First gut, clean and remove heads from fish, rinse
under cold water, then leave overnight in lightly
salted water in the fridge. Next day fillet the fish
neatly and remove fins, but do not remove the
skin. Cut fillets across into 1 cm (½ in) strips. Peel
and thinly slice onions. Mix sugar and spice
together. Put fish strips in glass jar with a good
sprinkle of sugar/spice and sliced onions between
each layer, then pour over vinegar to completely
cover the fish. Chill in fridge. Eat after 48 hours.

Potted mackerel or herring

6 mackerel or herring, filleted
½ teaspoon each of grated nutmeg, pounded cloves and
  ground ginger
2 tablespoons salt
6 bay leaves
lemon peel
250 g (½ lb) butter

The fish fillets need not be skinned. Mix the
spices together with salt, then rub into the fish
fillets. Lay these in an ovenproof dish, inter-
spersed with the bay leaves and strips of lemon
peel and knobs of butter. Cover with the
remaining butter, then cover the dish with foil
and a lid and bake in a low oven at 150°C (300°F,
Mark 2) for three hours. Remove any skin and
bones, as well as the bay leaves and peel, then
break the fish up roughly with a fork and leave to
cool. When cold, top with a layer of clarified
butter.

Potted shrimps

Made with fresh shrimps and new farm butter,
this is the apotheosis of potted fish. Best eaten
with dry toast or thin brown bread. It looks as
beautiful, with the whole shrimps merged in a
rosy paste, as it tastes.

100 g (4 oz) fresh shrimps (unshelled)
100 g (4 oz) whiting, dab, plaice or other delicate
  white fish
tiny pinch each of cayenne, mace or nutmeg
200 g (7 oz) unsalted butter
½ teaspoon anchovy sauce or ¼ anchovy fillet (optional)

Shell the shrimps. Put the shells and head in just
enough water to cover and simmer for 5 to 10
minutes, with the pan lid on. Strain the liquid
and use it to poach the white fish till tender –
about 10 minutes over a low flame. When cool
pick out any skin or bone and pound or blend the
white fish till smooth with spices, and butter. Put
the lot back into a pan, heat over a moderate
flame till thoroughly hot, stir in the whole
shrimps, and ladle the contents into small china
pots or dishes, leaving 1 cm (½ in) head room.
When quite cold cover with a thin layer of
clarified butter.

Meat

Meat: its cuts and cures

Meat is not only good eating but an outstandingly nutritious food. A mere 90 g ($3\frac{1}{2}$ oz) of cooked meat – or about 10 per cent of an adult male's daily calorie intake – provides him with 45 per cent of his day's protein requirements, 36 per cent of his iron, plus significant amounts of the essential B complex vitamins. Cooked meat also has what nutrition manuals prosaically describe as 'satiety value'; it leaves you feeling warmed, nourished and pleasantly full. One can easily work out a nutritious non-meat meal, but even when nicely cooked and satisfying it somehow fails to restore and comfort the inner man in quite the same way.

Meat is defined as the 'muscular flesh of edible animals' and broadly classified by colour – dark, red, pale – as well as type. Muscle itself is especially nourishing, which makes the meat of older, muscular animals good value, provided it is slowly and carefully cooked to make it tender. Freshly killed meat is tough, and indigestible; all meat sold commercially is hung in a cool place for at least a day or two to make it tender and improve its flavour. Tastes in meat change slowly but profoundly. Today's preference is universally for meat with the minimum of fat, and stock breeders naturally take note of this, producing lean pigs and trim steers which would appear undersized compared with the fatted-up animals of a century or more ago. In breeding out fatness, however, we may have bred out a fair bit of flavour too – fat, as it cooks, automatically bastes the lean, which adds to the flavour as well as succulence. I find that much of the meat sold today looks better than it tastes. Whether this is due to selective breeding, standardized foodstuffs, or over-use of steroids or other artificial meat-builders, is debatable. What is certain, happily, is that many of the old, traditional ways of preserving meat – salting, brining, drying, smoking – have a new relevance today, whether or not you are interested in their preservative value. They add flavour and interest to almost any type or cut of meat, and this includes the whole range of poultry, and frozen imported lamb and beef, as well as the traditional favourite, pork.

A spell in the brine tub, for instance, transforms any cut of pork, giving it a flavour and texture akin to gammon, which is particularly valuable in the case of fatty cuts, like pork belly, cheek or chaps, and what the English call 'hand', the French 'gorge'. Overnight dry curing with spices, salt and sugar, followed by a few hours cool smoking is the answer for anyone who finds turkey meat, especially frozen turkey meat, insipid eating. It makes the dark meat every bit as appetizing as the white, and is at its best eaten cold, the carcase making an exceptionally delicious soup. Dry spicing a fine round of beef for a week or two produces a cold cut of uniquely rich and racy flavour. At the other end of the price scale, there are all the time honoured ways of making the best of cheap, fatty cuts, scraps and trimmings and offal meat, ranging from the familiar pâtés and terrines to home-made sausage fillings, which can be bland and subtle, or ablaze with spice and garlic. These are pleasant and satisfying to make and can be stored in the deep freeze, or in many cases, dried and hung from the kitchen ceiling to be added to stews, paellas and thick soup as need arises.

I will not pretend that any of these traditional ruses are as simple as stashing stuff away in the freezer, but they greatly extend a cook's scope and many people will think the time and effort amply rewarded if it results in superb eating at very little extra cost – make one batch of home-made sausages and you will find yourself doing it for life.

The cheapest way to buy meat, as many freezer owners now do, is in bulk, a side of lamb or pork, or a quarter of beef at a time. Instead of freezing the lot, I would suggest that a more enlightened approach might be to reserve precious freezer space for choice roasting or grilling cuts, and use traditional preservation methods to deal with the remainder of the carcase, which might include along with such lesser cuts as heads, feet and tail, a variety of offal meats, including tongue, brains, heart and spleen. Most of these are the basis of excellent traditional recipes – pickled tongue, smoked heart, liver pâté, head cheese or brawn, faggots, salt trotters, smoked chap. If you have a cool smoker, or a suitable woodburning fireplace, it would be a pity not to try your hand at curing and smoking your own ham, since this is one of the most expensive meats to buy, and the techniques involved are quite simple if lengthy – after all home-cured hams were commonplace till electricity, gas and central heating did away with the old, roomy wood-burning hearth. A leg of lamb, incidentally, can be made into 'mutton ham', a delicacy little known outside Norway today but once made in all the sheep farming areas.

Having decided on your plan of campaign, draw up a list of what you hope to get from your side of lamb, pork, or quarter of beef, and then consult your butcher, or whoever is supplying the meat. It is a bit cheaper to cut up your carcase yourself, but this is such a skilful operation that it would be false economy for most people to try it. If you *must*, my butcher's advice is to start on something small like a side of lamb. Take it apart as if you were jointing an outsize rabbit, remembering – as with sawing wood – to cut across the grain, not along it. Otherwise leave it to the butcher, but let him know what cuts you want – hams for instance are cut quite differently from the conventional leg roasts.

More people keep poultry than raise livestock, so the possibility of a glut at certain times of year does arise here. Domestic fowl are plucked immediately after killing, then drawn. Hanging in a cold larder or cellar for a few days improves the flavour, but only when the weather is suitably crisp and cold and no flies are about. One of the most attractive traditional methods of dealing with surplus poultry is the celebrated *confit d'oie*, from the Périgord region of France, in which lightly salted and spiced goose joints are gently cooked and stored in their own rendered down fat, copious in the case of a goose. The method can be applied successfully to other birds, if their own fat is supplemented with clarified lard or dripping, and the result is meat of exceptional tenderness and flavour – miles away from the watery defrozen stuff – plus bowlfuls of delicous fat for cooking and frying. But make quite sure you do as the French always have: cook up the jars of *confit* every few months for the prescribed time – a few minutes in a low oven – to destroy any harmful toxins, and repeat this before finally eating the meat concerned. All poultry meat, home-raised or not, makes delicate and delicious terrines and galantines which will keep for months in a deep freeze.

Game

*'If there is one month worse than another for the amusement of shooting,
I should be apt to consider that it is November.
The warmer weather of September and October is then gone by,
and the birds become wild and cunning. The fall of the leaf,
with the sports of rabbit, woodcock, snipe and wildfowl shooting,
are not in general to be fully enjoyed till December and January.'*

Instructions to Young Sportsmen   Lt. Col. P. Hawker   1814

The meat which seems most in harmony with country living, vivid to taste and eye with all the concentrated essences of its wild habitats, is game, or the flesh of wild animals, such as venison, wild boar and hare, and the many varieties of game birds and wild fowl. A licence, or permission of some sort, is usually required to shoot any of these, and in most countries, a close season is observed in order to protect the animals and birds during their breeding times, and ensure that they are not hunted to extinction. Some wild creatures, like rabbits and pigeons, are classified as vermin in many countries, and can be shot at any time of the year. The distinction between game and vermin is finely drawn – not so long ago deer were considered vermin.

For most people, their first taste of game is positively startling, so richly coloured and strongly flavoured is it compared with butcher's meat, but carefully cooked and served with appropriate trimmings, game meat is noble fare and the basis for many superb, classic dishes. If you have never tasted game I suggest you begin with one of the milder flavoured meats – pheasant is a safe choice, or a fat rabbit – and ask the butcher to prepare it for cooking. Having once acquired a taste for this sort of meat, you can move on to the more robustly flavoured dark meats like hare and venison. Of the game sold in butchers' shops, hare is exceptional value for money, with enough meat to feed ten, or stretch to three meals – roast saddle, say, plus a pâté, pasty, or jugged dish. When buying game, look for signs of youth and health – bright plumage, sleek fur, supple uncalloused paws or claws. Or trust your butcher. Old game is usually cheaper, stronger flavoured, and meatier but needs long slow simmering *en casserole* to make it tender, as in those two classic dishes, jugged hare, or *perdrix au choux*. All game meat is extraordinarily rich, and needs an astringent contrast to be enjoyed fully; a sharp fruit jelly, a squeeze of orange juice, a dash of herb vinegar or a wine marinade are all traditional solutions. Most game meat, beast or bird, is dryish, since few wild creatures run to fat, so compensate when cooking – plain roasts should be basted with butter frequently, or larded with back fat, and game birds wrapped in streaky bacon.

A brace of pheasants on the butcher's block for plucking and drawing before cooking; hanging on butchers' hooks to ripen, still furred and feathered, are hare, quail and grouse. For first-time game cooks, pheasant is mild flavoured, hare robust dark meat.

Hanging

How long you do this depends on the weather (cold weather allows game to hang without spoiling for 1 to 3 weeks, while warm muggy weather means you should not leave it more than a few days), your tastes, and to some degree the age and size of the animal or bird. Old game is hung longer to tenderize it; large game like deer keep better longer than small birds. Note these rules. Except for rabbits, 'paunched' or disembowelled immediately they are killed, all game, furred or feathered, is hung with the guts in and the fur or feathers on. They keep better that way, oddly enough, and it is after they are made ready for cooking that they should not hang about too long. My butcher hangs venison for 2 weeks before paunching and skinning, and for a week after; game birds, on the other hand, are plucked and drawn the day before the customer wants to eat them. Game that is 'high' – smelly, in plain English – is quite safe to eat, provided you cook it thoroughly, but some claim it is indigestible.

Plucking and drawing

I do plucking sitting down, with the bird on my lap, and a large bucket for the feathers between my feet – even a small bird carries a mass of feathers. Take the bird in the left hand and begin pulling out the feathers from under the wing. Large feathers can generally be pulled out a few at a time, with a firm tug – pull the way the feather points – but breast feathers should be extracted one at a time to avoid tearing the delicate skin over the breast, so wasting valuable juice when it cooks. Obstinate feathers can be dealt with by singeing carefully over a gas flame. Wing tips are generally cut off before cooking, so do not bother plucking these. The same goes for head and neck. But the rest of your bird should be plucked smooth and bare as a bald pate. Where possible, extract any stray shot while plucking and drawing as these can be injurious to teeth if inadvertently chewed. Game birds and wild fowl are drawn like chickens, except for woodcock, which are cooked with the guts in. Cut off the head, feet and wingtips, and pull out the guts, retaining the liver to spread on toast under the bird.

Skinning and paunching

Skin first, then paunch, except for rabbit (see above). Professionals leave the head on, but you will find it is easier to cut the head off with the first joint of the legs, both fore and hind, which is the first step. Then slit the skin up the stomach and from there it is a bit like taking off a jacket. Using a sharp knife, cut and pull the legs clear of skin, then peel the skin back over the body of the animal, and give a good tug to release. To paunch make a cut up the belly, in the same direction as the skin was cut, and take out all the guts. Wipe out the cavity, or rinse out with clean cold water. Rabbit is often soaked in lightly salted water before cooking to whiten the meat and soak off any blood clots; hare's blood on the other hand is carefully saved, where possible, and added to the gravy or stock. If you are eating hare, rabbit or venison (or other game animals) regularly, and doing the skinning yourself it might be an idea to try your hand at curing and stretching the skins.

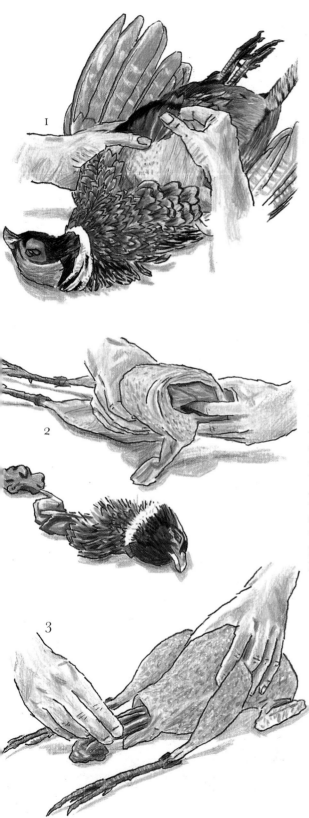

Plucking, drawing and trussing a pheasant

1. Hold the bird firmly in one hand to support its weight as you begin taking out the feathers. Always pull the way the feathers point. You can tug handfuls at a time, except over the delicate breastbone where the skin is likely to tear. Obstinate feathers can always be singed off over a gas flame. Leave on the feathers at the wingtip as you will trim these later.

2. Pull a fold of skin down the neck towards the body to give yourself a flap of skin once the head is removed. Then cut the head off, but before severing it, ease the knife blade round the inside of the neck passage to loosen the windpipe and the grain sack at the base. The whole matter should come away with the head.

3. To remove the entrails, heart, liver and guts, run your finger round the inside of the bird to loosen any matter from the bones. Then gradually ease the organs out of the bird. Do not hurry this process and peer inside later to see that everything has come away. The bits and pieces can be used for the stock, except for the liver which embitters any stock. Cook it separately while the bird is roasting and spread it on toast to serve underneath the bird, the way the French chefs do. Cut off the wingtips and the feet, above the knobbly socket.

4. Pull the flaps of skin both top and bottom over the openings. The bird is now ready for roasting. Once you have made a stuffing and placed it in the cavities, skewer the skin flaps in place and place larding strips of bacon over the bird as pheasant dries out when cooking.

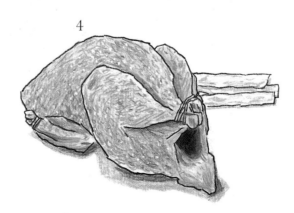

Pâtés, Pies & Galantines

"'There's cold chicken inside it," replied the Rat briefly;
"coldtonguecoldhamcoldbeefpickledgherkinssaladfrenchrollscress
sandwichespottedmeatgingerbeerlemonadesodawater –"
"Oh stop, stop," cried the Mole in ecstasies: "This is too much!"'

The Wind in the Willows   Kenneth Grahame   1908

I think of these made-up meat dishes as a sort of meat cake in which you can alter the texture by mincing everything several times, for smoothness, or inserting a layer of meat slivers, or stirring in a proportion of diced meat, or simply roughly chopping everything, for a coarse homespun effect. The main difference nowadays between a pâté and terrine would seem to be the frequent inclusion in terrines of slices or chunks of contrasting and different meats. A galantine, also a layered structure of meat, consists of either a boned, forcemeat-stuffed joint (a hand of pork or breast of veal), or a whole bird (chicken, turkey, pheasant), also boned and packed with forcemeat and good things, like truffles or pistachio nuts, before being stitched up and rolled in a floured pudding cloth. When cold and pressed, a galantine cuts as easily as a loaf of bread and looks spectacular, revealing its variegated filling. Finally, a good meaty mix can be enclosed in a sturdy edible container which makes a substantial and attractive pie. It is the surprise element in a pie that fascinates: the medieval banqueting showpiece piecrust held a whole aviary of birds boned and fitted inside each other. Today, there are many much simpler pies that can be made with a raised crust (a thick flour and water pastry) and the meat filling of your choice.

Ingredients can be cheap and basic, or as recherché and expensive as you like or can afford. I make a cheap, simple pâté regularly, using the least expensive liver and that most adaptable cheap cut, belly of pork – varying the seasonings according to what is growing, or how I feel. It is one of my most reliable stopgaps. All the cheaper, fatty, gristly, or strongly flavoured meats are potentially suited to pâtés and terrines because mincing refines the texture (always pick out stringy bits of gristle, chunks of fat as nasty surprises are another matter), prevents meat being tough, and a judicious use of bland flavoured meat like pork belly softens the most powerful tasting liver. I find the idea of a French pâté of lark's tongue unedifying but there is a place for the lavish set piece and the galantine fits the bill beautifully.

Cold meat dishes: Melton Mowbray raised pork pie and a veal and ham terrine larded with bacon (foreground); rabbit pâté, pork rillettes covered with butter and game pâté sprigged with sage (centre) and at the back, chicken galantine and simple daily pâté.

Pâtés and terrines

Pack a well seasoned forcemeat base of various meats, minced together with herbs or spices, juniper berries, maybe alcohol, garlic or onions, into a dish lined with streaky bacon or strips of fat (speck or hard back fat is best), cover it and bake gently. When making a terrine, a *salpicon*, or mixture of meat in strips or chunks, is sometimes added to the basic mixture to vary the texture. Stir it into the forcemeat, or keep it in a separate layer halfway up the dish. When cooked and pressed, it shows as a vein of marbling in a fine textured setting.

Take care to pick over the meats before and after mincing – cut off the gristle, membrane and any fibrous stuff which will not grind down properly and will not cook nicely either. A balance of flavour in the meat used helps both pâtés and terrines. Thus, some well flavoured lean meat, some bland fat meat and some meat of smooth texture with concentrated flavour, like liver, is a good combination. If you add a little bacon or ham to line the dish, go easy on the salt.

You can add a little flour or beaten egg to the mixture before cooking to bind it. Do not overdo it or the mixture can become stodgy. Dishes to be turned out can have a decorative spray of bay leaves laid on the bottom underneath the fat strip.

Equipment
An electric blender or chopper does make preparing minced meat mixtures very much easier and quicker, and some will deal with chopping onions, garlic and herbs finely as well. However, chopping by hand with a sharp *demi-lune* or cleaver is still the slow but sure way to the juiciest and freshest tasting pâtés and terrines. Electric gadgets do bash some of the natural springiness out of meat and the juice tends to get lost. Make several small pâtés rather than one large one so that you can seal some with lard to keep in the freezer. They are best made in traditional earthenware dishes, round or oval, the simpler the better. Lidded dishes are best.

Cooking pâtés and terrines
All pâtés and terrines should be cooked slowly and evenly, standing in a pan of hot water. Remove the lid to brown for the last half hour if they are not to be turned out. They are done when the meat shrinks away from the sides of the dish – do not be misled by a pinky tinge to the meat as any bacon colours the contents like that. To press out the fat, lay a plate with a small board on top, and weight with tins or kitchen weights overnight. Next day loosen round the edges with a knife, and turn out onto a dish. Pâtés and terrines will cut better when pressed.

For keeping longer (up to a few days) leave the dish to get cold then run a good layer of pure lard – 2 cm ($\frac{3}{4}$ in) deep – over the top to seal it well, making sure it adheres to the dish all round. Keep in the refrigerator. Or you could turn out the pâté when cold, scrape off all the fat on the outside, return to dish and pour in hot lard, enough to float it in. When cold pour a sealing layer on top. Or, lastly, pack the pâté into a Le Parfait preserving jar up to the level indicated, put on the soaked ring, clip shut and sterilize by putting into a pan with cold water to cover, bringing slowly to the boil and simmering for two hours.

Pies and galantines

Pies

The most handsome traditional pies are meaty fillings enclosed by hand-shaped raised crust pastry. The stock is poured in after the pie has been baked and cooled through a hole in the centre of the pastry lid.

The pastry case

Sieve strong plain white flour and salt into a deep bowl and make a well in the centre. Meanwhile, bring pure lard and water to the boil and when boiling, steadily tip into the bowl, mixing with a wooden spoon. As soon as the hot alabaster paste is cool enough to handle, work it vigorously till smooth – pummel, pound and knead. Leave in a warm place to rest for 15 minutes. Take up the pastry in a lump, and hollow it out from the middle with a coaxing finger, keeping it thick and solid till there is enough space to set inside a suitable mould, like a glass jar, to model round. Turn the mould upside down with the pastry over the base, and work downwards. Or you can place the pastry inside a hinged pie case and begin working up the sides gradually. Aim to keep the crust even throughout and no more than 6 mm ($\frac{1}{4}$ in) thick or the pastry will resemble the stodgy commercial efforts. When the crust reaches the top of the case, or sufficiently far down the jar, it is time to stop. To loosen the paste from the jar, lay it on its side and roll gently. Clip round the top with scissors to neaten. Pack with the prepared meat filling, closely but not ramming it in or you will make bulges in the crust. Roll a lid from the trimmings and damp the edges before laying the lid on top and nipping together firmly – use your thumb to make a piecrust edging. Now cut a neat hole in the middle of the lid and decorate with leaves, scrolls or acorns made from the leftover scraps of pastry. Damp these before placing on the lid. A tiny twist of paper set in the hole keeps it open while cooking. Brush over the outside of the pie with beaten egg for a golden finish. Cook in a moderate oven at 160°C (325°F, Mark 3) for 2 to 2$\frac{1}{2}$ hours. If the top is browning too much, cover with a loose lid of foil. Leave the pie to cool for an hour, while the crust stiffens, before pouring in the stock. The stock should be warm, not hot. If in doubt about the strength of the side, a foil belt helps. Leave to go quite cold overnight before serving.

Galantines

A boned chicken, pork hand, or breast of veal makes a neat pocket which you simply pack with the chosen ingredients, sew shut, then simmer, tied in a floured cloth. The meat envelope bastes the forcemeat as it cooks. Sliced when cold and pressed the galantine is an altogether excellent choice for party food.

Cooking galantines

Boning a chicken is not as difficult as it sounds (full instructions on page 153). The forcemeat and other ingredients are packed into the boned bird or joint, and built up with an eye to the effect when cooked and sliced through. Stitch the bird or joint into shape, parcel up in muslin or sheeting and cook in stock. Cool, lightly press, cut off wrapping and stitching and glaze with the reduced stock.

Pâtés, terrines and potted meats

There are many classic recipes in the field to use as a yardstick for gauging relative proportions of lean meat to fat, salty to bland, seasonings to overall bulk, but try now experimenting with a splash of brandy, another time fresh herbs or truffles.

Simple daily pâté
This pâté has the advantage of being cheap, tasty and endlessly variable. Add a little spice, herbs or brandy.

225 g (8 oz) streaky bacon
450 g (1 lb) pig, sheep or ox liver
450 g (1 lb) belly of pork
1 small onion
2 cloves garlic
2 teaspoons juniper berries
1 egg
1 teaspoon salt
¼ teaspoon pepper

Cut the rind off the bacon and line an earthenware dish with strips of bacon – reserving some for the cover. Finely mince the liver and the pork belly, which you have trimmed of skin and bone, with the onion and the garlic. Roughly crush the berries and stir them in with the well beaten egg, salt and pepper. Turn the mixture into the dish, cover with the remaining bacon strips, then the lid and bake in a *bain marie* for about one hour, or till the meat shrinks away from the sides of the dish, at 160°C (325°F, Mark 3).

Rabbit pâté
Rabbit meat, so often disappointing on its own (unless the rabbits are young, wild and herb scented), makes a light, pleasant pâté, eked out with veal and pork.

450 g (1 lb) rabbit meat (boned)
450 g (1 lb) veal
450 g (1 lb) belly of pork
1 onion
3 cloves garlic
120 ml (4 oz) white wine or wine vinegar
1 tablespoon each chopped parsley, thyme
rind of 1 lemon
225 g (8 oz) speck or hard back fat
a pinch of salt, pepper
1 tablespoon plain flour

Dice all the meats roughly (not the speck) removing gristle and membranes. Mince them together with the onion and the garlic. Meanwhile boil up any bones and scraps with a little white wine or wine vinegar to make a stock. Mix the chopped meats with the herbs, the grated lemon rind and the speck, cut into small cubes, and season with salt and pepper. Add a small glass of reduced stock, mixed with one tablespoon of plain flour. Pack into a dish, cover with foil, then the lid, stand in a pan of water and bake for 1½ to 2 hours at 160°C (325°F, Mark 3). Press with weights overnight.

Game pâté
French cooking is especially rich in pâtés made with game, and these are an excellent way of stretching an old bird, and relieving its dryness. Use pheasant, partridge, or capercaillie.

1 game bird
225 g (8 oz) veal
675 g (1½ lb) speck or hard back fat
3 eggs
150 ml (¼ pint) brandy or whisky
a handful of fresh parsley
1 tablespoon fresh thyme
1 teaspoon each juniper berries and coriander seeds
salt, pepper and nutmeg

Bone the bird carefully, reserving the best pieces whole. Mince the scraps with the veal and just over 450 g (1 lb) of speck, leaving enough to line the dish. Beat up the eggs and brandy (or whisky) and mix these into the forcemeat, with chopped herbs, crushed spices, salt, pepper and nutmeg. Leave in a cool place for a few hours for the flavours to mature. Then line a large terrine with strips of fat, and build up layers of alternate forcemeat and pieces of game, ending with forcemeat. Cover with more strips of fat, then foil, then a lid, stand in a pan of water and bake for 2½ hours at 160°C (325°F, Mark 3). Cool under a light weight and eat the next day.

Veal and ham terrine with fresh herbs

The charm of this summery pâté is the contrast between pink meat and tender green herbs – use a large handful of mixed fresh herbs from the garden, leaving out sage.

450 g (1 lb) ham
450 g (1 lb) belly of pork
450 g (1 lb) veal
3 cloves garlic
a handful of fresh herbs, finely chopped
a handful of fresh watercress or spinach, finely chopped
salt, pepper and nutmeg
small glass brandy or whisky
100 g (4 oz) streaky bacon
1 egg

Dice the ham small, mince the pork and the veal coarsely together, or chop by hand. Crush the garlic, and add to the mixed meats along with the herbs and watercress or spinach, salt, pepper, nutmeg and spirits. Leave for a few hours or overnight. Line a terrine with a lattice of bacon strips, cut in half. Stir a well beaten egg into the meat mixture and then pack it into the terrine, cover with more bacon lattices, then the lid and bake in a slow oven for 2 hours at 160°C (325°F, Mark 3). Leave to cool unpressed.

Rillettes

One of a clutch of dishes which are not strictly pâtés, or terrines, but more in the nature of potted meats. This dish of belly of pork cooked long and slowly and lightly flavoured is very good eaten with hot toast.

1 kg (2 lb) belly of pork
1 clove garlic
salt, pepper, nutmeg or mace
a sprig of fresh thyme or rosemary

Remove the skin and any bones from the meat, cut into small cubes and put them into a heavy cast iron pot with the other ingredients. Cook in the oven at the lowest setting or on top of the stove over a gentle heat, for at least four hours until all the fat is liquid and the meat is brown scraps. By then the pork bits should be just crisping and swimming in their own fat. Sieve off the fat into a pan. Pound the meat in a pestle and mortar. Season well. Pack into small jars and when cold pour over a thick layer – 2 cm ($\frac{3}{4}$ in) – of the strained fat. Cover with foil. Store in a cold dry place, the larder rather than the refrigerator.

Confit d'oie (preserved goose)

Though not many readers will have a surplus goose problem, this recipe ought to be included in any book on preserving food. The same technique may be used with other meats – rabbits, large pieces of pork, sausages. The pieces of meat are cooked very slowly in lard or their own fat (in the case of a goose) till tender, then packed into a deep stoneware or glass jar with a wide mouth and covered with hot fat, which makes a perfect seal when cold and hard. Covered with silver foil, these will keep for months in a cold dry place. A bonus is that the fat will be deliciously flavoured for frying potatoes, or cooking other meat. To retrieve the confit, heat the jar gently and hook out what you need, making sure the rest stays covered with lard. Before you eat it, you must heat the *confit* for three minutes at 70°C (158°F) to ensure potential bacteria are killed off.

1 goose (5 kg/10 lb), cut into six pieces with all fat removed
1 kg (2 lb) pure lard, enough to cover the goose pieces, together with the goose fat itself
To each 450 g (1 lb) of meat allow :
1 heaped tablespoon sea salt
$\frac{1}{4}$ teaspoon saltpetre
$\frac{1}{4}$ teaspoon dried thyme
1 crumbled bay leaf

Mix together the salt and other dry ingredients, rub into the pieces of goose and leave in a cool place covered for 24 hours. The next day, rinse the goose pieces free of salt and dry them. Then melt all the goose fat slowly in a heavy pan, add the pieces of meat, and enough pure lard to float the pieces. Cook very slowly for about $2\frac{1}{2}$ hours, till a skewer stuck in shows no juice bubbling out. Put a little fat into a large, cleaned and scalded preserve jar, then pack in the drained pieces of meat, and cover with hot fat. Leave to cool, till the meat is imprisoned in cold fat, then top up generously with more of the fat. Press silver foil down onto the lard and store in a cool place.

Pies and galantines

Galantines and the raised pie pastry case both make edible, sturdy containers for meat fillings. They seal in the meat juices while the dish cooks, as well as making it more substantial and attractive. Yield: 8–10 servings.

Melton Mowbray raised pork pie

The most celebrated raised pork pie, firm, juicy and made rosy by the use of a little anchovy essence in the stock.

Stock or jelly

1 pair trotters, veal knuckle, pig's ears or tail, odd bones or trimmings of the meat
a bundle of herbs – sage, marjoram, parsley, bay leaf
1 onion stuck with two cloves
a bowlful of apple cores (optional but traditional, the pips give a faint almond taste)
1 teaspoon anchovy essence
salt and pepper

Filling

1¼ kg (2¾ lb) pork (shoulder or hand)
225 g (8 oz) gammon, ham or salt pork
1 teaspoon each of salt and ground white peppercorns
3 leaves of sage and a sprig of marjoram

Pastry crust

600 g (1¼ lb) plain flour
250 g (9 oz) lard
200 g (7 oz) water
½ teaspoon salt

Start by making the stock. Put all the ingredients except the anchovy essence and salt and pepper, into a large pan with cold water to cover, bring to the boil, skim, then simmer for three or four hours, with the lid on. Strain off through a cloth into a new pan and boil hard till reduced to 600 ml (1 pint). Season with the anchovy essence, pepper and salt if needed. When cold, skim off the fat.

Meanwhile, prepare the filling. Trim the meat of gristle but leave on any firm white fat. Cut into neat small dice – about 2 cm (¾ in). Mince or finely chop ham or salt pork. Mix with the pork dice, sprinkle over the pepper, salt and herbs. Leave to mingle flavours overnight. Next day make the raised crust (see page 149). Fill the crust with the prepared meat and bake for 2½ hours at 160°C (325°F, Mark 3). Cover with foil for the first hour. When cooled, pour in the stock through the hole in the pastry case. Serve cold.

Galantine of pork, boned and stuffed

A coarser textured galantine than the next recipe, but full of flavour. A pork hand – the forehock – is a large, but not expensive, joint that makes a capacious cover for the stuffing.

1 hand of pork, boned

Forcemeat stuffing

1 pig's tongue (cooked)
450 g (1 lb) belly of pork
450 g (1 lb) veal
2 cloves garlic
1 truffle (optional)
225 g (8 oz) field mushrooms
a bunch of parsley
salt, pepper, nutmeg and cinnamon

Stock

2 pig's trotters
2 onions stuck with cloves
3 carrots
½ bottle white wine
3 cloves garlic
1 litre (1¾ pints) water

Open out the hand of pork, cut off any large chunks of meat which spoil its symmetry and mince these up with the three meats. (Or add the tongue separately as a *salpicon*, with whole mushrooms, bits of truffle.) Add crushed garlic, slivers of truffle, mushrooms, herbs, spices and seasonings to this mixture, and leave while you make the stock. Boil up the stock ingredients until well cooked and tasty, then add the wine. Lay out the pork, stuff with the forcemeat, and tie with string. Then cover with a cloth, tie and simmer in the stock for four to five hours, exceedingly gently. Leave to cool in the stock for a while, then remove, press and leave to grow cold. Use the jellied stock to glaze and decorate.
Note: It would be a pity not to use the truffle as the flavour is beautiful with pork, but for a cheaper alternative you might try adding peeled cooked chestnuts and stoned prunes (not too many) to the forcemeat, or some stoned black and green olives.

Chicken galantine

A resplendent dish for grand occasions. Use a fresh chicken or substitute a small turkey.

2–3 kg (6–7 lb) chicken, boned

Stock

2 pig's trotters
bones for stock
1 onion stuck with 2 cloves
1 carrot
½ bottle dry white wine
a bouquet garni
1 litre (1¾ pints) water

Salpicon layer

50 g (2 oz) pistachio nuts
225 g (8 oz) ham
a small tin foie gras
1 chicken liver
1 glass brandy, sherry or white wine

Forcemeat stuffing

1 kg (2 lb) lean pork and 450 g (1 lb) hard back pork
  or 450 g (1 lb) lean pork and 1 kg (2 lb) belly of pork
100 g (4 oz) streaky bacon
a sprig of thyme, marjoram and tarragon
salt, pepper, nutmeg, coriander
2 eggs

Put the chicken carcase, scraps and bones into a large pot with the other stock ingredients and simmer gently for 1 or 2 hours, covered. Strain and set aside.

Meanwhile make the *salpicon* layer. Blanch the pistachio nuts in boiling water and skin them. Cut the ham into strips. Cut the foie gras into cubes. Lightly fry the sliced liver and put all these into a bowl with the brandy or white wine mix and leave to marinate.

To make the forcemeat, finely mince up the lean and fat meats, without any skin and bones, together with the streaky bacon. Add the chopped herbs, spices, seasonings, and mix in the beaten eggs.

Now lay the boned bird breast down, seasoned lightly inside with salt and pepper, and pack it with a thick layer of forcemeat. Then add *salpicon* in a thick layer from front to back. Finish with forcemeat, stitch as shown below and wrap in a cloth. Put into the strained stock and gently simmer for 2 hours. Remove, press lightly between two boards to extract surplus liquid. Next day, remove wrapping and stitching and glaze with aspic. Decorate with bay leaves and truffles as shown on page 146.

To bone a chicken for a galantine, split the chicken with a sharp knife the entire length of the back. Loosen the carcase, being careful not to pierce the skin further. Gently detach the flesh from the bones. Leave the wing bones in, but prise the leg bone out of the socket with a knife. Lay the forcemeat upon the boned bird, breast side down on the board and sandwich with layers of *salpicon* for contrast. Wrap the skin back over the filling and stitch.

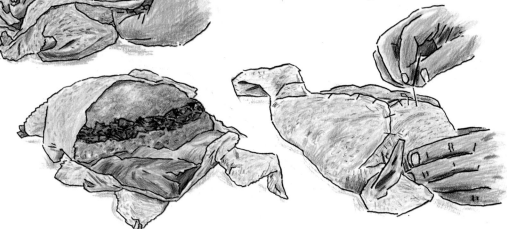

Sausages

'One gentle bite and it surrendered with an opulent pop
and a portion fell easily into the mouth.
It was a delicious mixture of tender meats
and mouth-melting fats concocted by an artist in gastronomy.'
101 Jubilee Road: A Book of London Yesterdays   Frederick Willis   1948

There is scarcely a country in the world which does not claim at least one distinctively national sausage, and some like France, Germany and Italy have developed sausage making into a highly specialized branch of charcuterie. Its popularity is hardly surprising when you consider that the sausage is probably as neat, handy and adaptable a food package as has ever been invented, and, if dried, keeps well too. In the days when every household was pressed for new ways of preserving food, dried sausages emerged as an excellent way of preserving meat, the gut casing allowing the natural moisture to dry out gradually while guarding the contents against dust, flies and bacteria. *Chorizo* made with wine, garlic and spices and dried in a warm airy place, keeps indefinitely and goes on getting more pungent and exciting all the time – one chunk of a well matured *chorizo* is enough to put new life into a bean casserole (and incidentally your kitchen too).

Home-made sausages stuffed with pure meat, fresh herbs or spices and laced with wine, garlic or whatever else the cook may feel inspired to try, are superb food, and a revelation to anyone brought up on the degraded factory product with its permitted 'cereal' content, standardized seasoning and distinct tang of preservative.

A certain insouciance seems to go with sausage making. Knowing that nothing can go wrong should encourage you to experiment, and invent – there are scores of traditional recipes to browse through of course but do not be shy of altering or adapting to suit your needs, likes and budget. If you dote on garlic, for instance, use twice as much; if you are trying to economize use a cheaper, fattier cut of pork, beef or whatever (a good proportion of fat makes any sausage more succulent); if the recipe says marjoram when your garden is buried in basil, make the switch, with confidence. You can always fry up a morsel to taste how it is going.

One sausage-making suggestion – the time and trouble which goes into making one's own sausages is likely to seem more justified when making something a bit different. That is not to say that pure pork sausages discreetly livened with nutmeg and herbs are not a joy to encounter, but you must expect the lot to disappear at a sitting, whereas the pungent *chorizo* imposes restraints and thus lasts for months.

Argentinian *chorizos* hang from the rafters, maturing; bowls of freshly minced sausage meat contain a rosy Scandinavian game mix based on venison (centre, back) and a pork sausage mix for the Pennsylvanian Dutch sausages (right) and in the centre are faggots, parcelled in lacy caul.

Sausage making

Equipment

A butcher's sausage machine pumps filling into gut at the rate of a foot a second, and costs a vast amount. An obliging butcher will sometimes fill sausage casings with your own prepared stuffing, but you would need to think big – 10 kilos (20 lbs) of meat, say – to make it worth his while. No domestic-sized machine can compete with these for speed and efficiency, as they have not got the push, but there are several modest models to choose from. Simplest, and cheapest, is an outsize syringe affair – the plunger forces meat out into gut threaded over the nozzle. Some brands of electric mixer come with a sausage-filling attachment. Smaller versions of the butcher's machine can be found quite cheaply, if they are old models reconditioned.

To fill sausage by hand you need only a plastic funnel and long smooth wooden stick, or spoon handle, to push the meat through into the gut. An electric mincer, or chopper, cuts down immensely on the time spent preparing the stuffing, but it can improve the texture of sausages to incorporate some coarser chopped meat, or fat cubes, and for this you need a very sharp knife. Large bowls are needed to take sausage-meat.

The most vital item, however, is of course the basic gut or casing, which comes in three sizes depending whether it belonged to a sheep (*chipolata* size), pig (standard banger size) or ox (hefty *mortadella* size). Pig casing is the easiest to buy – butchers who make their own sausages will usually sell you what you need. For sheep or ox gut you may have to contact butchers' suppliers – see your local classified directory. If ox gut is unobtainable you can substitute stitched cheesecloth tubes, made by yourself, Casings come dried and salted, and need soaking before use.

Ingredients

Almost any meat, or combination of meats, can be used for sausages, but pork is the universal favourite because of its bland flavour, texture and succulence. It is a perfect background for special effects with spices and wine. A hand of pork is a cheap cut, meaty and quite lean, or there is shoulder, leaner still. Belly of pork, usually about half fat, half lean, is the most economical and tasty basic sausage-meat and should always be added if you are making sausages from dry meat such as venison.

Cuts like beef-shin, which generally need prolonged cooking to tenderize them, are fine minced up for sausages as long as you remove carefully stringy tendons and membranes. Used with discretion, some cereal mixed in adds smoothness to a meat stuffing. Use home-made bread crumbs (not the packet sort), oatmeal or barley, or mashed potato.

For a complete change from all-meat, try an all-cereal sausage such as the traditional white pudding, well seasoned with herbs. It is pleasant sliced and fried with bacon. Blood sausages can be very good, but they are outside the scope of most people since the blood needs to be quite fresh and kept constantly stirred to prevent clotting. Faggots (or in France, *crépinettes*) are bundles of forcemeat wrapped in 'caul' – the pretty lacy fat lining the stomach, which bastes the meat as it cooks. Get caul fat from your butcher.

Herbs

Fresh or dried herbs can be used, remembering that fresh are much less pungent. Thyme, savory, marjoram, sage, basil are all good, used singly or mixed.

Spices

Whole spices, freshly ground have most potency. Coriander, mace, nutmeg, cloves, peppercorns and cinnamon are all used, in various combinations. Paprika has a special use in sausage making – adding colour as well as spiciness. If you want red or rosy sausages, and do not like the idea of using saltpetre, be generous with paprika, or its Spanish equivalent, pimento. Use fresh onions and garlic, rather than onion or garlic salt; however convenient they give that monosodium taste again.

Wine and spirits

A splash of wine adds excitement to any sausage mixture, and helps preserve it too; use the cheapest, or homemade. Cooking sherry or port gives alcoholic mellowness much more cheaply than brandy.

Storing and drying

To make the breaks between sausages, just twist the casings. For long term storage, tie with thread as shown on next page.

Sausages made from highly perishable meat, such as brains or liver, or intended to be eaten fresh should be kept in the fridge overnight for flavours to mature, then used as soon as possible. Since they do not contain preservative, fresh pork sausages should be eaten rather quicker than the commercial sort, and always stored in the fridge. Most sausages can be deep frozen for up to a month or six weeks, but the flavour and texture may not be quite so good. To dry sausages – these should be the spicy kind, preferably containing some beef which dries fast as well as pork, and wine too – simply hang them high up in a warm, dry but draughty spot. The opposite end of the kitchen from your cooker, range or boiler is as good as any. After three or four days they will have darkened and shrunk noticeably, and after ten days they should be quite hard and dry, and may be moved to a cool, dry place.

Another simple and attractive old method of storing sausages is to fry them first and then cover with melted lard, in a stoneware or glass jar – as with *confit d'oie* (see page 151). Make sure you cover them to a depth of 2.5 cm (1 in) at the top. Seal with aluminium foil. The charm of this method is that the lard will be flavoured nicely (use for frying) and the sausages tastier than if they were frozen. But you must heat these sausages for three minutes at 70°C (158°F) before eating them.

Smoking

This is a traditional way of flavouring and drying off some sausages, much used in Germany for their large *Würste*. A sausage for smoking should first be weighed, then dried off slowly for a few days in a warm dry place. Finally cool smoke for about five hours – when it has lost about 25 per cent weight it should be done.

Making farmhouse sausages, preserved in lard

1. The ideal gut casing for the ordinary frying 'banger' comes from the pig. A comfortable length to work with is $1\frac{3}{4}$ m (2 yd), kept moist and pliable by soaking in a bowl of water. Pork meat is traditionally used for country sausages. Take either 2 kg (4 lb) of pork belly, or for a leaner mixture, $1\frac{1}{2}$ kg (3 lb) of pork belly and 500 g (1 lb) of lean meat (shoulder for instance), and mince.

2. 225 g (8 oz) speck, or pork back fat may be added to the meat, cut into manageable cubes. When you get to the stuffing stage, it gives you a more solid filling.

3. Spices and herbs add original flavour to sausages, and here the cook can take the initiative: the standard mixture of spices is nutmeg, cloves and cinnamon, pounded in a mortar and pestle with salt and black peppercorns. For herbs, one handful of parsley, finely chopped is a staple, to be embellished with chopped thyme, marjoram, sage or basil. 500 g (1 lb) breadcrumbs may also be included to contribute a smoothness to the meat stuffing. Mix all these ingredients in a large bowl.

4. In the absence of sophisticated gadgetry to fill the casings, all you need is a simple funnel and a wooden spoon (it helps if the neck of the funnel and the handle of the spoon are roughly the same

diameter). Thread the entire length of soaked gut on to the neck of the funnel to form a ruff, and knot the end of the length.

5. Fill the funnel with sausagemeat, and push into the casing, forcing the meat down with the handle of the spoon until a respectable sized sausage is formed (about 10 cm/4 in long).

6. To eliminate air bubbles and pack the meat firmly into the case, use your hands. As sausages swell while cooking under rather than overfill.

7. There are various ways of fastening off sausages. The simplest is to twist the gut but this will not hold for smoking, or hanging sausages to dry. Using string, you can tie a knot at each intersection, or to give a professional finish, continue the string up the length of your whole run of sausages.

8. Your farmhouse sausages are now ready to be eaten straight away, or they may be preserved if the sausages are thoroughly cooked (fried is probably best).

9. Pour off the juices given off during cooking and fill a glass preserving jar with the sausages. Pour melted lard (half a packet will probably be enough) over the sausages. Allow the lard to set, imprisoning the sausages by 2.5 cm (1 in).

Note: Before eating the sausages, they must be heated through thoroughly for three minutes at 70°C (158°F).

Sausages

The sausage is one of the most convenient forms of packed food – a pleasure to make, delicious to eat in either its simplest form or with subtle variations and, if properly dried and possibly smoked, easy to keep.

Scandinavian game sausage
Venison is a good substitute for the traditional reindeer or elk. Not an everyday sausage but an exceptionally fine flavoured one – marvellous barbecue food.

1½ kg (3 lb) pork belly
2 kg (4 lb) venison
225 g (8 oz) speck, or hard back pork fat
1 tablespoon coriander
1 tablespoon allspice
1 teaspoon cloves
4 cloves garlic
4 tablespoons salt
2 tablespoons black peppercorns
300 ml (½ pint) red wine or port
pig casings

Remove the rind and rib bones from pork belly and put through your mincer with the game meat. Cut the speck into 2 cm (¾ in) cubes by hand and mix into the minced meat. Pound all the spices and mix into the meat mixture with crushed garlic, salt and pepper – use your hands to mix really thoroughly. Pour over the wine or port. Leave for a couple of hours, then stuff the skins, making short fat links. Leave in a cool place for 24 hours before eating, to allow the flavours to develop. Best broiled (fried) over charcoal.

Pennsylvanian Dutch sausage
Strongly spiced pure pork sausage to eat fresh, freeze, smoke or store in lard.

2 kg (4 lb) belly of pork
1 kg (2 lb) shoulder or hand of pork
2 tablespoons cloves
3 tablespoons coriander
1 teaspoon nutmeg
3 tablespoons salt
2 teaspoons pepper
a large handful of chopped fresh sage, or 6 tablespoons dry rubbed sage
pig casings

Cut the skin and rib bones from the pork belly, roughly chop all the meat then mince medium fine. Pound all the spices to powder, then add to the meat with salt, pepper and finely chopped fresh or dried sage. Stuff the casings, making short fat links – about 10 cm (4 in). Hang in a cool place overnight to develop flavour. Eat fresh or freeze. For smoking, leave the sausages to dry off in a cool airy place for two to three days, then smoke at 20°C (70°F) for five hours.

Schwäbischewurst
A fine textured, large sausage (use a muslin bag if you cannot get ox casing), good fresh or smoked. Spice with caraway seeds for a distinctly Continental flavour. This sausage is good eaten fresh with dill pickles, or smoked.

1 kg (2 lb) lean pork shoulder
450 kg (1 lb) speck or hard back fat
1 teaspoon sugar
2 tablespoons salt
½ tablespoon black pepper
3 cloves garlic
1 tablespoon caraway seeds
4 tablespoons white wine
ox casing

Roughly cut up the lean pork and speck, and put through your mincer once. Sprinkle over sugar, salt, ground pepper, working in well with both hands, then mince twice more, until pasty and smooth. Crush garlic and caraway seeds, and pound them with wine to a mush. Work this well into the meat. If you are using a blender give it another few seconds to blend. Stuff into soaked ox casings or two muslin or cheesecloth tubes about 30 cm (1 ft) long, 8 cm (3 in) diameter, tying both ends. Lower the *Würste* into simmering water, turn heat up until boiling, then turn down and simmer gently for 45 minutes. Drain and serve hot (cut off the covers of course), or leave to cool, then smoke for eight hours at 15–20°C (60–70°F).

Argentine chorizo

A first class sausage for drying, which concentrates the spicy, garlicky flavour. This is an old family recipe. Being Argentinian, it naturally includes beef which also helps the drying out process, as beef dries quicker than pork. Paprika gives the orangey-red colour.

2 kg (4 lb) belly of pork
300 ml (½ pint) red wine
6 cloves garlic
½ nutmeg
1 teaspoon cloves
1 tablespoon finely chopped fresh thyme or marjoram, or half tablespoon of dried herbs
3 tablespoons salt
½ tablespoon black peppercorns
2 tablespoons paprika or pimento
1 kg (2 lb) shin of beef
pig casing

Remove the rind and bones from pork belly and cut off the thick outer strip of fat. Dice the strip of fat and set the rest aside. Boil up the wine with crushed garlic, pounded spices and herbs, add salt, pepper and paprika and leave to cool. Cut off as much gristle from the shin of beef as possible, then roughly dice it with the lean pork belly and mince quite finely. Pick out any strings of membranous fat which refuse to be ground up. Strain the wine marinade and pour on to the minced meat. Mix in the diced fat and leave overnight. Next day stuff into 15 cm (6 in) links, twisting or tying off. Hang in a warm dry place for a week or two, till hard and knobbly, then transfer to a cool dry spot. As they dry harder, they will need longer cooking.

White pudding

Cooked and dried these oatmeal sausages keep for weeks. The best fat to use is 'flead' – a hard white fat surrounding the kidneys.

1 kg (2 lb) oatmeal (coarse porridge variety)
½ kg (1 lb) pig or sheep's flead
2 onions
3 tablespoons chopped parsley
mint, thyme (for mutton) or sage, rosemary (for pork)
salt and pepper
pig casing

Spread oats out on a baking tin and dry out thoroughly in the oven at the lowest setting for ten minutes. Very finely chop onion, herbs, and flead and add to oats, with salt and pepper. Stuff skins, leaving 2.5 cm (1 in) space in each link, for the oats to swell in cooking. Drop in boiling water and cook for 40 minutes, pricking here and there with a needle as they swell, to prevent bursting. Drain and hang up to dry.

Faggots

The answer for cooks who cannot get casings.

A variety on the theme: sausage-meat parcelled up in lacy caul fat instead of being stuffed into skins. The fat melts during cooking, and bastes the contents. Buy caul fat – usually frozen – from your butcher, and soak in salty water before use. 100 g (4 oz) wraps about 18 faggots.

450 g (1 lb) belly of pork
400 g (1 lb) pig's liver
1 large or 2 small onions
lard or butter
1 clove garlic
1 tablespoon dried sage
½ teaspoon each ground nutmeg, cinnamon
salt, black pepper
2 eggs
100 g (4 oz) fresh breadcrumbs
caul fat

Remove the skin and any rib bones from belly of pork, and put through coarse mincer with liver, onion and garlic. Tip the lot into a large frying pan with a nut of lard or butter and fry over gentle heat for 20 minutes, stirring now and then. Remove from the heat, drain any liquid off and mince again, more finely, adding herbs and spices and seasonings. Mix in the eggs, well beaten, then breadcrumbs made by giving a thick slice of bread a whirl in the blender. Wrap egg-sized lumps of meat in caul fat and arrange them in a greased shallow oven dish, touching each other. Add just enough water, stock or wine to cover the bottom of the tin. Bake for 45 minutes in a moderate oven (190°C, 375°F, Mark 5), pouring off all the liquid after half an hour. Blot the fat off with kitchen paper, return to dish. Eat hot or cold.

Dry Salted Meats

'Then my grandmother decided how much salt should be rubbed into each piece
before it was pressed with heavy stones in a huge, open-mouthed earthen jar
and left for ten days or more. After ten days or so
my grandmother asked the servants to take the pork out and look at it.
If it was still as red, or redder than originally, it would be very good.'

A Chinese Childhood   Chiang Yee   1940

There are two approaches to dry salting meat: one is mainly preservative, the other mainly for flavour. The preservative method, used in living memory to keep cut-up parts of the family pig over the winter, was simply to bury the joints in a snow drift of salt. Stone troughs were specially scooped out for the purpose (stone is naturally cool). Treated like this the meat stayed good for several months. Of course, certain rules were followed in all this: pigs were slaughtered (often by a local butcher who did the rounds) after the cold weather set in, never in muggy or unsettled weather. The whole family helped prepare the meat for the salt trough, and the pieces went in as quickly as possible. The trough itself was naturally kept in a cool place. As preservatives went, this was quick, cheap and reliable, but of course it did little for the meat except make it saltier, needing to be soaked for days to make it eatable.

The flavouring method of dry salting is the one most likely to appeal today.

Briefly, what dry salting, or dry curing or dry spicing as it's called in some old recipes, involves is rubbing the fresh meat liberally and thoroughly with a mixture, usually of coarse salt (sea salt gives finer flavour), sugar, spices and saltpetre (ascorbic acid, if you prefer). It is then kept in a cool place, turned and rubbed daily with the mixture (a little more liquid each day, as the natural lymph drains out) for varying lengths of time, depending on the size and the degree of flavouring wanted. The point of *dry* salting like this, as compared with the wet pickle (sometimes called wet salting, to confuse everyone a bit more) is that it strikes into a large piece of meat more quickly, encouraging the lymph, or natural fluids, to drain rapidly. For this reason it was often done to hams for a day or two before they went into a slow pickle cure. So much fluid is released from a large ham that the pickle would have been much diluted otherwise, and this risked spoiling the meat. In this case, salt alone was used, and the salted ham pressed overnight under a weighted board.

Various meats dry salted and spiced for flavour: dry salted tongue in the foreground; topside of beef rubbed with spices and juniper berries, ready to be cooked in pastry (centre) and, at the back, a bath chap (miniature ham), cooked and rolled in golden breadcrumbs.

Dry salting and spicing

Unlike pickling, which is good for preserving several pieces of meat at a time and takes up space, dry salting is ideal for a single large roll of beef, or pork, or a ham, and has the advantage that the meat can be kept in a bowl in the bottom of the fridge. Mix the specified ingredients in a large bowl, preferably a crock made of glass, china or glazed earthenware, and rub every get-at-able surface of your piece of meat vigorously for a minute or two. Rub the inside of birds, as well as the outside (you can always slip on rubber gloves). Push a good wodge of your mixture down into any bone or socket cavities, as round a bone is where trouble starts, so butchers will tell you, especially with big hunks like a ham. Tongues are sometimes dry cured, but I would emphasize that they must be very fresh (from recently slaughtered beasts), be pricked all over with a sterile needle to help the cure penetrate, then rubbed very thoroughly, then stored in the fridge. As tongues are laden with bacteria, you need to work fast, and thoroughly; do not leave one in its plastic bag in a warm room overnight while you meditate what to do with it. Having finished the dry rub, cover the meat, leave in a cool place. Turn and rub it well daily, and if you are not storing it in the fridge but in a basement or larder, *keep it covered*, with a proper old fashioned fly-cover of muslin stretched over wire. Or put it in a deeper container than a bowl, and secure a clean muslin cloth over the top. Flies are not often mentioned in books on home preserving, but I cannot imagine why, since they are a persistent pest in certain seasons and it only takes one fly a minute or so alone with a piece of meat to produce a maggoty thing you will not wish to touch let alone eat. So – either take care, or keep your dry salting for cold weather, when the fly risk is over. Go on for as long as your recipe suggests; the time usually varies with the weight as well as nature of the meat being treated. As the days pass some liquid will collect in the bowl – this is to be expected. The amount varies with the animal, and the cut. Leave it, just spoon the whole lot over several times as if basting and rub a bit less. When the meat is done, brush off the spices, wipe over with paper and cook/smoke or put into pickle, as the recipe bids.

To cure an ox tongue, ensure first that it is very fresh, then sterilize a sharp skewer by dipping it in boiling water. Prick the ox tongue all over, sprinkle with coarse salt, toss over a handful of juniper berries and stand overnight in a bowl. Rinse off the salt, put the tongue in a cast iron pan in the oven with a couple of onions (leave on their skins to colour the dish), chopped parsnips, celery stalks and peppercorns and cover with water. Simmer all day long, then strain the liquid through muslin. Skin and trim the tongue. Roll up and either eat hot, served with a piquant mustard sauce or capers or render down the stock by boiling it up till it thickens, add one tablespoonful of aspic gelatine and set the jelly round the cool tongue.

Dry salted meats

Also called dry curing, or dry-spicing, this method of preserving is a protracted form of marinade. All sorts of meat can be treated like this, and the results range from the rich mellow flavour of spiced beef to the exquisite delicacy of mutton ham.

Mutton ham

Smaller, cheaper and less unwieldy than a pork ham, a large leg of mutton (or more usually lamb these days) was traditionally smoked to keep longer. I often omit the smoking, and simply simmer, press and eat the spiced lamb cold.

225 g (8 oz) sea salt
100 g (4 oz) dark brown sugar
2 teaspoons saltpetre
1 tablespoon each peppercorns, coriander, allspice
1 large (2½ to 3 kg/5 to 6 lb) leg of lamb or mutton

Mix the salt, sugar and saltpetre with the crushed spices. Rub the leg thoroughly all over with this, pushing it in round the bone. Keep in a cool place for 10–14 days, rubbing daily with the spicy liquid which it yields, and turning it often.

Cook as for a ham, in a flavoured stock (or water with vegetables, garlic and a little wine), simmering very gently for 3 to 4 hours, depending on the size. Leave to cool in the cooking liquid. Then remove, wrap tightly in a clean cloth, lay a board on top and weight overnight.

Spiced or dry salted beef

5 kg (10 lb) topside or silverside
100 g (4 oz) brown sugar
½ teaspoon allspice
1 teaspoon nutmeg
2 teaspoons saltpetre
100 g (4 oz) sea salt
1 tablespoon each black pappercorns, juniper berries
1 kg (2 lb) plain white flour
beef suet

Rub the meat over with sugar to tenderize it, before the salt gets to work, put it in a bowl in a cool, clean place, covered, and leave for 2 days. Then crush the spices, mix them with the rest of the ingredients and rub the meat all over with this. Repeat daily, keeping the meat both cool and covered, for at least 10 days – this meat is better left longer than less time. To cook, wipe off the spices, then make a rough 'huff' paste with 1 kg (2 lb) plain flour and enough water to bind. Roll this out fairly thickly, lay the beef on top, then generously cover the meat with either grated beef suet, dripping or butter, close the pastry over it, wetting the edges and pinching shut. Bake in a tin in a very low oven (120°C, 250°F, Mark ½) for 1 hour per 450 g (1 lb) of beef. Leave to cool for 1–2 hours, then peel off the 'huff' and leave the joint under a weighted board overnight, wrapped in foil, clean cloth or greaseproof. Slice thinly.

Bath chaps

These miniature hams made from pig's cheek or jaw are cured along with the tongue which is rolled up in the middle of the finished 'chap'. Ask your butcher to cut and bone the jaw or jowl.

1 boned jowl of pork and tongue
175 g (6 oz) salt
100 g (4 oz) sugar
2 teaspoons saltpetre
2 teaspoon each coriander, peppercorns, allspice
1 onion stuck with 2 cloves
1 leek
1 bouquet garni

The tongue should be skinned before curing. Trim off the root, and gristle, prick with a sterile needle, then put into a bowl with the chap. Mix up the other ingredients, coarsely crushing the spices, and rub this well into the meat. Keep in a cool place covered and repeat daily for 1 week. At the end of this time roll up the chap with the tongue inside, tie with string to hold the shape, and cook like this – which is a fairly standard method for all salt meat. Put in a large pan of cold water, bring to the boil slowly (to remove excess salt), throw the salt away, cover again with cold water, adding herbs, vegetables for flavouring, bring to the boil slowly then simmer gently for 4 hours. Cool under a weight, and roll in crumbs.

Brined &
Pickled Meats

'To have sweet and fine bacon
the fitches must not be sopping in brine
which gives it the sort of taste that barrel pork and sea junk have,
than which nothing is more villainous.'

William Cobbett 1830

A brine or pickle tub, where cuts of meat submerged in strongly salted water can be stored for weeks, is a simple and effective old method of preservation that does not just keep meat from spoiling as a freezer would, but also adds to its flavour and makes it more tender. Some butchers keep a brine or pickle going in which tongues and cuts of pork and beef are left for several days to absorb piquant flavour and rosy colour. Brining is such a straightforward business that it would be a pity if you did not try out the process for yourself. Assuming the salt strength is checked from time to time and elementary hygiene observed, meat left in brine pretty well looks after itself. Brine provides a two-way protection since salt checks the bacterial activity, while water excludes air and flies, which are the home preserver's most tireless saboteur. All of which readily explains why pickling has been popular since the Romans imported hams from Gaul.

Brine is a basic salt and water solution while pickles (not to be confused with the vinegar solution for vegetables and fruit) are brine to which sugar or some other sweetener has been added. The reason for this is that salt and saltpetre (often used for the rosy colour it gives meat) have a decidedly hardening effect on meat as time goes on and sugar, which softens meat as well as mellowing the overall flavour, is the ideal antidote. Adding sugar (or honey, treacle or molasses) was just the start of improvements on the basic brine formula. People were soon titivating it in other ways, adding herbs or spices, or strongly flavoured berries that grow wild, like juniper. Alcohol, also a preservative, was bound to find its ways into a meat pickle sooner or later; wine from the wine-growing districts, beer and stout in other parts. Spanish *jamón serrano* and hams from Modena in Italy both spend weeks in white wine pickle while the famous Suffolk sweet cured hams in England were pickled for six weeks in stout or porter. A 'cure' in this context is the general term for whatever treatment meat (usually pork) undergoes in being turned into ham or bacon.

Pork curing in a pickling barrel: feet, ears, top of the head, ribs, all brine salted for immediate use in making brawn. The all-purpose pickle permeates the pork with piquant flavour and tenderizes the meat before cooking it.

Curing

Pork has always been the favourite meat for pickle tubs partly because pigs were plentiful, being the easiest animal to raise on a smallholding, partly because fatty pork is ideally suited to pickling, becoming more tender and delicate in texture. The fat soaks up the flavour – compare a rasher of green (that is, cured and not smoked) bacon with a slice of belly of pork. You can leave a joint of pork overnight in pickle just to improve the flavour and texture before roasting. A longer stay in the pickle makes the flavour change more emphatic; a couple of weeks makes the joint taste more like a ham, best simmered then glazed in the oven with honey and mustard, or cider and brown sugar. Like ham, it is especially succulent eaten cold.

Any cuts of pork can be pickled with advantage but most effective are the less expensive bits – belly of pork, trotters, pig's head (for brawn), chaps or cheek, even ears – because the fat and gelatinous meat is so much tastier after curing. Making bacon which tastes the way it did in the good old days is an enterprise which people buying half a carcase for the freezer might well consider. The pork for bacon must be hung for five days first otherwise the cure will not permeate. Then cure with the all-purpose pickle or the bacon pickle with white wine.

The benefits of a sweet pickle can also be extended usefully to other meats besides pork, especially when intended to be smoked later. Beef, game, poultry at the 'boiler' stage can all be softened and flavoured by a short pickle cure. Tongues – sheep's, pig's, ox – are traditionally pickled for flavour and tenderness and should be really fresh and pricked all over with a sterilized needle (hold it over a flame) to help the pickle penetrate, then immersed without delay. The smaller the cut of meat the less time it will take for the pickle to take effect, so when planning the contents of a pickle or brine tub allow for this. Use up the smaller pieces first but give something as large as a pig's haunch a week. Really large hams are best dry salted first (see page 170).

Equipment and ingredients
Traditionally, a brine tub or pickle barrel was used but today any large scrubbable container in plastic or china is suitable. A glazed stoneware crock is ideal. Sterilize everything before use by scalding with boiling water. You will need to keep the contents of the tub pressed down below the level of the pickle at all times. A wood or plastic lid weighted by a large stone is suitable. Scald these too.

The basic ingredients are water (preferably soft rain water) and salt (sea salt is best, block salt is cheapest). White or brown sugar can be used.

Saltpetre
Saltpetre, usually sodium nitrate, occasionally potassium nitrate which makes the meat look more appetizing, rosy rather than brownish grey, can be bought from chemists and small amounts used. There have been reservations about nitrates in food, the fear being that excessive amounts could be harmful. I continue using it because the amount called for in a pickle formula is insignificant and well within the safety factor. If you prefer, substitute ascorbic acid or vitamin C in crystal form. Buy from a chemist and use 1 g per 2 kg ($4\frac{1}{2}$ lb) meat instead of the saltpetre specified.

Using brines and pickles

Ingredients for the pickle should be boiled up (many writers in old cook-books dispense with this stage but it seems to be a sensible insurance against possible mishaps where fresh meat is concerned) and left to go quite cold. Bacteria breed in warmth. The cuts of meat should be packed in the bucket, or crock, and the pickle or brine mixture poured over. There should be enough to cover the meat by at least 2.5 cm (1 in). Then set your scalded board, or plastic lid, on top and a heavy stone or jar on top of that, so that the meat is well pressed down. The container should be kept in a cool place like a cellar, outhouse or basement. Pickling, in any case, is best undertaken in cool weather. Small-scale pickling can stay in the refrigerator. After a few days check the tub and contents and give them a stir with a scalded wooden spoon. Saltier water tends to drop in level so this helps even out the treatment. The meat can now be left for as long as a couple of weeks, provided you keep the salt level up. Salt is really the most effective disinfectant.

Testing the salt levels

The chief risk with brining occurs when a piece is removed from the brine. The salinity level drops accordingly so while a pair of trotters is unlikely to make any difference, a haunch will have absorbed much of the salt. The drill for these occasions involves testing the salt level by floating an egg on top before taking out the meat, then again afterwards. It should bob easily on the surface, not half drown. If it half sinks, the brine needs topping up. Make up a booster solution by boiling roughly one fifth the total of water with about 3 times as much salt per litre as in the original salt solution. Add a handful of spices too, and a tablespoon of sugar. Leave to get quite cold, then add to the brine. Repeat the egg test, which should now be favourable.

Better safe than sorry applies particularly with a food like meat, not so much because anything horrid is likely to happen but because we are unfamiliar with handling meat, compared to our ancestors, and so much more likely to panic if there is even the slightest hint of trouble. Remember: provided the salt content is high, there is nothing to worry about.

If at any time during the cure you find the brine has soured, it is no great expense or labour to take out the meat, rinse it, clean the tub and make up a whole new pickle solution. Scald the barrel or crock again, chill it thoroughly and return the meat, covering it with the fresh, chilly solution.

Curing times

A minimum of 28 days is needed for a large shoulder or haunch. As a rough rule of thumb, allow $3\frac{1}{2}$ to 4 days for each 450 g (1 lb) of ham or shoulder.

For small pieces like the loin or bacon strips, allow 20 days for a 5 kg (10 lb) piece of bacon but 25 days for a thicker piece, like the loin. The guideline here is 2 days per 450 g (1 lb).

The trotters, ears, and top of the pig's head can be brine salted for immediate use in making brawns.

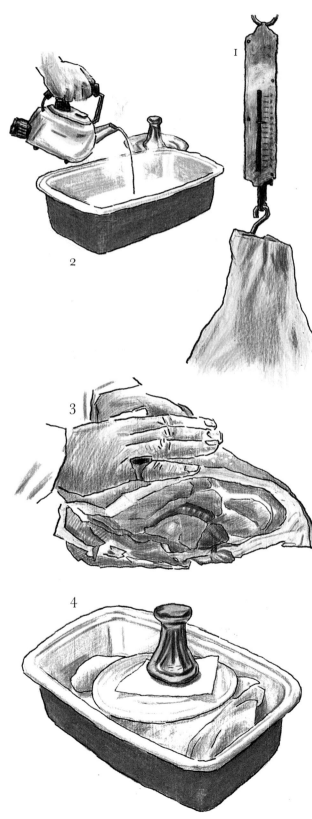

Curing a ham Italian style

Really large hams – about 5.5 kg (12 lb) are best dry-salted first, then given the slow pickle cure before smoking or drying. Dry salting encourages the lymph gland to release fluids – too much of that fluid in the sweet pickle later would dilute it and cause the meat to spoil. Smaller cuts, like those for bacon, can cure without this dry salting first.

1. Weigh the ham and record the weight. At the end of curing, the weight loss will tell you how long to continue smoking.

2. Scald a large crock, the wooden lid and the weight with boiling water.

3. Rub sea salt into the surface of the ham – 675 g ($1\frac{1}{2}$ lb) sea salt to every 5.5 kg (12 lb) of ham. Push the salt down into any bone or socket cavities.

4. Place the ham in the scalded bowl, put the lid on and weight it to encourage quick draining overnight.

5. Make up the Italian white wine pickle with: 2 litres (4 pints) water, 1 kg (2 lb) sea salt, 1 tablespoon bicarbonate of soda and 2 tablespoons saltpetre (or 3 grams of vitamin C, ascorbic acid) boiled together. Then add 2 litres (4 pints) white wine, 1 tablespoon allspice, $\frac{1}{2}$ tablespoon peppercorns and leave to get quite

cold: it is important that the ham, cold and compressed from the first salting, should go quickly into the pickle which should be just slightly warmer. If the pickle were colder than the ham, it would continue the extracting process, rather than the permeating one.

6. Drain the salt cure off the ham. Replace the ham in the bowl and pour over the pickle, straining it through a muslin bag.

7. Place on the lid, weight it down with a stone and leave for 28 days.

8. To test the brine or saltiness, at the end of each week float a fresh egg on the solution. If the egg half sinks, the salt level needs topping up. Boost by boiling up roughly one-fifth the total of water with three times as much salt per litre (2 pints) as in the original formula. Leave to get cool before adding.

9. Every four or five days, remove the ham and stir the brine with a scalded wooden spoon as the salt needs a stir-up. Quickly scald the board, lid and weight and replace them.

10. Remove the ham from the cure after 28 days, scrub off surface salt with a brush.

11. Hang in a cool airy place for about one week. Simmer for two hours in water, then with vegetables for flavour for another hour.

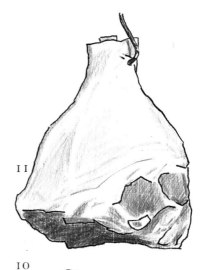

11

10

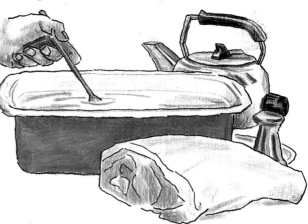

9

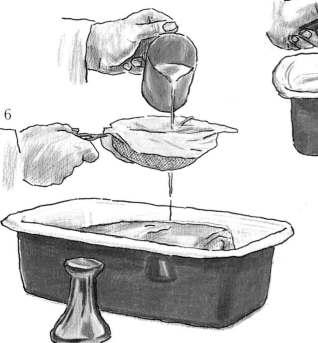

6

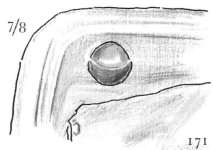

7/8

Meat

Brines and pickles

Soaking beef, pork or tongue in a brine (a basic salt and water solution) or a pickle (a brine to which a sweetener is added), gives the meat piquant flavour and rosy colour. It is a way both of preserving and tenderizing joints before cooking or smoking.

All-purpose pickle
This produces a mild, sweet cure suitable for bacon (or any cut of pork), or for poultry.

6 litres (1¼ gallons) water
1 kg (2 lb) salt
1 kg (2 lb) sugar
2 tablespoons saltpetre
1 tablespoon juniper berries
half a nutmeg
1 teaspoon each cloves and black peppercorns
1 large sprig of fresh thyme, rosemary or marjoram
3 bay leaves

Boil up the water, salt, sugar and saltpetre, slowly, stirring occasionally, with the other ingredients roughly crushed and tied up in muslin. Boil for three minutes, leave till quite cold then remove the spice bag and pour the liquid over the meat in a crock or tub. Weight cover to keep meat submerged.
Note: For mildly salted small pieces, three days in this pickle will be enough. Slightly larger joints – loin, belly – can stay for a week, if you want a mild cure. Shoulder or leg will be mild cured after ten days or so, but can of course be left much longer so long as you check on the salt level. They will get saltier, but slowly.

General brine
This is sweetened, but very slightly. Use it for beef, venison and poultry which is to be smoked. Leave meats in for two to five days depending on size, and dry overnight before smoking.

12 litres (3 gallons) water
1¼ kg (3 lb) salt
225 g (8 oz) sugar
2 teaspoons saltpetre
1 tablespoon juniper berries

Bring all the ingredients to the boil, the berries tied up in muslin. Leave till quite cold before pouring over the meats.

Sweet beer pickle
This is a hearty, robust tasting cure for a small ham, or bath chaps, or belly of pork to be smoked for bacon.

1 tablespoon allspice
1¼ litres (3 pints) strong beer
1¼ litres (3 pints) water
350 g (12 oz) sea salt
1 tablespoon saltpetre
225 g (8 oz) treacle

Tie the allspice, roughly crushed, in muslin and boil up with the remaining ingredients for five minutes. Skim if necessary, leave till cold, then pour over the meat. Small pieces will need 1 week or 10 days, larger ones can stay 3 weeks to a month for a good ham. Hams or bacon should be dried for 1–2 days after curing, and cool smoked for several days in a smoke house, or for several weeks in a chimney.

Italian white wine pickle
More delicate than the beer pickle, and unsweetened – ideal for a really special ham for Christmas or a boned, rolled shoulder, or loin of pork. The meat will have a fine flavour, and need not be smoked. Cook as you would ham, but rather plainly – in a stock flavoured with vegetables, but no fancy glazes which would obscure the steeped-in taste.

2 litres (4 pints) water
2 tablespoons saltpetre
1 kg (2 lb) sea salt
1 tablespoon bicarbonate of soda
2 litres (4 pints) white wine
1 tablespoon allspice
½ tablespoon peppercorns

Bring the water, salt, saltpetre and soda to the boil, remove from heat, add the wine and spices and leave to grow quite cold. Strain through muslin into a crock or a bin, over the meat. Leave

172

a smaller joint – shoulder, loin – two weeks; a ham, four weeks. Hang to dry in a cool airy place for about a week before cooking and eating. Italians store these hams – when unsmoked – by immersing them in olive oil – pure vegetable oil could substitute. Or smoke them. Full instructions for smoking hams are given on page 177.

Bacon

This is a basic dry salting recipe to which the white wine is added to pickle the pork for bacon. Eliza Acton, writing in the mid-19th century, makes enthusiastic claims for the addition of a bottle of good wine vinegar to the cure after 3 or 4 days and says it 'gives incomparable flavour'. A side of sweet cured bacon – smoked or green which is milder in flavour – keeps for a long time in a warm, dry place.

For 6 kg (12 lb) meat allow:
450 g (1 lb) coarse salt
450 g (1 lb) brown sugar
25 g (1 oz) saltpetre
25 g (1 oz) peppercorns
1 litre (1¾ pints) wine vinegar

Mix up all the dry ingredients and halve. After hanging the pork for 5 days after slaughtering, rub half the mixture into the meat and leave for four days, rubbing and turning daily. Then apply the rest of the ingredients mixed with wine vinegar. Keep turning and rubbing daily till done. For green bacon brush off any spices and salt and keep in a dry place (hung from the ceiling) at room temperature.

Recipes using pickled pork:
Brawn *(Fromage de tête)*
Though not an undertaking for the squeamish, a well made brawn is a dish with great style for a buffet supper or summer lunch party, especially when the pig's head is given three days in pickle first to heighten the flavour and some wine goes to flavour the jelly. It is a handsome dish – like pink marble set in clear jelly and quite absurdly cheap (pig's head is sold off at rock bottom prices for pet meat, mostly). In France, however, where sensibility never interferes with

good eating, *Fromage de tête* is a prized dish. This dish serves about 12 people.

1 pig's head
1 pair trotters
2 each of onions, carrots, leeks
a bouquet garni of thyme, parsley, bay leaf
1 teaspoon peppercorns
4 tablespoons wine vinegar
3 cloves garlic
1 litre (2 pints) white wine
lemon juice
a small pinch each of ground nutmeg, allspice
salt

Ask the butcher to prepare the head for brawn, leaving in the tongue – the brains can make a separate dish. Put the head and the trotters in an all-purpose pickle for two to three days. Then put in a pan and cover with cold water, bring to the boil and throw away the water – this removes any excess salt. Return to the pan, add the vegetables, cleaned and chopped herbs, pepper, vinegar and garlic. Add enough water to cover well, cover the pan and bring to the boil very slowly – the cool end of an old-fashioned range is ideal for cooking this type of dish. Simmer as slowly as possible, so the water hardly moves, for about five hours, or till the meat falls off the bones.

For the jelly you have to reduce 1½ litres (3 pints) of stock and white wine by one-third by boiling the water away. Drain off the liquid from the meat and measure 600 ml (1 pint) into a clean pan, add the 1 litre (2 pints) of wine and a squeeze of lemon and reduce by simmering till only 600 ml (1 pint) is left to make the jelly. Season to taste with spices, salt and pepper. Meanwhile sort out chunks of meat from the cooked head. The tongue stays whole, but should be skinned and trimmed neatly. Cut the meat into neat pieces, discarding any gristle and bone. Add the meat to the reduced stock, simmer very gently for about 15 minutes to let it absorb the flavour, then put to cool.

When cool, but before it sets, prepare the final 'cheese' by ladling a thick layer of meat over the bottom of a dish, set the tongue (whole or sliced, as you prefer) on top, cover with remaining meat and then pour over the liquid. Turn out when set. In France this is covered with breadcrumbs, but I prefer to see the brawn in all its simplicity.

Smoked meats

Meat is smoked both for flavour and for preservation. As it dries out very slowly over a period of days or weeks, up the chimney or in the smokehouse, it takes on a distinctive tang and assimilates minute amounts of preservative chemicals, which also deter flies and other pests. The snag, however, at least where a large joint like a ham is concerned, is the time that the smoking process takes – at the very least several days' continuous smoking, or several weeks of intermittent exposure.

If you live in an old house with one of those immense chimneys which used to take an open fire, range, or bread oven and you burn wood over the winter months, your smoking problem is solved – simply hook up the ham securely to a beam, or strong peg driven into the brickwork, at a point where it is as far away and high above the fire as it can be, but still in the path of the rising smoke. Distancing is necessary because if the ham itself is heated the fat will start to melt (dangerous flare-ups) and the lean to cook. This is of course how people have always smoked a ham or two without the trouble of keeping a smokehouse going, but it is necessary to keep a weather eye on even the simplest process. The wood burned needs to be of the right type i.e. hardwood – oak, beech, elm, sycamore etc. Resinous woods spoil the taste of the meat. A fire does not need to be kept going *permanently*, but of course the smoking process takes longer when it is intermittent.

There are no hard and fast rules about how long to smoke meat in this more casual fashion. Much depends on how strongly flavoured you want it to be, and how long you want it to keep for. A fairly reliable guide is weight loss – a large cut like a ham should lose between one quarter and one third of its initial weight (before curing that is) by the time it is smoked through, so remember to weigh the meat before and after curing and again after a week or two smoking.

Once your ham is smoked you can complete the good work of the 'cure' by stitching the ham into a stout cotton cover (they used to limewash these as extra protection) before hanging it in a dry, airy place. If thoroughly smoked, ham should keep like this for months, even a year or more. Old timers will tell you that they remember eating hams which had hung a couple of years and they were 'sweet as a nut', and 'beautiful tender eating'.

If you do not have an appropriate chimney for smoking hams, there are still many sorts of meat which can be smoked successfully and deliciously using a home-made cool smoker (see illustration on page 125). A ham *can* be smoked in one of these, of course, but I think that it would be more trouble than it is worth keeping the smoker going for the necessary length of time. Opt instead for meat which can be smoked much more rapidly, either because it is smaller in volume (a side of bacon takes far less time than a ham), or less fleshy (poultry – ducks, geese and turkeys specially) or small and tender (tenderloin, beef fillet).

Game is also a good candidate for the kiln, smoking being an interesting way of handling elderly game which responds particularly well to a few days in sweet pickle followed by smoking. Again, birds or small cuts take less time – a haunch of venison needs to be smoked for about a week. However, I should add that it is not vital to smoke meat continuously after it has begun drying off – an overnight break will not ruin the effect in the home smoker any more than in the chimney. But during the critical period before the preservative process has got a good hold, and the meat is dry to the touch and somewhat shrunken in weight, you do need to safeguard it against flies and other such pests and against sudden changes in temperature, like a sudden heatwave or spell of warm, damp weather. This means bringing the meat in at night and keeping it under cover meanwhile. One of those old style meat safes with flyscreen doors and ventilation holes would be a very useful adjunct to a smoker, for storing meat and fish.

Equipment
Your home-made smoker operates in exactly the same way for meat as for fish (see pages 126/7). Your 'tenters', however, will have to be strong enough to support greater weights. Plenty of butcher's S hooks are invaluable for suspending joints of meat, poultry and game. More sawdust will be needed, as most meat cuts take rather longer to smoke thoroughly. Hot smoking is more often used in finishing smoked meat than fish, and the design for your cool smoker should take into account the need to introduce a source of heat directly below the food being smoked. If this is altogether too much bother, it is quite in order to finish cool smoked meats in the ordinary domestic oven (set at 160°C, 325°F, Mark 3) after rubbing them over well with oil. For dry birds such as turkey, wrap foil round them to prevent drying out.

Method
All meat, game and poultry to be smoked are first put into a brine or pickle solution (see pages 172/3) or dry salted and spiced (see page 164), before being left to drain and dry off for a while. Timing varies with the variety and cut of meat, as described overleaf. The meat is then ready to be hung appropriately in the cool smoker to smoke for as long as necessary to preserve it, or if you are only concerned with *taste* and the meat is to be eaten soon, to give a pleasant flavour. Incidentally, most smoked food develops *more* flavour if left a few hours before eating. Smoked meats are almost always cooked after cool smoking. This is especially true of pork, because of the risk of trichinosis where uncooked pork is concerned (the raw ham curers have their own way round these difficulties).

A string of sausages for smoking is first weighed, then dried off slowly in a warm, dry place for a few days. Then the sausages are smoked for about five hours till they lose about 25 percent body weight.

Having tried smoking a variety of meats, my own feeling is that the fattiest meats are those which taste finest when smoked – succulent and with their own flavour enhanced rather than overpowered as can happen with delicately flavoured chicken, for instance. Besides which, the curing/smoking process definitely plays down their inherent greasiness, improves their texture and makes them much more digestible. In this list I would include pork, goose, duck, old fat pheasants and other elderly game birds. Some of the more exotic animals, too, would come under this heading – moose, elk, reindeer, wild boar.

Game animals

Venison and wild boar should be hung for a week or so before beginning the pre-smoking cure, but they should not be allowed to get 'high' at all. The haunch is the best cut to smoke with all these animals, but a well fleshed shoulder or saddle is another possibility. For the richest flavour, put the joints in a sweet pickle for a week, turning them often. Then rinse, and leave to dry off in a cool airy place for a day or two. Smoke for at least a week in a cool smoker (longer in short bursts), or until the surface is blackened. Rub drier meats with oil and finish in a low oven, or step up the temperature in the cool smoker to around $110°C$ ($225°F$, Mark $\frac{1}{4}-\frac{1}{2}$) and hot smoke for about three hours.

Game birds

Hang game birds for two or three days only – they should never be smoked 'high'. Small, young birds need only an hour or two in brine (make up a simple mixture of salt and water with only a little sugar added, as the usual sweet pickle spices would overpower the flavour) before cool smoking. Old dry birds go into a pickle pricked all over first. Small birds like quail need about 12 hours' cool smoking, larger ones like pheasant or elderly grouse need about three days', capercaillie four or five days'. If dry looking, the birds can be brushed over with vegetable oil several times before and during smoking. Hot smoke for an hour or two to finish, or transfer to a domestic oven and cook in foil at a low setting for a half to three hours, depending on the size.

Poultry

Ducks and geese smoke excellently, their meat never drying out. Some care needs to be taken with both birds however, to see that they are not over smoked because this turns the fat rancid and inedible. Ducks should be pricked all over before being placed in brine or a plainish pickle for three hours. Hang them to dry for a day and then cool smoke at between 23 and $26°C$ (75 and $80°F$) for 36 hours exactly. Finish in the oven at $160°C$ ($325°F$, Mark 3).

Smoked breast of goose is a Christmas feast dish in Germany, sliced thinly and eaten with rye bread and a scrape of clarified goose fat. Goose breast, divided into fillets, is rubbed with salt and a pinch of saltpetre, and left covered in a cool place for five days, the rubbing process continued often. Then it is dried for half a day and finally cool smoked till it looks and feels quite dry, which takes about 12 hours of continuous smoking, after which time it will look brown and slightly translucent, resembling ptarmigan.

Smoked turkey is an ideal bird for a party, as all the meat is tasty, and there is no danger of having smoky leftovers going mouldy in the fridge – incidentally, the carcases, bones and leftovers of all smoked birds make the most excellent stock for soup, cooked up just as you would usual leftovers. Turkey for smoking can be elderly hen birds, cheaper than young roasters. Prick the flesh with a fork, steep in brine for four hours, string up by the wings and drain for a day, then cool smoke for up to a week. Finish in the oven, as described above.

Beef fillet, pork tenderloin

Beef should be pricked and brined for about two hours, then tied up with a string noose and dried overnight. Weigh before smoking and cool smoke at 26°C (80°F) or less for around five days, or till blackened, and about 25 percent lighter. Tenderloin is delicious given 12 hours in sweet pickle, dried all day, then lightly cool smoked for up to 68 hours before baking, wrapped in puff pastry or brioche dough.

Corned beef

Tougher, fattier cuts of beef such as brisket, flank, shin, are all suitable for curing and smoking by this old fashioned method – the results are infinitely superior to the ubiquitous tinned article. The beef should be kept in a spiced sweet pickle (molasses can be used instead of brown sugar) for ten days, weighted down. Turn occasionally. Hang up to drain and dry for a day or two. Cool smoke for a week or until dark, dry and about 25 percent lighter than at first. Cook as you please.

Bacon

Mild cured bacon (see the cure on page 173) should be cool smoked at just below 21°C (70°F) for 24 hours, or up to a week for a strong one.

Rabbit

These are plentiful in most country places, but can be a bit tasteless. Curing and smoking changes all that. The rabbit should have been dead 3 days, hung in a cold place, or kept in the fridge. After skinning (it will have been gutted or 'paunched' as soon as shot) soak in salt water for a couple of hours to remove blood, then put into a brine or pickle for five hours. Cool smoke without drying, for a day.

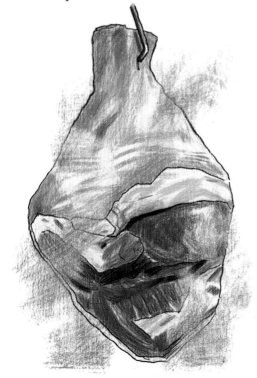

Smoking a ham

Casually, hung above the fire in a chimney a ham smokes well, but a large one needs smoking for so long in a home smoker that it is more trouble than it is worth. Smoking is ideal if you have one of those immense chimneys which used to take an open fire, bread oven or range. Simply hook up the ham to a beam or peg in the brickwork, far away and high above the fire, but still in the path of the rising smoke. Weight loss is the guide to how long the ham needs to be smoked. Large cuts like a ham should lose between a quarter and a third of their initial weight. Once smoked, stitch the ham into a stout cotton cover (these were traditionally lime-washed for extra protection) and hang in a dry airy place for months. The muslin helps keep the moisture in the ham and protects it.

Fruit & Vegetables

Harvesting the crop

Few sights do more to restore a cook's equanimity, and induce self-complacency than a cupboard ranged with jars and bottles, polished and labelled, in which the scents and flavours, colours and textures of summer kitchen garden, autumn orchard and hedgerow are distilled, imprisoned and perfected. No treasure hoard was ever come by so innocently, assembled so lovingly, or dismantled so enjoyably. Biting into a fat red strawberry, or a crisp young cucumber is a delight, but to meet them again in mid-winter, bobbing in a sugary syrup, or piquant with herbs and vinegar, is luxury. My grandmother used to bottle fruit as a matter of course, hoards of great rose-flushed Victoria plums ending up in row upon row of dignified jars in the larder shelves, the fruit bronze like goldfish within their transparent bellies. The sumptuous flavour of those bottled plums haunted me for years, and it was not till fate arranged the coincidence of a bumper harvest and the discovery of a crate of dusty preserving jars in a local junk shop, that I discovered what my granny always knew – that certain fruit of luscious texture are more delicious preserved in a light syrup even than when eaten straight from the tree.

Nowadays, we can afford to think of preserves as luxuries, delicious non-essentials all the nicer – and of course cheaper – for being home-made. But it is only a hundred years or so since a well stocked store cupboard was a bastion, the housewife's arsenal, and the surest proof of her skill. Winter must have fallen upon the land like a seizure, in grim contrast to the ease and plenty of summer and autumn. It was a time when hens went off lay, cows gave little or no milk (if they were not slaughtered for meat) and fresh food was limited to such hardy vegetables as could stand up to severe frosts. Shops were few and far between, their stocks restricted in any case largely to dry goods. In most households, especially in remote country areas, work began early in summer, salting down butter and making cheeses, waxing or pickling eggs, making soft fruit into preserves, with sugar, honey or spiced vinegar, pickling vegetables or turning them into powerfully seasoned sauces, ketchups and chutneys. As the months passed there would be barley and malt to brew for beer and ale, wheat to be milled and stored in mouseproof bins – rats, mice, weevils, cockroaches and similar voracious pests were a perennial headache – fish and meat to be salted, dried, cured or smoked, orchard fruit to be dried or bottled (in simple corked jars, cooked in the oven) beans and cabbages to be salted, root vegetables to be stored in 'clamps', herbs hung in bunches from the roof beams, walnuts husked and buried in wet salt. To think that they also found time to gather wild flowers and fruit for country wines and liqueurs, to grow, gather and distil herbs for – often effective – remedies or 'simples', not to mention making all their own soap, candles, household linen and clothes! Small wonder that 'strong and strapping' was high praise where a marriageable wench was concerned, and that the untimely death of one of those powerful women plunged her family and household into chaos and confusion from which the looked-for escape was for the widower to find a successor as soon as custom allowed. 'Huswifery' in those times was, indisputably, a highly and variously skilled occupation.

All the same, I cannot help feeling relieved that we can take life more easily today, thanks to modern conveniences. To preserve or not to preserve is a proposition one can toy with, safe from the rather alarming consequences that might well have followed on neglect or incompetence in these matters once upon a time – scurvy, for instance, due to lack of the vitamins which even preserved foods supply quite generously; rickets, from calcium deficiency (cheese is a pre-eminent source of calcium), and other deficiency diseases from which today most of us are comfortably insulated.

Whatever the motivation might be – economy, nostalgia, revolt against overpriced, tasteless commercial products – there is sure evidence that the old fashioned methods of preserving food, and especially fruit and vegetables, are enjoying a considerable revival. The disappearance of distilled vinegar, preserving sugar and preserving equipment generally from shop shelves in the late summer is exasperating proof. This is not to say that everyone has suddenly fallen in love with the idea of home-made jams, jellies and pickles but that more and more people are making their own hedge against inflation by growing as many fruit and vegetables as their gardens can sustain. What this leads to, as every gardener knows, is over-production, runner beans, courgettes and tomatoes fruiting in the extravagant way they do, not to mention the gooseberry bushes sagging with fruit, the strawberry beds running amok and all the other agreeable problems gardens give rise to. Much of this surplus can go straight into the freezer of course, and simple, safe and effective a method it is too. But not very interesting or imaginative, dare I say, compared with the rich variety of treatments, each contributing distinctive texture, flavouring and character, perfected by our ancestors. Besides, even freezers get overcrowded, and some fresh produce – courgettes, tomatoes, orchard fruit – just does not stand up to freezing well. There is a place in any kitchen for bottled fruit, home-made jams and jellies, pickles and chutney, unusual delicacies like damson cheese and apple butter, the surprising pungency of dried mushrooms or morello cherries, the epicureanism of whole fruit conserves in brandy flavoured syrups, or the lively individuality of fruit vinegars, marmalades, home-made mustard, spiced crab apples, elderflower wine, sloe gin and raspberry cordial.

The dearth in our eating today is not one of variety and quantity – a short stroll around any supermarket shows a greater range of foodstuffs than many of our ancestors encountered in a lifetime. But that there is a sameness, a processed 'tastiness' about it all, nobody could deny. The real value of home-made foods and preserves, as with all things made by people rather than machines, is that they redress the balance in favour of *non*-conformity, the things taste of themselves, the ground they grew in, the air they breathed, the way you cooked them, a whole host of variables which make the opening of each new jar, or pot, something of an event. Late ripening blackberries picked along the seashore taste quite different, when made into jelly, from fat squashy berries culled along sheltered hedgerows inland. It is small surprises like these which make the hours of picking, the tedious coring, peeling or otherwise preparing, seem like nothing in retrospect. The rewards are so real that a passing enthusiasm can easily grow into a lifelong hobby.

Food from the wild

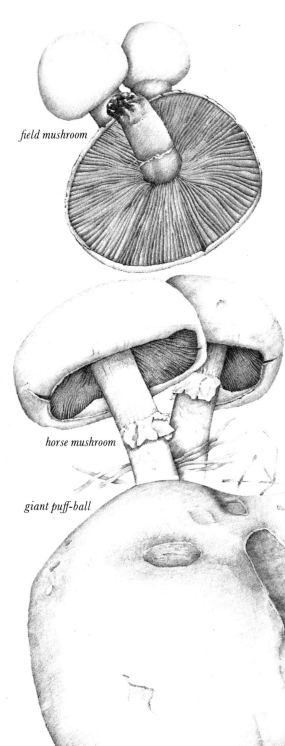

field mushroom

horse mushroom

giant puff-ball

common puff-ball

Collecting mushrooms and other edible fungi

In early autumn, mild damp weather will bring out the mushrooms and fungi. Some places are better than others – rough ground for grazing is best – but fungi are capricious and one year may see a field white with puff-balls never to appear again.

Limit yourself to a few well known species and take care to identify mature specimens. All mushrooms are fragile so carry them in rigid containers. Begin by searching for the *Agaricaceae*, which most closely resemble the familiar cultivated mushroom. Go for the mature specimens with brown gills and whitish caps, not the tight unopened ones in case you confuse them with the noxious *Amanitas* which has white gills. The field mushroom, *Agaricus campestris*, is usually found in open fields, its gills white at first, soon turning pink then dark brown as it ages. Its white cap between 7 and 18 cm (3 and 7 in) in diameter is connected by a membrane to the stem. As it grows, this membrane tears till all you can see in an older mushroom is the narrow ring round the stem. Horse mushrooms (*A. arvensis*) are found in both woodlands and fields, resembling field mushrooms except their white flesh goes vivid yellow when bruised and they have greyish gills.

The giant puff-ball (*Calvatia gigantea*) is quite unmistakable in meadow or woodland – it has virtually no stalk and can be as large as 90 cm (3 ft) across. Eat them young as the flesh goes soggy as it ages. The common puff-ball (*Lycoperdon perlatum*) covering a field is a promise of treats in store. Rarely more than 7 cm (3 in) in circumference, its white body is covered in small spines.

Blewits often appear in late autumn, later than other fungi. *Lepista saeva* is mushroom shaped, has a beige cap 5 to 15 cm (2 to 6 in) in diameter, white to greyish pink gills and a violet tinge to the stout and ringless stem. It is found in fields. Wood blewits (*Lepista nuda*) are an astonishing purplish bruised colour when young, though cap and gills often go beige as the fungus ages. Another woodland species, chanterelle (*Cantharellus cibarius*), has a tawny yellow body and funnel shaped cap, 3 to 10 cm (1 to 4 in) in diameter, which makes them unmistakable.

Coniferous woods in summer and autumn can yield a delicacy: cep or *Boletus edulis*, with its dark brown, moist, shiny cap 5 to 20 cm (2 to 8 in) in diameter and spongy mass of tubes beneath. White at first, these turn green/yellow later. All members of the *Boletus* family are identified by these vertical tubes resembling foam beneath the caps. Beware of the *Boletus satanas* – identifiable by its red stem and tubes – as it is poisonous when eaten raw.

Parasol mushrooms (*Lepiota procera*) are well worth looking out for. They occur in clearings, or the fringes of woods. The caps are veiled when young but later can open out to as much as 25 cm (10 in) across in an umbrella shape, and the long, striped stem has a loose double ring. The cap is covered in large dark scales, the gills are white and detached from the stem and the spores are colourless. The shaggy parasol (*Lepiota rhacodes*) has a less scaly cap than the other, the stipe or stem is smooth and if its surface is scratched, particularly near the base, it soon turns yellow, then reddish. Both fungi are strongly flavoured and delicious eaten fresh or dried. For details on drying mushrooms turn to page 196.

chanterelle

cep

blewit

parasol mushroom

Fruit and vegetables

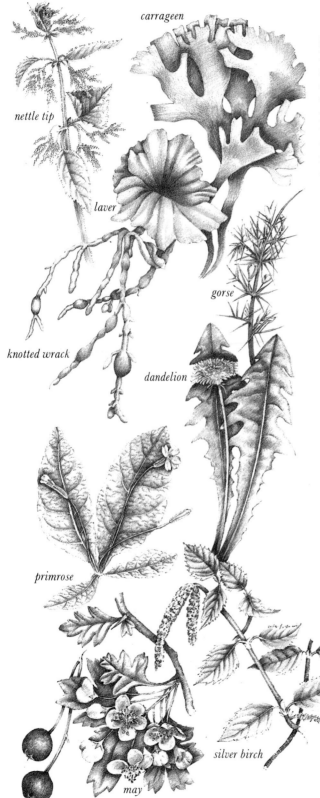

nettle tip

carrageen

laver

knotted wrack

gorse

dandelion

primrose

may

silver birch

elder

Spring

Birch sap rises just before spring's official start, and this is the time to tap trees carefully for an exhilarating wine. Early spring is a sucession of wild flowers, all yellow, and excellent for wine: primroses, gorse, dandelions. Do not pick more than a litre (2 pints) of primroses, and only then if you happen on a mass at once. Brave gorse thorns for the coconut-smelling flowers which make a delicate golden wine of great distinction. Dandelion petals make a fine wine.

Edible seaweeds like laver (*Porphyta umbilicalis*), carrageen or Irish moss (*Chondrus crispus*), and knotted wrack (*Aescophyllum nodosum*) are all commonly found in temperate waters in the late spring. Laver fronds are purplish, thin and irregularly shaped. Washed and boiled until it looks like dark-brown spinach purée, this seaweed can be cooked in butter and rolled in oats for breakfast scones. Carrageen or 'Irish moss' which is purple-brown, more clump than moss, and knotted wrack with its branching fronds are both traditionally used to set jellies and blanc-manges. Rock samphire (*Chrithmum maritimum*), a handsome pale-green clump of fleshy forked leaves with yellow flower cushions, clings to cliff sides, has a fieryacid taste and can be boiled with vinegar for pickles, or blanched for salads.

Inland, meanwhile, pick a bucket or two of may blossom for wine, filmy young beech leaves for *noyau* and hawthorn buds for an equally potent liqueur. Wild greens are sprouting in profusion; pick nettle *tips*, in gloves, to make a sharp, tonic broth with sorrel, spinach and cream. Put a flowerpot over a convenient dandelion to blanch young leaves for a salad. Allow yourself a few wild violets to crystallize.

Summer

Early to mid-summer is elderblossom time. A mere litre (2 pints) of the creamy talcum scented blossom make 4 litres (1 gallon) of elderflower wine, most fragrant and brilliant of country wines. A few heads will give you elderflower champagne which is frothy, quick and fun. A few more dipped with gooseberries and strawberries make beautiful muscat flavoured jam. Or, simplest of all, dip the heads in batter for a flower fritter, scented and charming. Lime blossom may be dried to make a sedative and refreshing tisane.

Wild horseradish, a tallish plant with a white spire of flowers and big crinkled dock-like leaves, grows in sunny sheltered waste land. The root – dig down and cut a length off – is pungent enough to make several jars of sauce. Or grate a mound and eat fresh with or without cream to eat with beef. Search along stream beds in shady places for wild garlic, or ramsons, a starry white flower with green blade leaves. The smell is unmistakable. It can be used just like the cultivated sort but more freely, leaves, stems and all chopped into salads or soft cheeses.

Mid-summer is the time to search for wild soft berries: raspberries and strawberries, tiny, sweet and beautiful with curd cream. Look for them in light woodland, grassy heath and in sunny sheltered corners. The raspberry can be distinguished from red bramble berries by its smooth stems. Wild strawberries creep down low in grass and bracken so need to be hunted for. Just a few or either will transform a pudding or a jam. On high ground, hunt for the thinly scattered bilberries (also called blaeberries, 'hurts' or wortleberries). They are marvellously juicy and good in tarts or with cream.

horseradish

bilberry

wild strawberry

sweet violet

ramsons (wild garlic)

sloe

crab apple

elderberry

haw

truffle

hazel

Autumn

Gardeners are almost too busy to chase up all the wild fruits on offer in the pauses between preserving all the cultivated ones, like apples and pears. Elderberries and blackberries ripen about the same time: elderberries are ready to pick for wine, syrup or sauce when the flat heads of juicy berries hang down like tassels. Wild blackberries are everywhere. The first of the season are best for eating raw, the mid-season fruits make nice tarts, jams and wine and the late autumn ones can be sieved with apple for blackberry jelly. Coastal blackberries ripen later but have a keener flavour. In the fields, brambles on the sheltered side may be twice as big as those in the other, so look around. Do not forget the bright haws, fruit of the hawthorn. They have a smoky, strange flavour which grows on you, although too dry to use for anything but jelly or wine. The same is true of rowan berries, fruit of the mountain ash, which should ripen around this time of year and the crabapple. The green berries of the cranberry ripen in late autumn, ready for bottling into the much loved cranberry sauce to serve with the Christmas turkey. Hickory nuts, cobnuts and walnuts must be picked early in autumn if they are to be pickled green, a treat in store for the grey winter months ahead.

Winter

Mild damp weather can raise a flush of fungi in fields and woods, so take a plastic bag in your pocket when you go out for a walk. After a downpour the odd truffle may sometimes – rarely – be discerned just surfacing through leafmould at the foot of beech trees. Truffles are hunted and found by trained dogs and greedy pigs all over Europe. Black and white truffles are roughly spherical, mostly about the size of a ping pong ball, with warty and crinkled skin. They usually grow some inches below ground but heavy rain can uncover them.

After the frosts is the best time to pick rosehips for wine, syrups and jellies as they are more tender and have a better flavour. This also applies to sloes for making into the crimson sloe gin. Sloes cling to the branches but you cannot mistake their misty blue bloom among the green leaves in early winter.

A few nuts such as hazel or cobnuts may have escaped the squirrels while the bigger nuts from the hickory are improved after being left out for a winter, ready for an early spring pickling. While in the colder climates winter offers little in the way of edible food to be picked out of doors, it is a good time of the year for putting away the fruits of sunnier climes.

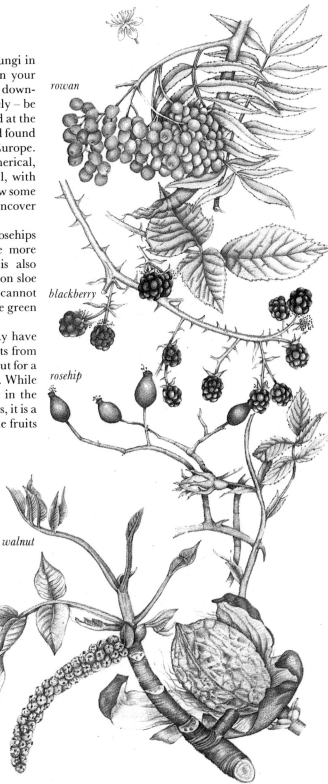

rowan

blackberry

rosehip

sweet chestnut

walnut

Salted vegetables

Salting is a cheap and effective way of preserving some vegetables – an ideal method for those who do not have, or want, deep freezes.

Salting beans

Preserving raw green beans of the runner, or French, varieties in salt is uncomplicated – the beans are merely buried in lots of salt. Also useful is the fact that more beans can be added as the season progresses. They keep well like this for six months. Rinse well in cold running water before use, though, and do not salt the cooking water.

You will need an earthenware crock, or glass jars, and block or kitchen salt, table salt is not suitable. Allow 450 g (1 lb) of salt to $1\frac{1}{2}$ kg (3 lb) beans. Alternate layers of salt and layers of beans in the jar or crock, beginning and ending with salt. Press the beans down well, and cover with waxed paper or polythene.

Salting cabbage

Sauerkraut – German for pickled cabbage – is a deservedly popular traditional method of preserving cabbage by fermenting it in salt, a process which not only keeps moulds and bacteria at bay but turns the shredded cabbage into a piquant vegetable delicacy. Use it as a winter salad, or serve it in the plain, hearty style of Alsace, where a mound of sauerkraut is dished up with steaming boiled potatoes and carrots, a selection of smoked sausages and lots of spicy mustard.

Equipment

To make a bulk amount of sauerkraut, you need a large crock or glass jars, a wooden board to fit down inside the container like a lid, a large smooth, scalded stone, and a very sharp knife to shred the cabbage finely. The shredding attachment to your electric blender will perform this task admirably. Also, you need a generous supply of hard white cabbages (no others will do) and coarse kitchen salt or block salt. Iodized salt is unsuitable. Several large sheets of clean white cloth or muslin are needed, too.

If in doubt as to how many cabbages your crock will hold, start small – 8 to 10 kg (15 to 20 lb) – and add more later.

Heat processing: the quick water bath method

Sauerkraut will keep for up to two months so long as you make sure the cabbage is covered with brine, and the muslin cover is scalded and washed regularly. But to keep longer, it must be heat processed. Pack the sauerkraut into large, clean jars, filling to within 5 cm (2 in) of the rim. Stand the jars (without lids) on a layer of cloth in a large deep pan up to their shoulders in cold water. Bring the water gently to the boil. Remove from the heat. Wipe the jar rims and top up with extra boiling brine made up from $1\frac{1}{2}$ tablespoons of salt to 1 litre (1 quart) water. Screw on the lids lightly, allowing air to escape with expansion. Bring back to the boil and simmer gently for 30 minutes. Remove, cool on a wooden board and seal when completely cold.

Sauerkraut making

1. Peel coarse outer leaves and shred the cabbage very finely.

2. Weigh it as you shred, and pack down into a large crock or earthenware jar – at least 60 cm (12 in) in diameter at the mouth – 1 kg (2 lb) at a time, mixing in 25 g (1 oz) of salt to each layer. A little crushed cumin or caraway seed can be added for flavour. Layer until 7 cm (3 in) from the top. By this time the cabbage should have yielded a fair bit of juice. Press down until the juice easily covers the cabbage.

Cover the crock with several layers of scalded muslin. Then choose a scalded wooden board which can fit down inside the container. Weight it down with a smooth, scalded stone so that the air is excluded. Keep the crock in a warm place (21°C/70°F) to encourage the fermentation evidenced by busy bubbling beneath a skin. After a few days, even the lid should be submerged. Keep the kraut at this temperature for two to three weeks, regularly washing and scalding the cloth and board and skimming off the skin. When the bubbles stop, transfer the crock to a cool place (10°C/50°F) to store. It may be eaten now and will keep for two or three months.

3. To preserve sauerkraut for longer, pack it down tightly into large, clean, glass jars and heat process, by boiling the jars in water for 30 minutes. Cool, seal tightly when cold and store.

Dried Fruit

'Of the two downstairs rooms, one was used as a kind of kitchen storeroom,
with pots and pans and a big red crockery water vessel at one end,
and potatoes in sacks and peas and beans spread out to dry at the other.
The apple crop was stored on racks suspended beneath the ceiling,
and bunches of herbs dangled below.'

Lark Rise to Candleford   Flora Thompson   1945

Preserving fruit by drying is the oldest, easiest and most natural way of all. It is also the most satisfactory for long-term storage as the various moulds, yeasts and bacteria which spoil fruit need moisture to thrive and multiply. By drying out whatever natural moisture is in the fruit, the action of the bacteria is stopped.

The easy, cheap way to dry fruit is in the sun's heat but it needs to be a hot sun burning out of a cloudless sky for the process to continue unchecked. Sun drying, as well as costing nothing and being highly convenient, produces fruit with the truest flavour: sun-dried apricots from Kashmir are the best in the world.

So much for drying under optimum conditions. People living in more variable climates can still dry fruit successfully by making the best use of such natural sunshine and wind as comes their way, together with a judicious back-up from artificial sources of heat. Festoons of apple rings slowly turning leathery in the heat of the old kitchen stove used to be a common feature of northern country kitchens; in sunnier climates there would be trays of plums and cherries.

In the case of foods that dry particularly well, this is a straightforward and satisfactory way of taking care of a sudden glut, or of dealing with food left over from bottling or pickling. The enormous advantage of dried food is that it takes up so little room – a hoard of fresh plums will fit into a glass jar when dried into prunes and several jars will last the winter through. Containers for drying fruit must, however, be airtight, since anything dried is likely to absorb whatever moisture is floating about in the air. Apple rings over a kitchen range in constant use are one thing, apple rings in a damp kitchen full of steam quite another.

In theory anything may be dried. In practice, I think the field can be limited to perhaps half a dozen different sorts of fruit. The ones I have chosen are the ones I think most people would find most useful, and which stand up to drying best.

Late summer sunshine steadily warms and dries prepared fruits: plump apricots; windfall apples, peeled, cored and skewered; and pears, halved and brushed with ascorbic acid to prevent discolouration. The plums and nuts have been harvested for indoor drying.

Fruit drying

Equipment

For drying in the sun, some kind of large, light tray to spread out the produce, is needed. The air must be able to circulate freely, so light, rigid, wooden frames covered with wire, gauze or cheesecloth stapled on for strength are a handy solution. Make them so they can be stacked on top of each other indoors, allowing air to circulate, above an artificial heat source: convector heater, hot plate, radiator. If you are drying fruit out of doors, provide some sort of protection against flies too – fine muslin sheets thrown over the top of the trays. Bring it all indoors if it rains. Another expedient, useful where the weather is variable, is to set the food out under glass, which concentrates the sun's heat – use a glazed cold frame, or the shelves of a greenhouse.

For indoor drying, equipment can range from your own cooker, turned to a low setting to expensive, but convenient, electrically powered drying cabinets with thermometers, fans to circulate air and slatted shelves. In my experience an ordinary domestic oven will dry average amounts of food quite satisfactorily and inexpensively. Depending on the size of the fruit, it can be dried on the usual oven grids, with a piece of muslin laid over the trays, or in baking tins, or in specially made stacking trays designed to fit the oven.

Not vital to success, but handy, is a thermometer for checking oven temperature or heat over the drying trays.

Some fruits tend to darken or discolour as they dry; it is arguable whether this affects the flavour but, in some people's view, it makes them unattractive. There are various ways of checking this. The simplest is a salt water dip, which is suitable for apples. Or you can use ascorbic acid, available in crystal form from chemists. Added to water at the rate of 1 teaspoon per 600 ml (1 pint) and sprinkled over the prepared fruit (apricots, peaches, pears, apples) it helps preserve their natural colour without altering the flavour.

Peaches and nectarines

Peel, halve and stone the peaches and nectarines. Sprinkle with ascorbic acid to prevent darkening. Lay on trays, hollow side uppermost (sugary juice collects here at first), and dry at a very mild heat (51°C/125°F to 65°C/150°F). Lower the heat towards the end to prevent them scorching. After about fifteen hours they will be dry but pliable and leathery.

Apricots

Slit the top carefully, remove the stone but do not peel. Sprinkle with ascorbic acid to prevent discolouration then dry. As for peaches, except they need less time and less heat.

Grapes

Dry these in bunches, after picking off any bad ones. Dip them in boiling water to speed things up. A mild heat as for peaches, then dry out for eight hours.

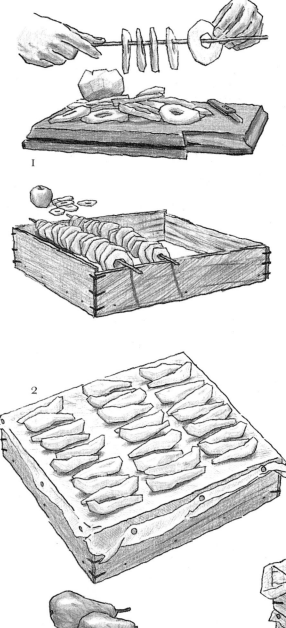

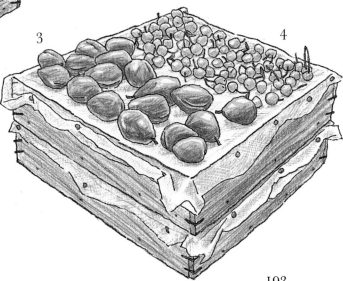

Drying fruit

First clean, wash and trim the fruit, cutting into manageable slices or pieces unless really small. To dry the fruit out entirely you need a steady source of heat – the sun is best, but sadly usually unreliable – plus a slight draught if possible. Fruit can be dried in short bursts, as it contains enough acid and sugar to inhibit moulds. When the fruit has dried, leave it at room temperature overnight to 'condition', and then store.

1. Apples. Use ripe apples, eaters or cookers. Peel, core and slice into 6 mm ($\frac{1}{4}$ in) rings, dropping them into lightly salted water (2 tablespoons per 4 litres/1 gallon) to prevent browning. Shake off the water, and thread on sticks or spread on trays. The sticks can then be propped up above the stove, or supported on trays in the oven. The oven heat should be no more than 60°C (140°F). If heat is continuous, the rings take 4–6 hours to dry; if intermittent, two to three days. They are ready when their texture is like chamois leather.

2. Pears. Pears should be peeled, quartered and cored, sprinkled with ascorbic acid to prevent darkening, and spread on stacking trays covered with cheesecloth. Dry as for apples, never allowing the temperature to exceed 65°C (150°F).

3. Plums. If small, dry whole, first scalding with boiling water to split the skins. Large plums can be halved and stoned. Proceed as for pears.

4. Cherries. Sour or Morello cherries dry best, with the most flavour. Leave the stalks on, do not stone, and spread on trays and dry at 54°C (130°F) for six hours.

194

Dried Vegetables

'Other jams, jellies and pickles already stood on the pantry shelves. Big yellow vegetable marrows dangled from hooks and bunches of drying thyme and sage. The faggot pile was being replenished and the lamp was lighted after tea.'

Lark Rise to Candleford   Flora Thompson   1945

Vegetables are a little trickier to dry than fruit, as they contain less acid and almost no natural sugar. If the drying process is interrupted, or does not get going properly, they can go mouldy before they dry. I find that onions, peppers and mushrooms are the best vegetables – pulses excepted – to dry, and seem to avoid this problem.

Cut vegetables smaller than fruits when preparing them for drying as more water will be lost and the process takes longer. When they are quite dried, leave the vegetables at room temperature overnight to 'condition', and then store in airtight containers, in a cool, dark place. Obviously some things dry faster than others, and the type of heat used makes a difference too, so it is impossible to give precise times. Keep an eye on your vegetables to begin with, looking over your handiwork every hour or so, and change the trays round to encourage everything to dry evenly.

Nearly all garden herbs, except parsley and chives, can be dried successfully. The best time to pick herbs for drying is early in the summer, just before they flower. They should be cut in the morning on a fine day. Small leaved herbs – thyme, savory, marjoram – need only be tied loosely in bundles and hung up to dry in a warm place, preferably wrapped in a loose muslin cover to keep off the dust. Bunches of herbs can be hung outdoors in the half shade during the warmest part of the day for several days. Large leaved herbs like sage, may be dipped in boiling water for one minute, then removed, the water shaken off, and dried in a cool oven until brittle. Basil can be dried as for thyme – it tastes different dry, but is still good for cooking. If you are drying for seeds – fennel, dill, coriander – cut the stems with the seed heads as soon as they are ripe. Dry the whole stalk then thresh them out over a sheet of clean paper. Dry the seeds for a further two hours in the sun or in a warm, dry place.

Run a roller over dried herbs to crush them, pick out stalks and store in dark glass jars or tins, away from the light. Keep different herbs separate or their flavours will blend, with disappointing results.

A warm, dry barn for drying the autumn crop of vegetables and herbs: onions knotted in bunches, garlanded in rings from the rafters; threaded mushrooms to flavour winter soups; broad beans left to dry in their pods; bunches of herbs; and sweet peppers ready to be sliced for drying.

Vegetable drying

Garlic

Dry, string and store homegrown garlic bulbs exactly as for onions. Because of their natural oil, garlic bulbs keep perfectly in a dry place for months.

Tomatoes

This is a Tunisian method of preserving ripe tomatoes in the form of a salty paste. Cut the tomatoes in half, scoop out the seeds and remove the skins. Mix three handfuls of salt with the thick, red juice, turn into a jellybag and leave to drip all night over a basin. Next day, scrape off the red paste, mix with one handful of salt, spread on flat earthenware dishes or plates (do not use metal plates) and leave in the sun or in a cool oven to evaporate the remaining moisture. It should not be allowed to dry hard, but remain pasty and soft. Cool. Spoon into jars, cover with 1 cm ($\frac{1}{2}$ in) of oil, cover and store. Add no salt when cooking with this paste.

Sweet peppers

Buy peppers at their cheapest in summer, and dry them to use throughout the year. Home-grown peppers also dry well and retain their flavour better than commercially dried peppers. Prepare the peppers – red and green – by slicing across into rings, removing the stalk, seeds and partitions. Best to spread on trays and dry in the oven – they take approximately three hours in the oven. They are ready when brittle. Condition, pack and store.

Edible fungi

The right weather conditions raise wild fungi like dragon seed – too much at once. Drying is the best way to preserve wild mushrooms and other edible fungi and their flavour is concentrated enough for one of two dried specimens to flavour a whole stew. To dry, simply rub any dirt off the stalks, discarding really tough ones, spread out on trays and dry slowly, at not more than 49°C (120°F), in the sun or an oven till dry and leathery. Or thread them on strings without stalks and suspend them over the range, or in another warm, dry place.

Note: If the oven is too warm, or the mushrooms exceptionally juicy, you may find precious juice oozing out of them, so it is a good idea to put a tin beneath to catch it. Boiled up with nutmeg, mace, cayenne and a spoonful of brandy, and sterilized in boiling water for 15 minutes, this makes superb ketchup. You *must* sterilize mushroom ketchup as it grows mould very quickly otherwise.

Pulses

All the pulse family (chick peas, soya beans, lentils, peas and haricots) are dried in much the same way. Leave them on the plant to dry naturally as long as possible, then take the pods indoors or into a greenhouse to dry for another few days. Finally, shell them, spread them out on trays and allow them to dry completely hard in the sun or an oven. It takes many plants to get much to show for your work. Mature beans and peas dry easily out of doors.

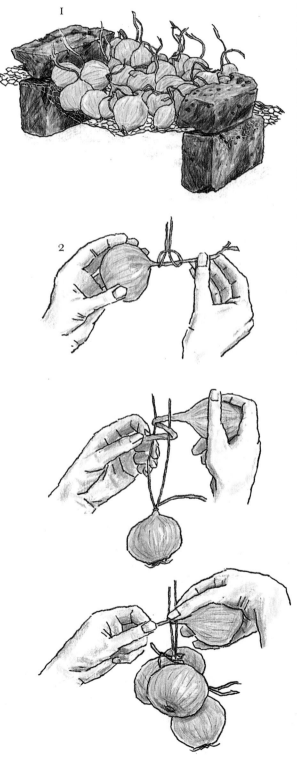

Drying onions

Onions can be dried either whole and strung up in skeins, or peeled and sliced. The bulbs themselves will keep for months in a dry place, as will the slices in an airtight container.

1. For the first method, spread out the onion bulbs (still on their stems) on raised wire mesh to allow the air to circulate and leave them to dry for several days out of doors in the sun. Cover them if it rains. They are ready when their skins are bronzed and papery and the stalks have shrivelled.

2. To string onions, take a length of stout string or twine and tie it to form a loop. Hang the loop over a hook at a convenient height for working.

Knot the first few onions as shown in the illustration. Continue until the string has been used up. Alternatively push the onions into old stockings to store them. Hang the bunches in a warm dry place. Dryness is the vital factor, they will sprout in a damp spot.

3. Only sound onions are suitable for stringing up whole, since those with soft patches will rot. Any that are bruised or damaged can be dried in peeled slices of 1 cm ($\frac{1}{2}$ in) thickness. Spread them on trays covered with muslin and dry for three hours in an oven, or eight hours in the sun. They are ready when brittle.

Leave them overnight at room temperature to 'condition', then store them in plastic bags. Use as a convenience food in stews and soups; they are marvellously tasty fried for a second or two.

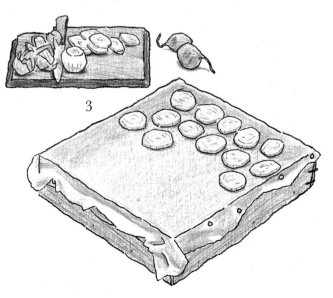

Bottled Fruit

With the advent of canning and, in latter years, freezing, the thrifty practice of packing away ripe orchard fruit in bottles for winter use seems to have fallen from favour. This is a pity, I think, because the fruit that bottles well tastes fresher and truer to itself preserved that way than any other. Fruit of luscious texture are even more delicious preserved in a light syrup than when eaten straight from the tree. I would put peaches, apricots, nectarines, pears and cherries in this class, and in other climates I imagine mangoes, guavas and lychees would respond well too. It is a waste of time bottling soft fruit such as gooseberries, strawberries and raspberries because they emerge tough, or flimsy, and seem to be all pip. Blackberries, sieved to a purée and bottled with puréed apple, are an honourable exception. Bottled apple purée is a good standby, and useful and pleasant to have on hand for turning into charlottes, crumbles and pies at a moment's notice. Rhubarb, too, bottles excellently due to its high acid content.

It is the natural acid in fruit which makes it so perfect for bottling. *Clostridium botulinum*, the bogey of home bottling, cannot survive in acid conditions though it can survive heat processing and airless vacuum seals. Vegetables, due to their low acid content, are risky subjects for home bottling except where vinegar, lemon juice or some other acid is supplied, as in pickling. Properly bottled fruit will keep safely for a long time, but it should be heat processed to destroy the enzymes and micro-organisms which could spoil the flavour and the fruit.

This is not difficult to do, but it is one of those kitchen activities which need full concentration, proper equipment, careful preparation and a conscientious eye on the clock. Do not try to weave it in with the usual day's routine, but set aside a whole morning or afternoon for the job, at least for the first few times. You will find full instructions overleaf.

Rosy damsons and golden plums float within the transparent bottling jars; large pears soak up clear sugary syrup, more delicious even than when eaten straight from the tree; and apple purée has been bottled with cinnamon and lemon peel as a useful standby for pies and crumbles.

Fruit bottling

Equipment

The *sine qua non* of bottling is proper jars, made of glass strong enough to withstand high temperatures, large enough to contain a reasonable quantity of fruit (enough to fill a pie dish, say), and supplied with suitable lids for creating a vacuum seal. Purpose made preserving jars fulfil these requirements and will last for years if you look after them, but they are expensive initially, and the rubber rings need replacing every time they are used. A cheaper solution is to collect *thick* glass jars in large sizes, and seal them with a commercial plastic sealing material which can be saved and re-used. Secondhand preserving jars come cheap, but you must check that rubber rings are still being manufactured to fit their lids.

Other equipment you should have includes a thermometer, a pan deep enough to stand jars in completely submerged (for the quick water bath method), and kitchen tongs to lift out the jars. Finally, a wooden board is necessary to stand the hot jars on – and do not forget a clock.

Making syrup

Make the syrup with water and ordinary granulated sugar, adding a little honey to bottled pears, if you feel like it. Do not make the syrup too strong because the fruit will crowd at the top of the jar if you do. As an average guide use 225 g (8 oz) sugar to 600 ml (1 pint) of water. Melt the sugar in the water by stirring over a low heat before bringing it up to the boil, then simmer for a couple of minutes. It should be added, hot, to the warm jars for the quick water bath method of heat processing, and boiling for the moderate oven method. Add a little cinnamon or lemon peel to the syrup.

Preparing and packing the fruit

Fruit should be cleaned and trimmed of brown or squashy bits. They can be bottled whole or peeled, cored and quartered – cut-up fruit packs down tighter. Pears and apples should be kept in a large bowl of slightly salted water with a squeeze of lemon juice until you are ready to pack them down, to stop them browning.

Heat processing: the moderate oven method

Although this method uses an extravagant amount of fuel it does dispense with the problem of filling *hot* jars with boiling syrup. Preheat the oven to 150°C (300°F, Mark 2) and put the jars in to warm. Begin boiling the syrup. Remove the jars, stand them on a wooden board, pack them quickly with the prepared fruit, fill to within 3 cm (1 in) of the top with boiling syrup and put the metal tops on loosely or cover the jars with saucers. The syrup may boil over in the oven so the jars are not sealed till after processing. Transfer the jars to a large baking tin lined with a folded sheet of newspaper then slide the tin carefully into the middle of the oven. Give sliced apple and rhubarb, whole plums, damsons, apricots and cherries 40 minutes, and allow an hour for the tighter packed cut-up fruit. Remove the jars from the oven, screw on caps, clip down lids or tie on covers. Do this at once while the contents are piping hot. Leave to cool on a wooden board for 24 hours before testing the seal.

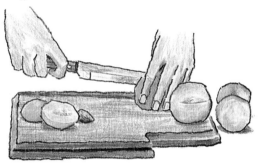

Bottling peaches:
The quick water bath process

1. Make a syrup from 1 litre (2 pints) of water and 450 g (1 lb) of granulated sugar.

2. Clean and trim the peaches, which can be bottled whole or peeled, halved and stoned. If you cut up the fruit it will pack down tighter.

3. Warm the jars and bottles and pack them to the top with peaches (they will soften and shrink later). Push the fruit down with a wooden spoon, fill to the brim with hot (60°C/140°F) syrup, give the jars a quick shake to release any trapped air and cover. Screw-on lids should be screwed tight, then unscrewed a half turn, to let air escape.

4. Put a trivet, wire rack or some other type of false bottom in a large deep pan. Stand the jars on it and completely fill the pan with warm water (38°C/100°F), submerging the bottles. Bring the water to simmering point (88°C/190°F) slowly over 30 minutes and maintain the heat for 20 minutes. Remove the jars from the pan, tighten the seals and leave to cool.

Note: If you are using jars without screw- or clip-on lids they should not be submerged but covered up to the shoulder in water.

Preserves

If preserves did not exist it would be a priority matter to invent them because they provide the simplest, longest lasting method of preserving a quantity of fruit in a small compass. This was discovered way back in medieval times – indeed Chaucer was present at the coronation banquet for Henry IV, at which comfits of candied quince, among other dainties, regaled the company.

In those times fruit seems usually to have been made into fruit cheeses – sliced rather than spread – instead of jams and jellies, because this method, being so highly concentrated, makes the most of whatever natural sugar may be in the fruit itself (a fact New England farmers' wives thriftily turned to account a few centuries later) and thus requires less extra sweetening in the way of sugar or honey.

It was not until the West Indian sugarcane plantations were in full swing that sugar became cheap and commonplace enough to be used extravagantly. Sugar was a luxury until then, sold in apothecary shops by the ounce and the poor had to satisfy their craving for sweetness with honey and dried fruit.

Home-made preserves today, however luxurious they may be, are not necessarily expensive. Hedgerow jams, jellies, butters and cheeses can be made from all the wild fruits and berries – blackberries, blueberries, cloudberries, hips and haws, elderberries – which are there for the picking, on country expeditions, weekend walks and if you look carefully, in many of the less formal parks and commons. Preserves like these have a fresh, innocent wild savour all their own and are one of the nearest things I know to a free treat. Fruit farms where you pick your own raspberries, strawberries and other soft fruit are well worth a visit as the prices are rock bottom, but ring up first to check that they still have what you want, as soft fruit seasons are short.

I have been using the word 'preserve' very loosely to cover the whole range of jams and their more refined, more clearly defined compatriots such as jellies, butters and cheeses. However, I should add that a 'preserve' is in fact a distinctive type of jam. If this sounds confusing, I had better quickly say that cooks are not linguistic philosophers and pass on to some of the basic definitions.

Damson fruit cheese, foreground left, and sweet black butter, right, made from any surplus soft fruits in summer. Then, at the back, crabapple jellies with the fruits suspended in amber jelly, lemon curd, beside rowan and redcurrant jellies, and two jars of purpled damson jam.

Preserving

Jams: whole fruit or fruit pulp boiled with sugar till such time as the acid and pectin in the fruit combine with the thickening sugar syrup to make the mixture set or jell.

Preserves: in its specific, rather than generic, meaning this refers to a rather stately sort of jam, intended for 'best' rather than everyday eating, to which nuts, candied peel, dried fruit, lemon or orange slices, ginger or alcohol are added.

Conserves: whole fruit preserved in a fair amount of syrup or a light jelly to be eaten with a spoon together with fresh curd cream at the end of a good meal. This is a peculiarly French type of preserve and the word descends, I would guess, from the French 'compote de fruits en conserve'.

Jellies: essentially the same as jam, except that the cooked fruit pulp is strained in a bag, and the strained juice alone boiled up with sugar till it reaches setting point. A good way of getting rid of pips, stones and extracting the flavour of certain dry berries like hips, haws and rowanberries and certain juicy ones like cranberries or elderberries though it has a lower yield per 450 g (1 lb) of fruit than jam.

Fruit cheeses and butters: descendants of the medieval sweetmeats, the fruit pulp cooked slowly with sugar till stiff, solid and almost dry. Fruit butters are cooked for a shorter time till thick but not stiff, and are used for spreads whereas fruit cheeses are eaten in small slices.

Marmalades: normally a preserve made with citrus fruit, in which the cut peel is embedded in a jelly flavoured with the juice. It is the ideal breakfast time preserve as the astringent flavour helps to unclog a drowsy palate.

Equipment
The single most important piece of equipment is a suitable pan for cooking up preserves. It needs to be large (6 to 9 litre/$1\frac{1}{2}$ to 2 gallon capacity), shallow but wide to help evaporation and solid to distribute heat and guard against sticking and burning. This may seem very large but the golden rule in jam making is never to have the pan more than half full. Boiling sugar splutters, foams and boils up with alarming suddenness. A good quality, aluminium preserving pan, with a thick bottom, is not cheap but it is a well designed piece of equipment which lasts for years. A conventional pan of 2 litre (4 pint) capacity is useful for cooking up small quantities of jelly.

Also vital are kitchen scales, for weighing fruit, sugar, and pulp or juice, a long handled wooden spoon for stirring (most jams should be stirred in the last few minutes to prevent scorching). A jam making thermometer is useful. Other items which will be needed are a hair or nylon sieve, a ladle, a plastic funnel and a jug for transferring the cooked jam into pots. A commercial or home-made jellybag is the neatest way of straining fruit pulp for jellies. More advanced jam makers will probably want to try the pectin test, to work out the setting capacity of a particular batch of fruit, and for this a little methylated spirits will be needed.

Almost any glass jar in good condition will do for storing preserves, though fruit cheeses should be pressed into oiled pottery dishes or moulds so they can be turned out easily. For the everyday type of jam, I find the standard 450 g (1 lb) jar is the best size. For the special herb scented or wild berry jellies to eat with game and meat, very small glass jars are best, as they provide just enough for one meal. These make really attractive presents.

To keep well, all preserves should be given an airtight seal immediately on top of the jam itself either with waxed paper discs sold in sizes to fit standard jars, or by melting paraffin wax. The jar itself can be covered with sober greaseproof, pretty paper doilies, or smart rounds of check gingham. Polish the jars inside and out, label them neatly with the name of the jam and the date. A good, home-made jam or preserve should look elegant and individual.

Making preserves

Some methodology is helpful. Let us deal first with the pectin and acid question: pectin is a gummy substance naturally found in fruit, in some fruit more than others. Ditto for acid. Acid helps leach out the pectin during cooking. The pectin then combines with the sugar to produce a good jell or set, so it follows that fruit high in both is good for jam.

Green cooking apples, blackcurrants, redcurrants, damsons, plums, gooseberries and quinces are all high in pectin and acid. All these jell, or jam, effortlessly.

Fresh apricots, loganberries, raspberries, greengages and early blackberries have a medium pectin/acid content.

Strawberries, rhubarb, marrow, late blackberries, pears, cherries and pumpkin have a low pectin/acid content.

Slightly underripe fruit is at its peak for pectin/acid and this is the best to use. Testing fruit for pectin is simple and can be useful in deciding how much sugar to use. A simple rule of thumb is that high pectin sets more sugar equals more jam. However, a more accurate version with measures is:

High pectin fruits – 575–675 g ($1\frac{1}{4}$–$1\frac{1}{2}$ lb) sugar to 450 g (1 lb) fruit
Medium pectin fruits – 450 g (1 lb) sugar to 450 g (1 lb) fruit
Low pectin fruits – 350 g (12 oz) sugar to 450 g (1 lb) fruit

To test for pectin, take one teaspoon of juices from the pre-cooked fruit (before adding the sugar) and put it into a small glass jar with three teaspoons of methylated spirits. Shake. If one jelly blob forms, the fruit is rich in pectin; if two or three smaller ones, it is moderately well off; if small beads, or none at all, it is so low that you must mix it with a high pectin fruit, or commercial pectin. A lack of acid is easily made up by a squeeze of lemon juice, lemon slices or a little citric acid. Commercial pectin can be added to any jam of doubtful setting properties.

Medium to low pectin fruit, as the following recipes will show, generally uses a greater weight of fruit than sugar.

Making everyday strawberry jam

1. Take 2 kg (4 lb) of ripe but sound fruit, pick over for stalks and leaves and remove the hulls.

2. Strawberries should not be washed, but should be wiped instead with a clean cloth.

3. Put the prepared fruit into a preserving pan with the squeezed juice of four lemons. Strawberries are low in pectin/acid, and the sharp juice helps the jam to set. Simmer over a low heat until the strawberries are quite soft and mushy – about 30 minutes. Warm the sugar before adding it to the fruit. Granulated sugar is quite adequate, but for special preserves the preserving sugar gives finer colour. Draw the pan off the flame for a minute, add $1\frac{3}{4}$ kg ($3\frac{1}{2}$ lb) warmed sugar to the softened fruit, stir vigorously to dissolve, turn up the heat, return the pan and bring quickly back to the boil. This jam takes approximately 15 minutes to reach a set.

4. A jam-making thermometer is not essential, but helps to give you an instant progress report, telling at a glance if the jam is ready to set. Before plunging it into boiling jam, it should always be warmed in a jug of hot water. The red line will shoot up to within a couple of degrees of 'setting point', 105°C (221°F), the last degree

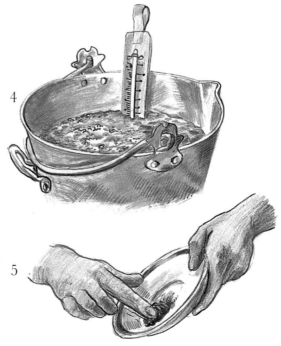

always taking the longest to reach. When the jam is nearly done, unclip the thermometer, and take the reading from the centre of the pan for accuracy.

5. Alternatively if you do not have a jam thermometer, do the saucer test. Drop a tiny bit of boiling jam on to a clean saucer, blow to cool, push with your fingertip, and if it crinkles because a skin has formed on top, the jam is done.

6. When the jam is judged ready, remove the pan from the heat. Your jam jars should be washed, dried, warmed in a low oven (they can go in when the sugar comes out) and standing by on a large (preferably wood – to prevent cracking) chopping board or tray. Leave jam to cool and set slightly for 20 minutes and then ladle into a jug, and either funnel or pour into the jars to within 6 mm ($\frac{1}{4}$ in) of the rim. Wipe off drips and stickiness with a hot damp cloth.

7. Place a waxed paper disc on the jam surface to seal.

8. An alternative method of sealing is to run a tablespoon of melted paraffin wax on top of the jam.

9. Cover the mouth of the jar with a cellophane cover, anchored down with an elastic band.

Jams

Home-made jam has never really lost ground to the commercial product. A good jam appeals to the artist in every cook; fine colour and brilliance count for almost as much as good flavour.

Damson jam

Damsons are a natural jam fruit, and make a jam of episcopal purple, firm texture and intense plummy flavour – splendid with buttered toast and scones. The stones are one of the small inconveniences one has to put up with to enjoy the rest – do not attempt to stone the raw fruit, just skim off as many as you can as they rise while cooking.

2½ kg (5 lb) damsons
900 ml (1½ pints) water
3 kg (6 lb) sugar

Put the damsons in a large bowl, fill with cold water to float off stalks and leaves. Pick off any remaining stalks. Turn into a preserving pan with the water and simmer till quite soft. Add warmed sugar, bring to the boil and boil hard till the jam sets, skimming off any stones as they rise, with a slotted spoon. Pot and seal as usual. This will make approximately 5 kg (10 lb) of jam.
Note : a refinement is to crack some of the damson stones and add the kernels for a hint of bitter almonds.

Raspberry jam

Seeds or no, this is one of the most perfect jams, as fragrant as it is richly flavoured and royally crimson.

2 kg (4 lb) raspberries
2 kg (4 lb) castor sugar

I think it is worth spending a little extra on a finer sugar for this preserve because it melts quicker and helps prevent the berries getting crushed. To make the jam, put both sugar and raspberries into a bowl in a medium oven for 10 to 15 minutes. Then turn them into the preserving pan bring to the boil and cook, stirring slowly, for three to five minutes or till it reaches setting point. Pot, seal, cover as usual. This will make approximately 3 kg (6 lb) of jam.

Strawberry jam II

Unlike the everyday strawberry jam, this uses commercial pectin, the best choice if strawberries are scarce and expensive and you do not want to risk a flop. It looks handsome too because the fruit remains whole.

2 kg (4 lb) strawberries
3 kg (6 lb) sugar
1 small bottle of commercial pectin

Put the fruit in the pan and bring slowly to the boil. Add the warmed sugar, stir well but gently till the sugar is dissolved, then boil for six minutes. Remove from the heat. Add the pectin, stir for 10 minutes. Skim. Leave to cool for 15 minutes. Pot and seal at once. This will make approximately 5 kg (10 lb) of jam.

Rose petal jam

This jam is a fitting end for any richly scented roses (preferably red). Spread the petals out on newspaper and dry them in a cool place. You need the same weight of petals as sugar, not less than 225 g (8 oz) to justify the trouble involved. An old fashioned, sweet, fragrant jam to grace a poet's tea.

225 g (8 oz) rose petals
225 g (8 oz) loaf sugar
150 ml (¼ pint) rosewater (available from chemists)
1 tablespoon orangeflower water

Put the dried petals into a large bowl and pour a kettleful of boiling water on them. After a minute, drain off the water, shake the petals and leave them to dry off.

Make a syrup from the loaf sugar and the rosewater. Use just enough rosewater to melt the sugar. When the sugar is quite melted, stir in rose petals and one tablespoonful of orangeflower water and boil till the jam has reached setting point. Leave to cool for a few minutes then spoon into small jars, seal and cover.

Dumpsideary jam

A traditional English country jam, made with mixed orchard fruit – apples, plums, pears – which are ripe at the same time. The Irish version, 'Mixty Maxty', is much the same except that it omits the spices.

1 kg (2 lb) apples (green cookers)
1 kg (2 lb) pears
1 kg (2 lb) plums
600 ml (1 pint) water
2 lemons
6 cloves
1 small stick cinnamon
4½ kg (9 lb) sugar

Quarter the apples, slicing off the core and any brown parts. Do not peel. Chop the pears somewhat smaller, also removing soft or brown parts. Put them all, with the whole plums, into a large pan, with 600 ml (1 pint) of water and cook gently and slowly till the flesh is all soft. Turn into a large hair sieve, and rub through into a preserving pan. Keep some of the plum stones, cracking them with a hammer to extract the kernels. Weigh the pulp and warm the sugar. Add grated lemon rind and squeezed juice to the fruit. Tie bruised spices in a muslin bag and add. Stir in the warmed sugar, set over a moderate heat, stirring till the sugar melts, then boil rapidly, stirring often, till it reaches setting point. Stir in the plum kernels, pot and cover.

Blackcurrant jam

A classic and unfailingly successful jam. One of the most economical too, as the yield in jam is two and a half times the weight in fruit.

2 kg (4 lb) blackcurrants
1¾ litres (3 pints) water
3 kg (6 lb) sugar

Pick over the fruit, removing stalks and leaves. Run quickly under cold tap, then turn into a pan with the water and simmer gently till the skins are soft, stirring now and then. This may take 45 minutes. Add the warmed sugar, boil rapidly till setting point is reached. Pot, seal and cover.
Note: unripe green grapes can be used instead, but with an equal weight of sugar and fruit.

Gooseberry and elderflower jam

Elderflower heads dipped into cooking gooseberries confer an elusive, elegant muscatel grape flavour. If you cannot manage the elderflowers try a sprig of rosemary, a few blackcurrant leaves or a teaspoon of crushed coriander seed, all aromatic in their different ways. Unadorned, gooseberries still make one of the best jams, of keen flavour, tawny port colour and good set.

Note the large proportion of sugar to fruit – gooseberries are high in acid and pectin so perfect for jam.

2 kg (4 lb) gooseberries
5 heads of elderflower
water
3 kg (6 lb) sugar

Top and tail the berries, then put them with enough water to cover in a preserving pan and cook gently for 20 to 40 minutes, till the skins are quite tender. Add the warmed sugar, and elderflower heads, rosemary, blackcurrant leaves or coriander tied in a small piece of muslin. Stir to melt the sugar, bring to the boil, then boil hard till the jam sets. Remove the muslin bag, pot and seal at once. This will make approximately 5 kg (10 lb) of jam.

Dried apricot jam

The best all-the-year-round jam as dried apricots have no season, and they make a rich strongly flavoured preserve. The grapefruit supplies acid – two lemons can be substituted.

350 g (12 oz) dried apricots
1¾ litres (3 pints) boiling water
1 kg (2 lb) sugar
1 large grapefruit or two lemons

Wash the fruit, put them in a large bowl and pour over boiling water. Leave for one to three days, till swollen and soft. Turn into a pan and simmer till tender. Add sugar and squeezed grapefruit juice, bring to the boil and boil till it sets. Pot, seal and cover. This will make approximately 1½ kg (3 lb) of jam.
Note: a few shredded almonds are often added with the sugar.

Rhubarb, marrow and ginger jam

Marrow makes a dull jam on its own, even with the help of ginger. The addition of rhubarb enlivens the flavour considerably.

1½ kg (3 lb) hard, yellow marrow
1½ kg (3 lb) rhubarb
3 kg (6 lb) sugar
75g (3 oz) preserved ginger
3 lemons

Skin and cube the marrow. Cut the rhubarb into short segments, and layer the marrow, rhubarb and sugar into a large bowl. Leave overnight to draw the juices out. Turn the lot into the preserving pan, with the chopped ginger, squeezed lemon juice and the lemon rind tied up in muslin. Bring to the boil rapidly and boil for approximately 30 minutes, or until the jam reaches setting point. Remove the muslin bag containing the rinds. Pot, seal and cover. This will make approximately 2½ kg (5 lb) of jam.

Hedgerow jam

This is the attractive, omnibus name for jam made from a mixture of wild fruits, the sort you might bring back from a casual country stroll in the autumn. Sloes, bilberries and elderberries can be cooked up together to make a wine-dark jam of intense, wild fruit flavour. Strengthen this if you like with a handful of hips and haws, but the jam must be sieved, because rose hip seeds are like infinitesimal burrs. In any case sieving is advisable, to get rid of the sloe stones and blackberry pips. To make your wild fruit go further, add a few cooking apples, or wild crab apples.

2 kg (4 lb) wild fruit of your choice
sugar
water

Remove the stalks and dry leaves, and chop apple into quarters. Put all the fruit into a pan with enough water to barely cover and gently simmer till soft – 30 minutes. Put through a sieve. Weigh pulp, and return to the pan with an equal weight of sugar. Stir to dissolve the sugar, bring to the boil and boil hard until the jam reaches setting point. Pot, cover and seal.

Blackberry and apple jam

Blackberry seeds add nothing to a jam (and are torture to denture wearers) so I usually sieve this classic mixture, to make a smooth pulp halfway to a jelly. The proportions of apple to blackberry can be varied depending on your haul – more blackberry than apple gives stronger flavour and needs more sugar to compensate for the lack of pectin in the berries. Include some red (unripe) berries to sharpen the flavour.

2 kg (4 lb) blackberries
1 kg (2 lb) apples
300 ml (½ pint) water
sugar

Pick over the berries, removing the leaves and stalks. Cut unpeeled apples into quarters, removing any brown parts. Combine the fruit in a pan with approximately 300 ml (½ pint) water, simmer very slowly till the fruit is soft and the apple peel floats loose. Turn into a hair sieve, and rub through into a preserving pan. Weigh the pulp, and add an equal weight of sugar. Stir to dissolve. Bring to the boil rapidly, boil hard till it sets – about 10 minutes. Pot, seal and cover.

Lemon curd

Not really a jam, so much as a lemony custard but too good, and useful to leave out. It makes a delicious tart filling. Children love it on anything in the bun, bread or teacake line.

75 g (3 oz) unsalted butter
350 g (12 oz) sugar
2 large lemons
3 eggs

Make the curd in the top of a double boiler. Melt the butter with the sugar, add the lemon juice and grated rind of both lemons. Stir over simmering water till the sugar is melted, then add the eggs (lightly whisked) and stir constantly till thick. Pot at once, seal and store in a cool dry place.
Note : Lemon curd does not last as long as jams and jellies and should be eaten within three to four months. This will make approximately 500 g (just over one pound) of curd.

Conserves

Conserves and preserves are elegant jams with sophisticated additions like ginger, nuts, brandy or rum, or exquisite refinements like de-seeding each gooseberry. The method and equipment are the same as for jams and jellies.

Currant conserve Bar-le-Duc

The gourmet version is made from currants as big as cherries (from specially pruned bushes) pipped with a goose quill. More realistically, we can substitute a medley of red and white currants and leave the pips in – but take care not to squash or mash the fruit.

1 kg (2 lb) red and white currants
1 kg (2 lb) preserving sugar

Pick over the fruit, removing the stalks and leaves. Do not squash. Put them into a pan, heat very gradually till the fruit is soft, shaking the pan instead of stirring. Now sprinkle on the warmed sugar little by little so one lot dissolves before adding the next. Shake the pan to prevent sticking. Bring just to boiling point, no more, then turn immediately into small warmed jars or glasses. Seal, cover and store. This will make approximately 1½ kg (3 lb) of conserve.

Raisiné

A Burgundian preserve, and very choice.

2 kg (4 lb) ripe juicy grapes
1 kg (2 lb) dessert pears
sugar

Put the grapes into a pan and simmer very slowly till the juices flow, mashing from time to time. When soft, turn into a hair sieve and press the juice out into a bowl. Meanwhile peel, quarter, core and thinly slice the pears and poach them for three or four minutes in just enough simmering water to cover. Drain when just tender. Weigh the grape juice and allow half as much weight of sugar to juice. Put the juice and the sugar into a preserving pan, bring to the boil and simmer till reduced by about one third. Add drained pear slices and go on simmering, stirring constantly, till the mixture is thick. Turn into pots, seal, cover and store. This will make approximately 2½ kg (5 lb) of raisiné.

Plum, orange, walnut preserve

2 oranges
1½ kg (3 lb) plums
1 kg (2 lb) sugar
100 g (4 oz) walnuts

Wash the unpeeled oranges, and mince them finely, saving the juice. Stone the plums and tie the stones in a muslin bag. Put the plums, the minced oranges, the juice and the sugar into a pan and heat slowly to boiling point, stirring once or twice to make sure the sugar melts. Simmer over a gentle heat for an hour, or till the fruit and peel are soft. Add roughly chopped, blanched and skinned walnuts and simmer for another 30 to 40 minutes. Pot, seal, cover. This will make approximately 1½ kg (3 lb) of preserve.

Apples in wine and brandy

If you can substitute some quinces – three or four – for apples, the flavour will be sumptuous. This is the quintessence of a conserve.

6 lemons
600 ml (1 pint) white wine
2 kg (4 lb) sugar
2 kg (4 lb) apples
2 tablespoons brandy

Finely peel the lemons and marinate the peel in the wine plus an equal quantity of boiling water, for 30 minutes. Put this mixture plus the lemon juice and sugar into a pan and boil hard for about eight minutes, till slightly syrupy. Strain the syrup and return to pan. Drop in thinly sliced apples, which have been peeled, cored and quartered, and simmer for 40 minutes till the apples are tender and the syrup thick. Add the brandy, pour into hot jars, seal and cover. Eat with cream. This will make approximately 3 kg (6 lb) of conserve.
Note: It is a good idea to put a melted wax seal over any preserve using alcohol.

Jelly making

Jellies are the most pleasing and insouciant of all preserves to make. The fruit needs little or no preparation, the basic formula is easy to keep in one's head, and they always seem to turn out right, setting well and keeping perfectly. They are *beautiful* to look at, as vividly translucent as stained glass: amber, rose, gold, cornelian, ruby, purple. Wild fruits and berries, or the often disregarded fruit of decorative garden shrubs and trees – japonica, berberis, crab apple – make some of the best jellies, with a distinctive and appealing sharpness and intensity of flavour, and a subtle variation in colour which gives the cook an almost painterly satisfaction to contemplate. Jelly making *feels* casual, no need to pick till one's arms ache because a few handfuls of fruit or berries, eked out perhaps with some windfall apples, will make many tiny pots of jelly to eat with meat or game, or stuff into pancakes, or spread on toasted crumpets for tea.

Ingredients

Once you have mastered the absurdly simple basic procedure, you can make jelly from most things, starting with the free, wild offerings of woods, fields and hedgerows – brambles, sloes, elderberries, rowan berries, hips and haws, bilberries, cranberries – and moving on to the domesticated flavours of your own garden – green grapes, unripe figs and guavas, currants white, black and red. Fruit sweet enough to enjoy without sugar makes insipid jelly, thus crab apples are better than apples, redcurrants than raspberries, damsons than plums. Sugar is added to strained juice either weight for weight, or (marginally sweeter) at the rate of 450 g (1 lb) sugar to 600 ml (1 pint) juice. Both jell equally well, and are blessedly simple to remember. Seal with wax, or waxed paper discs.

Method

Jelly making can be informal, or full dress, depending on your mood and the rarity of the ingredient. For an everyday sort of jelly, do not bother with strigging (taking off stalks), or lengthy straining through a jellybag – simmer the fruit as it comes then turn it into a large hair sieve, and press the last drop through with a wooden spoon. Do not rub – that is going too far. For immaculate jelly turn to the jellybag, bought, home-made or improvised with a clean cotton square tied securely by all four corners to the four legs of an up-ended stool or chair so the juice drips into the pan beneath. The bag, or square, should first be scalded by pouring over boiling water. Wring out, then use – the dampness helps the juice pass through. Jars should be wide mouthed (the traditional jelly glass looks most elegant), not too big, and warmed before filling. Have them standing by – some jellies jell in a wink. Should the reverse occur – which it rarely does – simply tip it all back into the pan and boil up for a few minutes longer.

To test when your jelly is ready to set, take the temperature of the boiling brew from the centre of the pan with a jam thermometer, when the reading reaches 105°C (220°F) you are there. Alternatively try the saucer test. Spoon a few drops on to a saucer, and if they wrinkle when pushed with a finger, the jelly is done. Seal with wax, or waxed paper discs.

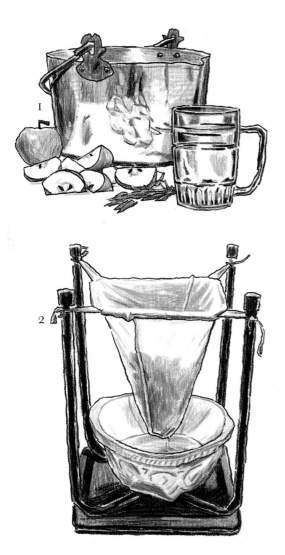

Making basic apple jelly with herbs

1. Take a mixed bag of apples – cookers, eaters, crabapples, windfalls – for the best flavoured jelly. Quarter 2 kg (4 lb) of fruit, removing any bruised, discoloured or brown parts, and chop roughly (no need to peel and core). Place in a preserving pan with a handful of fresh herbs tied in a bunch, either mint or tarragon, or a large sprig of rosemary or thyme, Pour over enough water barely to cover, and simmer slowly until the fruit is soft.

2. Remove the herbs and strain the remaining fruit and juice into a bowl through a scalded sieve or jellybag.

3. The amount of sugar to be added is determined by the quantity or weight of the juice. The proportions are either weight for weight of juice and sugar, or for a slightly sweeter jelly, add 450 g (1 lb) sugar to 600 ml (1 pint) of juice. Return the extracted juice and sugar to the preserving pan and bring to the boil, stirring with a wooden spoon to dissolve the sugar.

4. Have warmed jars ready to be filled (small jars are best, as one can be finished at one meal), standing on a baking tray. Fill with a jug and seal with waxed discs, either commercially supplied to fit the jars, or cut yourself from sheets. Cover the necks with cellophane, or more attractively, gingham squares secured with rubber bands. Serve rosemary and thyme jellies with pork or beef, mint with lamb, tarragon with roast chicken or chops.

Jellies

The fruit for jelly – unlike jam – is cooked until very soft then strained through a jelly bag, cheesecloth or muslin. The juice is then weighed and cooked with the required amount of sugar as stated in the recipes.

Crab apple jelly

Cornelian coloured, sharp and delicious. If you ask around you may find a neighbour who has a crab apple tree, with fruit to spare, as they crop prolifically.

2 kg (4 lb) crab apples
1 litre (2 pints) water
sugar

Wash and quarter the apples without peeling or coring. Put into a pan with the water and cook gently till quite soft, which takes an hour or so. Check to see that the water does not boil away. Strain the apples, either through a jellybag or hair sieve. Measure the juice and return to the pan, with 450 g (1 lb) sugar for each 600 ml (1 pint) juice, bring to the boil and boil briskly for about 10 minutes, or till it reaches setting point. Pot, seal and cover.

Lemon and honey jelly

An excellent and unusual jelly, with a sweet flavour as refreshing to the palate as a fine marmalade. It is delicious on hot toast, or with scones, or as a filling in sponge cake. It needs commercial pectin to assist setting. Or you could substitute your own apple jelly base.

180 ml (6 fl oz) lemon juice
1 tablespoon grated lemon rind
450 g (1 lb) honey
½ bottle (or 75 g, 3 oz) commercial pectin

Strain the lemon juice to remove any pulp. Stir the juice with grated lemon rind and honey in a pan over a moderate heat until fluid and well mixed, then bring to the boil. When bubbling hard, add the commercial pectin and boil for one minute, stirring constantly. Remove from the heat, stir for three minutes longer and pour into clean, hot jelly jars or glasses, seal with waxed paper discs and cover. Makes about 900 ml (1½ pints) jelly, or 3 jars.

Rowan jelly

Rowans are the brave scarlet berries of the mountain ash: so decorative it is a surprise to find they are edible. As the berries are dryish, it is best to add apples for bulk. Rowan jelly has an interesting smoky flavour, and is traditionally served with venison in Scotland.

3 kg (6 lb) rowan berries
1¼ kg (3 lb) sharp apples
water
sugar

Pull the stalks off the berries. Put the berries with the quartered apples (do not peel or core these) in a pan, add enough water just to cover and simmer gently till quite soft – about one hour. Tip into scalded jellybag, and leave to drip overnight. Measure the juice and add 450 g (1 lb) sugar to each 600 ml (1 pint) of juice. Put them both in the pan, stir to melt the sugar, bring to the boil and boil hard till it reaches setting point – this jelly does not set hard so use the drop on a saucer test alongside the thermometer reading. Pot, seal and cover as usual.

Cranberry jelly

Cranberries, traditional accompaniment to the Thanksgiving turkey, make an agreeably tart jelly. Apples help the set.

1¼ kg (3 lb) cooking apples
1 kg (2 lb) cranberries
water
sugar

Put the roughly chopped apples (do not peel or core) and the cranberries into a pan with enough water just to cover them. Simmer till soft. Turn into a jellybag and leave to drip through overnight. Measure the juice, and return to the pan with 450 g (1 lb) of sugar to every 600 ml (1 pint of liquid. Bring to the boil and boil hard till setting point is reached. Pot, seal and cover.

Hips and haws jelly

A handsome red jelly of strange, striking flavour: a little smoky, astringent and reminiscent of autumn hedgerows after rain.

450 g (1 lb) hips and haws (in equal proportions)
water
sugar
1 lemon

Rinse the berries under a cold tap and remove bits of stalk and leaves. Put into a pan with water just to cover. Simmer until soft and strain through a jellybag overnight. Weigh the juice and return to the pan with an equal weight of sugar, plus the juice of the squeezed lemon. Stir, bring to the boil, and boil to setting point. Pot, seal, cover.

Bramble jelly

This tastes of autumn to me, of damp earth, mist and woodsmoke. Add some red, unripe berries to help the set.

2 kg (4 lb) blackberries
450 ml (¾ pint) water
sugar
2 lemons

Put the blackberries with the water in a pan and simmer for 30 minutes, or till quite soft. Turn into a hair sieve and press to extract all the juice. Measure the juice, and add 450 g (1 lb) of sugar to each 600 ml (1 pint) of juice. Put the juice, the sugar and the squeezed lemon juice into a pan, bring to the boil and boil till it will set. Pot, seal and cover.
Note: if the blackberries are late ones, add a few hard cooking apples to help the jelly set firm.

Redcurrant jelly

A rich, red, finely flavoured accompaniment to venison, roast lamb and saddle of hare. This is the most extravagant way of making it, as it uses no water, but the gain in flavour makes it worthwhile.

3 kg (6 lb) redcurrants
sugar

Put the fruit into the pan and heat slowly, squashing with a wooden spoon to help the juice flow. Continue simmering and squashing for about 45 minutes, till the fruit is quite pulped. Turn into a jellybag and leave to drip for several hours. Weigh the extract and return to the preserving pan. Add an equal weight of warmed sugar, stir to dissolve, then bring back to the boil and boil hard for five minutes. Have warmed jars and waxed paper discs standing by, because this jelly sets almost at once. Transfer immediately into pots, seal and cover.

Guava jelly

Reputed to be the most distinguished jelly of all for serving with cold meat.

2 kg (4 lb) green guavas
sugar
water

Wash the fruit, remove the stems, and slice thinly. Place them in a pan with enough water just to cover, and simmer till quite soft. Leave overnight in a jellybag to drip through. Return the juice to the pan with an equal weight of sugar. Bring to the boil, and boil hard till the mixture sets. Pot, seal and cover.

Japonica jelly

Many people do not realize that the small apple-like fruit of the japonica can be used to make an attractive, tawny jelly, but in some country districts they are also known as 'jelly apples'.

1 kg (2 lb) japonica fruit
1 lemon
sugar
water

Wash the japonica apples, remove stalks and cut into quarters. Finely peel the yellow lemon rind. Put the rind and the apples into a pan, add enough water just to cover the fruit and simmer till soft. Strain the pulp – using a jellybag or sieve – then weigh, and weigh out an equal amount of sugar. Put the juice, the sugar and the lemon juice into a pan and bring to the boil. Boil fast for about six minutes, or till it will set. Pot, seal, cover.

Fruit butters and cheeses

Fruit cheeses and butters are simple, sugared fruit purées or jams with all the moisture cooked out of them. The cheeses, which use more sugar, are cooked till stiff enough to hold the impression of a spoon, and set firm when cooled. Butters are cooked till they can 'hold a trail' and although thick, soft and dryish they spread easily.

Traditionally fruit cheeses appeared at Christmas, flanking the Stilton and crusted port. On one side the damson cheese, wickedly black, glossy and unadorned (though people tipped a little port over their slice sometimes), on the other, the russet quince or apple cheese, bristling with slivered almonds and flounced with whipped cream. Such aristocratic preserves were never *spread*, but cut into small fingers or cubes to nibble at along with the nuts, the ripe Stilton and the port or madeira. Fruit butters, as the name suggests, are more utilitarian, designed to be spread on toast, scones or used to fill tarts and pancakes.

Cheeses and butters must be cooked slowly otherwise they have a tendency to burn. Given a really good quality thick bottomed pan, you can produce a successful cheese or butter provided you simmer the sieved fruit long and slowly till almost dry *before* adding the sugar, as fruit alone is less likely to burn, and stir constantly *after* adding the sugar, as this helps drive out the remaining moisture rapidly, as well as preventing the mixture sticking to the pan. Woven wire mats would be useful under the pan to diffuse the heat.

Cooking either of these delicacies is a process not to be hurried, and one which needs watching over, but the results are distinguished and delicious.

Finishing, covering and storing cheeses and butters

Do *not* store fruit cheese in a jam jar, or you will lose the pleasure of turning it out onto a plate. Any fairly small, shallow container will do, such as a little pie dish or casserole, cereal bowls and even old teacups. Wash the container well, dry and rub over with a little almond oil or glycerine to prevent the cheese sticking. Fill with cheese and press waxed paper cut to fit down onto the hot cheese, waxed side down. The wax melts on contact with the hot preserve to make an airtight seal. To make certain, you can invert the container to force out air. Then cover the pot or jelly glass with ordinary cellophane, or plastic film, and tie down with string. Store in a cool dry place. Keep for three months before eating, as the flavour improves with keeping. Fruit butter does not keep so well as cheese, as it contains less sugar and more moisture, so start eating it fairly promptly. It can be stored in ordinary jam jars, as it is soft enough to spoon out easily. Cover with waxed paper to seal, then with cellophane as for cheeses.

Melted paraffin wax, poured over while the preserve is very hot, makes the most perfect airtight seal, but has the disadvantage that you cannot see how the preserve looks till you break the seal.

For one reason or another – curiosity, pleasure in the quaint names, a feeling for tradition – every imaginative cook I know is intrigued by any mention of fruit cheese and butter.

Comfits and sweetmeats, or what we now think of as fruit cheeses and butters, seem to have been the earliest sort of jam. Dating from medieval times, they enjoyed success in the Royal court and in the countrywoman's kitchen.

Apple butter

This recipe converts a pile of windfalls into an excellent, russet coloured, rich tasting spread, which is popular with children. The yield is less than with jams, but being more condensed a little goes a lot further. Cider is not essential, but improves the taste. Use crab apples instead of some of the apples if you can for more flavour.

2 kg (4 lb) apples
600 ml (1 pint) cider
water
5 cloves
3 cm (1 in) cinnamon stick
sugar
1 lemon

Quarter the apples, remove the stalks and any brown parts but do not peel or core. Put them into a pan, pour over the cider, then enough water just to cover, add spices and simmer till the apples are soft and mushy. Sieve and weigh the pulp. Return to the pan and continue simmering till thick and dryish before adding the warmed sugar – 350 g (12 oz) of sugar to each 450 g (1 lb) of pulp. Remove from heat while stirring in sugar. When the sugar has quite dissolved, add squeezed lemon juice, and grated rind, return to heat and cook slowly, stirring all the time, till drawing a spoon across the surface leaves a trail. Spoon into wide mouthed jars. Press down waxed paper, or plastic film onto the butter surface, and reverse onto plates to force out air. When cool, cover with cellophane, tie down and store in a cool dry place.

Sweet black butter

Make this from any surplus soft fruits in season – strawberries, redcurrants, raspberries, gooseberries, black currants – mixed together in varying proportions. For 'blackness', the blackcurrants should predominate slightly. This is rich and sticky, a real nursery treat. As the fruit is so sweet, this recipe uses less sugar.

1 kg (2 lb) mixed soft fruit
450 g (1 lb) sugar

Put the soft fruit into a pan, without water and heat gently till the juices flow, mashing now and then. Simmer till soft, sieve, weigh the pulp and return with the sugar to the pan. Cook, stirring, till thick enough to leave a trail. Pot, seal, cover as usual.

Damson cheese

2 kg (4 lb) damsons
300 ml (½ pint) water
sugar

Rinse the damsons under the cold tap. Put them in the pan with the water and simmer gently till quite soft, mashing occasionally. Sieve. Weigh the pulp, and measure out 350 g (12 oz) sugar to every 450 g (1 lb) pulp. Return the pulp to the pan (do not put the sugar in yet) and cook very gently till thick, with no visible liquid. Pour in the warmed sugar, stirring hard to dissolve it, then turn up the heat just a little and go on cooking and stirring till pressing the spoon down on top of the mixture leaves a mark. This gives a cheese firm enough to turn out of a mould and slice. For a very firm, almost candied consistency, go on cooking till a spoon drawn across the pan parts the mixture and the bottom shows very clearly. Turn into oiled moulds and seal.

Cranberry cheese

1 kg (2 lb) cranberries
1 kg (2 lb) sugar
900 ml (1½ pints) water

Pick over the cranberries, rinse them under a cold tap then simmer them in water till quite soft. Cook as for damson cheese (above), but stop short at the spoon marking stage. Pot and seal.

Marmalade making

For an explanation of why Scotland's renowned orange preserve should have borrowed a foreign name for a completely different fruit, we must visit the town of Dundee in the last years of the 19th century where a certain John Keiller, grocer, was wondering whether he had not acted a bit rashly in buying up a shipload of Seville oranges on the cheap. Fortunately, it occurred to his wife that by cooking them up according to her mother's recipe for quince 'marmalet' (from the Portuguese 'marmelo' or quince), the best part of the cargo might be preserved. She experimented. The results were so gratifying that news of Mrs Keiller's orange preserve or marmalet soon spread. Thus the Keillers made their name and fortune, Seville oranges found their noblest use and marmalade became permanently associated with Scotland and citrus fruit – an unlikely partnership on the face of it.

Marmalade is a jam or preserve made from citrus fruit: lime, lemon, grapefruit, sweet and Seville oranges. In the traditional marmalade no particle of the fruit is wasted – the juice flavours the syrup or jelly, pith and pips contribute pectin and their own bitter tang, while the peel, sliced thick or fine according to taste, lends the preserve its distinctive taste, texture and appearance. Save the peel from Christmas tangerines and add it to your marmalade; it adds a scented tang of its own. A spoonful of coriander seeds lends a spicy warmth too.

Equipment
The equipment is the same as for jam, except that a really sharp knife is essential for slicing the peel, and an efficient vegetable peeler saves time in thinly paring off the outer rind. Old fashioned gadgets for shredding peel sometimes turn up, and are efficient and labour saving. Some electric mixers have a slicing and shredding attachment which can be used for this most arduous part of the process, but they do not make such a neat job of it as a sharp knife and a pair of hands. A very large bowl is needed for soaking the peel. A pressure cooker cuts down the time spent on preliminary softening of the peel from hours to minutes. Be sure to provide yourself with plenty of clean, hot jars, waxed discs and cellophane covers: quantities of marmalade can result from what looks like a handful of fruit.

Method
The first step in marmalade making is to scrub the fruit well, to remove dirt and fungicides. Use a small stiff brush and plain warm water. There are various ways of preparing the fruit. Sometimes the fruit is simmered whole, before slicing; sometimes the outer rind is pared off finely and cooked separately before being added to the fruit; and sometimes the fruit is cut in half and squeezed, then the peel sliced, and the whole lot cooked together. The reasons for this have to do with varying traditions, cooks' caprices, and the coarseness and pithiness of the orange skins. Marmalade making is basically no more complicated than jam making, except that as the peel is so very thick and hard it needs long preliminary softening (by soaking overnight, long cooking, or a short spell in a pressure cooker) before the sugar is added. As with jam the golden rule is slow gentle cooking *before*, fast boiling *after*, adding sugar.

Making pressure-cooked marmalade

1. Take 1 kg (2 lb) Seville oranges and 1 lemon and scrub the skins with a soft brush in water to remove any dirt and fungicides. Pare off the rind thinly with a sharp knife and slice into thin strips.

2. Peel off the pith and put by.

3. Place all the fruit on a large plate and cut up roughly, trying to keep all the juice and saving the pips. Fill a small muslin bag with the pips and the pith, and tie up securely. The chopped fruit, juice, sliced rind, pips and pith are now ready to be cooked under pressure. Bring to 5 kg (10 lb) pressure and cook for ten minutes, after which time the hard peel should be soft enough to crush in your fingers – if not, cook a little longer as once peel meets sugar no further softening takes place.

4. Leave to cool at room temperature and remove the muslin bag. (Use the pressure cooker if more convenient for the next stage of cooking, but *leave the lid off*.) Add 2 kg (4 lb) sugar and 1 litre (2 pints) of water and heat, stirring to melt the sugar. Bring the marmalade to the boil and boil fast until it reaches setting point.

5. Remove the pan from the heat and let the marmalade stand for 15 minutes to thicken slightly. Stir to distribute rind, and pour into warmed jars, cover the preserve with a waxed disc, and seal.

Marmalades

Home-made marmalade is cheaper and better than any other. Now, with the aid of modern gadgets such as pressure cookers and shredding machines, the complete process has become uncomplicated and pleasurable.

Seville marmalade

This is the whole fruit method – easiest to grasp and the least tiring to prepare.

1 kg (2 lb) Seville oranges
2 litres (4 pints) water
juice of one large lemon
2 kg (4 lb) sugar (granulated or preserving)

Wash the oranges, put them into a pan with the water and simmer for about two hours, till the peel can be easily pierced with a fork. Take the oranges out, and when they are cool enough to handle cut them up, into thick or fine shreds as you prefer, reserving all the pips. Put the fruit aside in a preserving pan. Tie the pips in a muslin bag, return this to the cooking liquid in the pan, add squeezed lemon juice and boil for five minutes. Strain the liquid, add it to the sliced fruit and boil till the contents are reduced by one third – draw a line on the outside of the pan to guide you. Add the sugar, stir to dissolve, then bring to the boil and boil fast until the setting point is reached. Cool for 15 minutes before potting, to prevent the fruit rising to the top. Stir, pot and seal as usual.

Lime marmalade

Made with fresh limes, this is a special and delicious marmalade. It is a particularly good recipe for the tropics.

12 limes
1½ litres (3 pints) water
1½ kg (3 lb) sugar

Peel the fruit, halve and squeeze out the juice. Slice peel thinly. Chop the fruit pulp and tie in a muslin bag with the pips. Put the muslin bag, peel, juice and water into a pan and simmer for 1 hour. Remove the muslin bag, squeezing hard. Stir in the sugar, bring to the boil and boil hard for 10 minutes. Stand for a few minutes, stir, pot, seal and cover.

Superior Scotch marmalade

Here is a thoroughly old fashioned recipe, slow and painstaking in the making – in marked contrast to the corner-cutting recipe below – but giving a preserve of outstanding flavour.

2 kg (4 lb) Seville oranges
2¼ kg (5 lb) sugar
3 lemons

Wash the oranges, halve and squeeze out the juice into a bowl, reserving the pips. Scrape off any pulp clinging to the skins, and add this to the juice. Boil the skins in water to cover. After half an hour, change the water – this makes the preserve less bitter – and boil again in water to cover until the skins are tender enough to pierce with a matchstick. When quite cool, scrape any white thready bits off the skins and slice the skins thinly. Put the juice, pulp, sliced peel and muslin bag with the pips into a pan. Heat slowly, adding warmed sugar after a few minutes. Stir to dissolve the sugar and bring to the boil. After it has boiled for ten minutes add the squeezed, strained juice and finely grated rind of the lemons. Boil for a further 20 minutes or until the marmalade has reached setting point. This can be judged either with a jam thermometer (the setting point is 105°C, 221°F) or by doing the saucer test. Cool for 15 minutes, then pot, seal and cover. Yield about 10 jars.

Grapefruit and lemon marmalade

Sharp but refreshing.

3 grapefruit
4 lemons
2 litres (4 pints) water
1½ kg (3 lb) sugar

The method is precisely as for the three fruit marmalade. For a gingery snap, add about 175 g (6 oz) crystallized ginger, finely chopped, just after adding the sugar.

Mincer marmalade

The most objectionable part of marmalade making for most people is cutting up the peel. Mincing it (using either the old fashioned hand mincer, or an attachment on an electric mixer) saves time and an aching wrist, though the resulting marmalade will not be crystal clear.

8 Seville oranges
2 lemons
4 litres (7 pints) water
3 kg (6 lb) sugar

Wash and halve the fruit, then squeeze the juice into a large bowl. Collect the pips and tie in a muslin bag. Mince all the rinds, collecting up any juice, and add to the bowl with the water. Leave to soak overnight. Next day put the lot into a pan with the bag of pips and gently simmer for about two hours or until the peel is quite soft and the liquid well reduced. Remove the pips, add the warmed sugar, stir to melt the sugar, then bring to the boil fast and cook for about 25 minutes or till setting point is reached. Cool for ten minutes, then pot, seal and cover as usual. Yield 10 jars.

Tangerine and lemon marmalade

A clean, sharp marmalade, less bitter than Seville, and with the pleasant sweet scent of tangerines. Add more peel from any tangerines you eat.

1 kg (2 lb) tangerines
3 lemons
2 litres (3½ pints) water
1½ kg (3 lb) sugar

Peel both fruit, removing white pith and strings. Slice the peel thinly and put it into a muslin bag. Chop all fruit roughly, put it into a pan with the water and the muslin bags and simmer gently for 45 minutes, then remove the peel and reserve it and continue cooking for a further hour. Tip the cooked fruit pulp into a jellybag and leave to drip overnight. Next day put the strained juice and warmed sugar into a pan and bring to the boil, stirring to dissolve the sugar. Empty the muslin bag and add the reserved peel shreds. Boil fast to setting point. Leave to cool for 15 minutes before potting. Seal and cover. Yield 5 jars.

Three fruit marmalade

The best all-year-round mixture.

2 grapefruit
2 sweet oranges
4 lemons
3 litres (6 pints) water
3 kg (6 lb) sugar

Peel all the fruit, quite finely, then cut them in half and extract the pips. Put these, with the thick pith from the grapefruit and the oranges (if there is any) into a muslin bag. Chop the fruit roughly on a plate. Cut all the peel finely into shreds. Put everything into a preserving pan with water and simmer for one and a half hours, or till soft – you should be able to crush the peel in your fingers. Remove the muslin bag, squeezing out any liquid. Stir in the sugar, bring to the boil, and boil fast till setting point is reached. Cool for 15 minutes, stir, pot, seal and cover as usual.
Note: Vary this recipe by including a spoonful of coriander seeds in the muslin bag.

Pineapple and lime marmalade

Here's a true exotic for warm climates, or as a special treat elsewhere.

1 large pineapple, ripe but sound
2 kg (4 lb) sugar
4 limes or lemons
1 litre (2 pints) water

Peel and thinly slice the pineapple. Cut out the core and reserve. Chop the flesh into small pieces. Put in a bowl with half the sugar sprinkled over and leave overnight to extract the juice. Wash the limes or lemons, then slice them thinly, putting the pips with the bits of pineapple core into a piece of muslin. Put the lime, or lemon, slices and water into a pan, with the muslin bag, and simmer till the peel is soft. Squeeze the pip bag and remove, add the pineapple and the remaining sugar, stir over a low heat till the sugar is dissolved, then boil fast till setting point is reached. Skim, pot and seal. Yield about 6 jars.
Note: If you use the pressure cooker method for any marmalade, a labour-saving tip is to cook the fruit in quarters; when softened slice up in an egg slicer. There is no need to separate the pith.

Pickles
& Chutneys

'I chose my wife as she did her wedding gown,
not for a fine glossy surface, but such qualities as would wear well.
She could read any English book without much spelling:
but for pickling, preserving and cookery, none could excel her.'
The Vicar of Wakefield   Oliver Goldsmith   1858

The first thing to be said about pickles and chutneys is that they are both endearingly *easy* to make. Jam making, even for the experienced, has its tensions and pitfalls, but making chutneys and pickles is a relaxing and rewarding business, nicely attuned to the mellow, winding-down atmosphere of autumn. The methods are simple, the materials are (or should be) cheap, and the results reliably excellent. A shelf packed with interesting, varied, home-made 'condiments' is immensely useful. It is remarkable what spiced pickled peaches will do for tinned ham, and the difference a seasoned chutney (all chutneys improve with age) makes to sausages and meat balls, not to mention the cheering effect a plate of crisp pickles has on cheese and bread.

Pickles and chutneys both make use of vinegar and spices to flavour and preserve. But the pickle is international in character, with an honoured place in the cooking of almost every country, whereas all chutneys are descended from a purely national invention, the Indian *chatni*. This is a spiced relish served alongside the bland *dal* or lentil dishes. Indians like their *chatni* both cooked and uncooked, and usually serve a bowl of each. For storage, however, the cooked chutney, a medley of ingredients simmered till reduced to a sort of savoury jam, is more suitable.

One of the great delights of chutneys and pickles is their good tempered adaptability. Quantities are not really critical in chutney making, so there is no need to abandon the idea because you have not quite as much sugar as the recipe asks for, or only sugar of a different colour. One dried fruit does as well as another and an extra handful will make up for any missing sugar. Equally with spices; it will not ruin a chutney to use, say, cloves and cinnamon instead of coriander seeds, or ground mustard instead of mustard seed, or preserved ginger instead of fresh. It will just be a slightly different – maybe better – chutney. Use the recipes as a guide to relative proportions and quantities of ingredients, by all means, but do not feel that you are imprisoned by them.

Foreground, left, sweet pepper pickle beside a jar of tomato chutney and, centre, dill pickle sealed with oilskin. Jars of pickled onions cluster beside bottles of clear vinegar flavoured with herb cuttings of tarragon and marjoram and a small jar of amber spiced pickled fruit.

Making pickles and chutneys

Equipment

The important point to be noted here is that chutneys and pickles contain a fair amount of vinegar and vinegar contains acetic acid which instantly attacks metals such as brass, copper, iron, and produces a taste as bitter as wormwood. It will also corrode any metal it is in contact with, in time. So use aluminium, or unchipped enamel pans for cooking chutneys and for boiling spiced vinegar for pickles. Use a nylon or hair sieve rather than a wire one for straining. Glass containers are safest for anything containing vinegar and the simplest lid, which must be airtight, is either screw-on plastic, or a circle of greaseproof paper covered by cotton dipped in melted paraffin wax. The cover must be airtight because vinegar evaporates in time and this shrinks and dries out your precious chutney and pickles. I find those attractive French glass jars with spring clip lids are unsuitable as it only needs a little vinegar to touch the wire spring for corrosion to start, slowly but surely, discolouring the pickles most unpleasantly.

Other standard items of equipment which may be needed are a large bowl, weighing machine, ladle, sharp knife and chopping board. Some chutney recipes call for ingredients to be minced, or finely chopped – obviously a mincer, operated by hand or electricity, will save time and effort here.

Pickle ingredients

The choice internationally is wide. But probably the most appealing pickles to Western palates are either crisp, onions, shallots, red cabbage, baby cucumbers or gherkins, or sweet, beetroots, plums, peaches. Pickled walnuts are excellent if you can get hold of green walnuts, but other green nuts – hazel, cob, filbert – can be used instead. Some celebrated pickles – the Italian Mostarda di Cremona, Piccalilli – use a mixture of fruits or vegetables, highly seasoned. Sweet peppers, turnips and garlic can all be pickled and are both good and unusual. Ingredients for pickles should be as fresh and crisp as possible, and firm and sound.

Chutney ingredients

Chutneys are even more obliging than pickles in respect of ingredients as these need not be perfect, super fresh, or intrinsically tasty. Those huge overgrown courgettes, marrows, pumpkins and squashes which are a problem to keep up with at the height of the growing season, make excellent chutney, with a luscious texture. Windfall apples, rhubarb past its prime, green tomatoes are obvious candidates too. Green gooseberries, under-ripe plums, green mangoes, hard peaches and apricots are all excellent if you have enough to spare. Use good malt vinegar for everyday chutney, a finer grade (wine or cider) for more delicate fruit chutneys. White or brown sugar are equally suitable, brown gives a deeper colour and slight caramel taste. More important to a good chutney is to use whole, that is unground, spices, cheapest and freshest bought loose from an Indian grocer. The difference in pungency between these and the relatively costly powdered spices put up commercially in pretty little jars is quite astonishing.

Making pickles and chutneys

Pickles, broadly speaking, are edibles of one sort or another stored in a liquid which preserves and flavours: vinegar, brine, oil. They preserve by excluding air and by destroying bacteria. Sugar is another preservative and, when added to pickling vinegar, acts as a further safeguard besides greatly improving the flavour.

There are various ways of pickling fruit and vegetables. The simplest, and one of the most popular methods, is to pack the jars with selected fruit or vegetables, and pour over enough spiced, sweetened vinegar to cover them. For crisp, sharp pickles – onions, cabbage, gherkins – the vinegar may be poured over cold, for others which need softening, it is poured over boiling hot. In some cases this is repeated a few times over a period of days, draining off the vinegar, re-boiling and pouring over again. This both softens the pickle, and concentrates all the flavours. Alternatively, the pickle ingredient itself may be simmered till tender in water before going into the vinegar. This is essential with whole baby beets, for instance, some other vegetables, and with hard fruit like crab apples.

Chutney-making is simpler still: usually all the ingredients are very gently simmered together in a pan for several hours. The brew is stirred occasionally – *more* often when the chutney begins to thicken – and transferred into warm pots when thick like jam.

Brining or salting before pickling

Salt has a way of drawing out moisture which is why sliced aubergines are salted as a matter of course before cooking. Salting vegetables before pickling them has the same effect, drawing out the moisture which would otherwise dilute the pickle and lessen its preservative properties. The salt can be applied straight on top of the vegetables – dry salting – or the vegetables can be steeped in a saline solution – wet salting. In dry salting the cleaned, peeled or otherwise prepared vegetables are packed in layers in a large bowl with salt sprinkled in between – approximately 50 g (2 oz) salt to 450 g (1 lb) vegetables. The vegetables are then covered and left for between 12 to 24 hours as a rule. Now noticeably softer, and slightly shrunken, the vegetables are rinsed under running water and dried before pickling. For wet salting, mix up a saline solution, using 225 g (8 oz) salt to 2 litres (4 pints) water – you will need about 600 ml (1 pint) of salt solution to each 450 g (1 lb) of vegetables. Immerse the prepared vegetables, cover them with a weighted plate and leave for the stated time. Some traditional recipes from Central Europe and the Middle East leave the ingredients in brine long enough to allow natural fermentation to start, which not only drives out unwanted bacteria but creates a distinct, pleasant change in taste and texture of the vegetables concerned, making them mellow and rich.

It is important to keep the vegetables completely immersed throughout this lengthy brining, and to check now and then to make sure the solution has not been diluted too much by the moisture extracted from the vegetables. Before going into pickle, wet salted vegetables should also be well rinsed, and dried off. If you do not they will taste very strongly of salt.

Vinegar

Malt vinegar is the cheapest available, and a decent brand (buy plastic, 4 litre/1 gallon containers) is fine for the more robust type of pickle such as eggs, onions, beets and cabbage, especially if you add enough sugar to soften the flavour. Keep the more expensive vinegars – cider, distilled malt, wine vinegar – for fancier efforts, where you are aiming for a subtler sweet-sour flavour, pickled fruits, for instance. Vinegar is usually spiced as well as sweetened, to add interest to pickles. Pickling spices are sold ready mixed, but it is usually cheaper and more interesting to mix up your own. For a change use just one spice instead of a mixture – coriander has a pungent, orangey taste which is delicious with cabbage; cloves and peppercorns are excellent with onions; a few cardamom pods complement pickled peaches. If you are planning to pickle on a lavish scale, save time by making up 4 litres (1 gallon) of spiced vinegar and leaving the spices to infuse for several weeks before use. A good basic spice mixture for 4 litres (1 gallon) of vinegar would be: 25 g (1 oz) each of allspice, cloves, black peppercorns, coriander, mustard seed, 25 g (1 oz) fresh root ginger or ground ginger, 3 dried chilies, 6 to 10 cloves garlic, 225 g (8 oz) sugar. To maximize the flavour, bruise the spices lightly (tie them up in a cloth and hit them with a rolling pin), bring to boiling point in vinegar, then cool and store till needed. For people who only want to make a few jars at a time, it is more fun to mix up different spices to suit each batch of pickles, cooking them up with the vinegar as above. You can leave them in or take them out before pickling, depending on how aromatic you want the pickle to finish up. I leave them in myself, but some people prefer their pickles free from seeds, pods or grains. The same applies to garlic cloves, ginger and chilies, all of which contribute a distinctive note to a harmonious pickle.

Warning note

The American FDA (Food and Drug Association) has recommended that all pickles be heat-processed (see Bottled Fruit) for 30 minutes before storage, to triple check against spoilage, infection or botulism. My own view is that this is excessive in the case of pickles in vinegar and oil, which are pretty powerful preservatives in their own right, though it might be sensible in the case of food pickled in a vinegar plus brine solution, like some Middle Eastern pickles. Brine is a less efficient long term preservative than vinegar. On the other hand, these milder pickles are definitely intended to be eaten rapidly – within six weeks as a rule, so the risk should not arise. This is something for the individual cook to make up his or her own mind about, I think. Heat-processed pickles will not, of course, be quite the same in point of texture.

Chutneys present fewer problems since the large amounts of vinegar and sugar used in making them are about as effective a preservative – next to alcohol – as could be devised.

Melon, marrows, courgettes and pumpkin ripe for pickling and chutney making. Golden pumpkins and green marrows are simmered slowly with spices into a rich, mild chutney; huge rosy watermelon yields pithy rind for a spicy pickle.

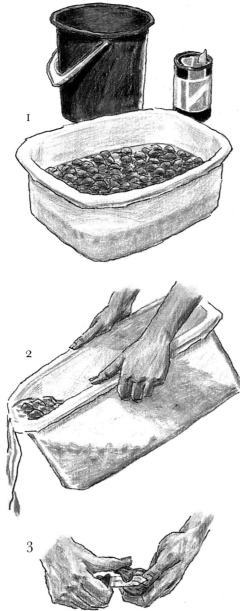

Pickling onions

Delicious with bread and cheese, this pickle can be made with either small pickling onions or shallots. This method of draining off the brine and pouring it on again both softens the pickle and concentrates all the flavour.

1. Make a brine solution of 450 g (1 lb) salt added to 4 litres (1 gallon) water in a plastic household bucket. Half the solution will be used immediately and half kept until later. This saline solution draws out the moisture from the onions which would otherwise dilute the pickle and lessen its preservative qualities. Put 2 kg (4 lb) unpeeled pickling onions – or shallots which connoisseurs prefer – in a washing-up bowl and cover with half the brine solution. Leave overnight.

2. Next day, pour off the first brine solution.

3. Peel the onions.

4. Put them back in the bowl with the second half of the brine. Test to see if it is sufficiently salty by floating a fresh egg on top – if it floats, the solution is salty enough. If it sinks or half bobs, top up with more salt. Weight the onions down with a plate and heavy tin, or jar, so that they are completely covered by the salt solution. Leave for 2–3 days.

5. The onions are ready after 2–3 days to go into a solution of prepared cold vinegar. Take the onions from the brine, drain through a colander

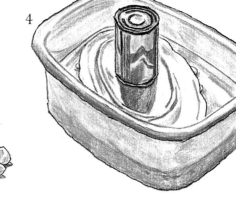

and rinse well – if you don't they will taste of not much besides salt. Leave to dry off on towels.

6. Meanwhile make up the vinegar solution. To get the most flavour first bruise your pickling spices – 1 level tablespoon cloves, 1 tablespoon white peppercorns, 2 dried red chilies – by tying them in a cloth and bashing them with a rolling pin. Then boil them up in an aluminium saucepan with 100 g (4 oz) sugar and 2 litres (4 pints) malt vinegar. Remove from the heat and leave to get cold.

7. Pack the onions into glass screw-top jars and pour over the prepared cold vinegar, making sure the vinegar covers the onions. For a crisp, sharp pickle like this one, the vinegar is always poured over when cold. I leave the spices in to make the pickle more aromatic. Some people prefer their pickles free from seeds and pods in which case strain the solution first through a nylon sieve before adding to the pickle jars.

8. Seal to make the jars airtight. Vinegar evaporates in no time and shrinks or darkens the precious chutney and pickles. Don't use the plastic film sold for covering jam pots for this reason. The best seal is a circle of greaseproof covered by cotton dipped in melted paraffin wax. Or you could use clip-on plastic lids bought separately in various sizes. Avoid anything metal, as it only needs a little vinegar to touch the metal or wire spring for corrosion to start.

Pickles

There is room in any well stocked cupboard for a variety of pickles and I have added some Middle Eastern as well as traditional recipes. They are not difficult to make so present them with quiet triumph to complement a plate of cold meat.

Sweet pepper pickle

Pickle a medley of red, yellow and green peppers when they are cheap to cheer you later in mid-winter. This is a Turkish recipe, good with kebabs, hors d'oeuvres, and pilaffs.

6 red peppers
6 green peppers
6 yellow peppers
white vinegar
salt
sugar
sherry

Slice the peppers across, removing the seeds and centres. Pack them into jars, and cover with a spiced vinegar made by stirring 1 teaspoon of salt, 4 teaspoons of sugar and a small sherry glass of sherry into every 600 ml (1 pint) of vinegar. Cover, store.

Spiced pickled fruit

This is a sweet-sour pickle, delicious eaten with game, cold ham and pâtés. The syrup makes a good sauce for steamed puddings. Use brown sugar for peaches, white for pears or plums.

2 kg (4 lb) small ripe peaches, or small hard pears or
  small under-ripe plums
1 tablespoon each : allspice, cloves, cinnamon (powder
  or stick) and coriander seeds
1 kg (2 lb) sugar
600 ml (1 pint) white vinegar

To prepare the fruit, wash and wipe but leave them whole, only cutting off any soft or brown parts. Tie the spices into muslin, crush them slightly and boil up with the vinegar and the sugar, stirring to dissolve the sugar. Add the fruit and simmer very gently till tender. Lift out with a slotted spoon and pack into warmed jars. Boil the vinegar hard for a few minutes to reduce it to a syrupy consistency, then pour it over the fruit, and cover at once. Store in cool dry place.

Spiced crab apples

Too often these most decorative fruits are left to drop and rot. Cooked, they have a delicate tartness and superb colour. Use them to stuff roast goose or duck, or eat with meat or game.

2 kg (4 lb) crab apples
water
lemon
white wine vinegar or white malt vinegar
sugar
coriander seeds, cinnamon, peppercorns

Remove the stalks and any blemishes, wash the apples and put them into enough boiling water to just cover. Add strips of lemon peel. Simmer till just tender. Strain off the cooking water, and to each 600 ml (1 pint) add 450 g (1 lb) sugar, 150 ml ($\frac{1}{4}$ pint) vinegar and 1 teaspoon mixed spices, either ground or tied into muslin whole. Boil this mixture up, stirring well to melt the sugar, then add the crab apples and simmer uncovered over a gentle heat till the syrup is much reduced and the crab apples almost transparent. This will take about 40 minutes. Ladle into warmed jars, cover with syrup, seal and store.
Note: Medieval recipes invariably added a little pepper to spiced mixtures like these.

Pickled grapes

The small, seedless variety of grapes are good for this pickle. Serve with smoked fish.

300 ml ($\frac{1}{2}$ pint) white vinegar
600 ml (1 pint) water
225 g (8 oz) sugar
1 teaspoon mixed cloves, cinnamon and allspice
1 kg (2 lb) grapes

Boil up the vinegar, the water and the sugar with the spices and leave to cool. Wash the grapes, picking out any blemished ones, and dry them off before packing into jars. Pour the cold spiced vinegar over them, seal and store.

Dill pickle

Ideally you should use tiny cucumbers 10 to 12 cm (4 to 5 in) specially grown for pickling, but ordinary cucumbers cut into sticks can be substituted, though they will not be so crisp.

brine solution
2 kg (4 lb) small pickling cucumbers
6 cloves garlic
several sprays of fresh dill
1 teaspoon each allspice, cloves, cinnamon and caraway
  seeds
1 to 1½ litres (2 to 3 pints) white, distilled vinegar
100 g (4 oz) sugar

Make up 4 litres (1 gallon) of brine (see page 226). Wash the cucumbers carefully, remove any flowers, pack them into the brine and leave covered and weighted down for three days. Remove, drain, pack into jars, with the garlic cloves and dill distributed among them. Boil up the spices (tied in a cloth bag) and the sugar with the vinegar. Stir to dissolve the sugar. Pour the spiced vinegar boiling hot over the cucumbers. Cover tightly and leave in warm place for 24 hours. Drain off the vinegar, boil it up again, and pour over the cucumbers once more. Cover and leave in a warm place for another 24 hours. Repeat this again if necessary until the cucumbers are a fine green colour. Top up with fresh vinegar before sealing and storing.

Pickled eggs

Excellent with winter salads and cold meats.

12 hardboiled eggs
900 ml (1½ pints) malt vinegar or white, distilled malt
  vinegar
6 cloves garlic
1 level tablespoon white peppercorns
1 level tablespoon allspice
small piece fresh ginger root (optional)

Boil the eggs for 10 minutes, then leave to cool in cold water. Shell. Simmer the vinegar with all the other ingredients for 10 minutes. Leave to go cold. Pack the eggs into a wide mouthed jar and pour over the vinegar which may be either strained or used complete with spices. Cover and store. They can be eaten after one month.

Pickled walnuts

Pickled walnuts are the most elegant accompaniment to a really good cheese. Wear fine rubber gloves to handle the walnuts – the stain is near indelible.

2 kg (4 lb) green walnuts (or cob or hazel nuts)
salt
water
spiced vinegar as for pickled eggs

Leave the walnuts in enough brine (see previous page) to cover them. Keep them submerged for five days, then drain, and cover with fresh brine for another week. Drain and spread out on trays in the sun, turning occasionally till they are quite black, and dry – about a day. Pack into jars and cover with spiced vinegar poured over hot. Cover and store. Eat after a month.

Pickled watermelon rind

This classic American pickle uses the part of the melon which is normally thrown away, the white strip between flesh and skin.

2 litres (4 pints) cubed watermelon rind
100 g (4 oz) salt
1 teaspoon powdered alum
water
1 cinnamon stick
10 cloves
450 g (1 lb) sugar
900 ml (1½ pints) white or wine vinegar

To make the cubes, pare off the green outer skin (the red inside has all been eaten of course) and cut the white, hard flesh into 1 cm (½ inch) cubes. Put them all into a large bowl. Mix salt, alum and 1 litre (2 pints) of cold water together, pour over the rind and add enough cold water to cover. Put a weighted plate on top and leave overnight. Drain, rinse under running water and shake off as much moisture as possible. Put the spices and half the sugar into vinegar and simmer for 10 minutes. Add the watermelon cubes, bring to simmering point, remove from heat and cool. Add the rest of the sugar, bring to simmering point and cook gently till the cubes are transparent, stirring occasionally. Put into hot jars, seal and store.

Chutneys

Uncooked chutneys must be eaten within a month, but the cooked chutney, a medley of ingredients simmered until reduced to a sort of savoury jam, is an ideal case for preserving, and actually improves on keeping.

Pumpkin, marrow or courgette chutney

One of the best home-made chutney recipes, rich but mild.

2¼ kg (5 lb) pumpkin, marrow or courgettes
1 kg (2 lb) fresh or tinned tomatoes
450 g (1 lb) onions
6 to 8 cloves garlic
1½ kg (3 lb) soft, pale brown sugar
175 g (6 oz) sultanas
4 tablespoons salt
1 tablespoon each : peppercorns, allspice, ground ginger
* (or 1 piece crushed fresh ginger)*
1 litre (2 pints) malt or white vinegar

Peel the pumpkin or the marrow, but leave the skin on the courgettes. Slice thickly, remove the cottony centres and the seeds and cut lengthways into strips 2 cm (1 in) square and 1 cm (½in) thick (if the fruit is too thick it might not soften in cooking). Roughly chop the tomatoes, if fresh. Slice the onions and chop the garlic. Put all the ingredients into a large pan, bring slowly to the boil, stirring to dissolve the sugar. Cook slowly but steadily for one to two hours, till the mixture is tender (but not disintegrated) and thick, but not too dry. Ladle into pots, cover and store.

Apple chutney

A mild, fresh tasting chutney which improves with keeping. Children like it. I use windfalls and do not bother peeling them.

2 kg (4 lb) sharp, green apples
1 kg (2 lb) onions
2 tablespoons yellow mustard seed
1 tablespoon ground ginger or 1 knob of fresh ginger
* root*
225 g (8 oz) sultanas
450 g (1 lb) soft brown sugar
6 red chilies or 1 teaspoon cayenne pepper
900 ml (1½ pints) malt vinegar
1 tablespoon salt

Quarter the apples, core and chop roughly. Peel and chop the onions. Heat the mustard seed lightly in a heavy pan then grind to a powder in a mortar. Chop the ginger finely if using fresh root. Put all the ingredients into a large heavy pan and cook for several hours very gently till pulpy, and brown. Pot, cover and store.

Note: Old recipes give an uncooked – or largely uncooked – variation on this chutney under the title of Bengal chutney. Usually all the ingredients are put through a mincer, stirred up with vinegar, spices and sugar then bottled.

Tamatarr (tomato) chutney

A hot, spicy chutney which makes use of both green and red tomatoes. It should be stored for six months to allow the flavours to develop.

1 kg (2 lb) each red and green tomatoes
450 g (1 lb) onions
1 whole head of garlic
2 teaspoons fenugreek
3 tablespoons coriander
1 teaspoon each ground nutmeg, cardamom pods,
* chopped fresh basil*
2 litres (4 pints) malt vinegar or white vinegar
450 g (1 lb) raisins
450 g (1 lb) soft brown sugar
1 tablespoon cayenne pepper
4 tablespoons salt
100 g (4 oz) capers

Chop the tomatoes roughly, peel and chop onions and garlic. Roast the fenugreek and the coriander for a few minutes in the oven, then grind finely. Take the seeds from the cardamom pods. Cook the tomatoes in half the vinegar over a low heat till reduced to a thick mush – make sure it does not burn. Cook the raisins, the chopped onion, the garlic, sugar, spices, capers, cayenne pepper and salt in the rest of the vinegar till the onion is tender and the consistency reduced. Add the tomato mush, stir to mix, simmer for 10 minutes. Pot, cover and store.

Ketchup

The best way of dealing with a glut of ripe tomatoes, or field mushrooms is to simmer them down into highly flavoured sauces and ketchups. These are a safe and easy way of preserving surplus vegetables, and take up very little space.

Tomato ketchup

5 kg (12 lb) ripe outdoor tomatoes
450 g (1 lb) sugar
600 ml (1 pint) white vinegar
1 tablespoon salt
1 teaspoon each ground ginger, cloves, nutmeg, paprika
* and cayenne*

Cut the tomatoes into quarters and either cook gently on the top of the stove, or bake at a low heat in the oven till soft enough to sieve. You should not need to add water if the tomatoes are juicy enough. Sieve the tomatoes. Then simmer the pulp in a large pan with all the remaining ingredients till thickened – it will thicken more when cool. Pour at once into Kilner jars and heat process (see Bottling Fruit) for 30 minutes at 76°C (170°F) to sterilize the ketchup and prevent it fermenting later in the store cupboard.
Note: Kilner jars or plastic screw-capped bottles are suitable for storing tomato ketchup.

Pontack sauce

This is a proper, pungent old fashioned 'store sauce'. Traditionally it was kept for seven years to allow the true bouquet to mature.

450 g (1 lb) ripe elderberries
450 ml ($\frac{3}{4}$ pint) vinegar
1 tablespoon black peppercorns
$\frac{1}{2}$ tablespoon allspice
1 teaspoon cloves
$\frac{1}{2}$ teaspoon grated nutmeg or mace
1 teaspoon salt
8 shallots

Put the berries into an earthenware jar or pot, cover with vinegar and set in a warm oven for two hours to extract all the juice. Strain into a pan, add the spices, the seasonings, the shallots and simmer for 30 minutes. Strain, return to the pan and simmer for five minutes. Pour into hot bottles and seal at once. Leave for two months to mature.

Mushroom ketchup

Wild mushrooms make the best ketchup of all – a few drops in soups, sauces and gravy makes an astonishing difference. Use sound mushrooms only – a good sized bucket or basket at least.

Weigh the mushrooms, then break them up and layer them in a crock with 1 tablespoon of salt to every 450 g (1 lb). Leave them to sweat out their juices for two or three days, pressing now and then. Then put the jar in a cool oven at the lowest setting) for three hours to extract the last drops. Turn them into a nylon sieve over a bowl and squeeze as much juice from the mushrooms as possible. To every litre (1 quart) of mushroom liquor allow:

1 teaspoon allspice
$\frac{1}{2}$ teaspoon grated nutmeg
3 cloves chopped garlic
1 red chili
$\frac{1}{2}$ teaspoon ground ginger
300 ml ($\frac{1}{2}$ pint) red wine (home-made elderberry)

Put the spices and the garlic into muslin, then add them to a saucepan with the mushroom liquor and the wine. Simmer slowly for two or three hours till thickened. Turn into Kilner jars or bottles and heat process for 20 minutes.

Mustard

Those fashionable old style mustards are simple to make at home. Wine vinegar simmered with the dregs from a wine bottle till slightly reduced makes a good base. Use a mixture of yellow and black mustard seed (available from Indian grocers) in a ratio of two yellow to one black. Pound or blend about half the mixture to a powder, more if you do not like the mixture too grainy. Stir the whole seed into the powdered seed, then add a pinch of sugar and blend in the reduced liquid. Using vinegar flavoured with herbs or spices will vary the flavour, as will adding a little minced garlic, powdered turmeric and coriander, or peppercorns.

Wines

' "I want you to hev a look at my wine, gel; I ain't sure about it."
Prissy went to the old man's house and her verdict was instantaneous:
"You want to take that there mould off the top right quick, you dew!
Thet will spoil it. Thet at the bottom's all right . . ." '

Ask the Fellows who Cut the Hay   George Ewart Evans   *1956*

Home wine making has become one of the most popular hobbies, supported by a flourishing small industry turning out recipe books, magazines, and equipment ranging from the simplest cork to the most streamlined insulated heater to keep the fermenting bin at the ideal temperature. This popularity has brought about a timely reappraisal of amateur wine-making methods; one result is the proliferation of grape concentrates, which are about the closest one can get to an instant wine mix. The traditional, country wine recipes based on the local fruits and flowers which were a frugal peasant's first choice, have been revised to produce wines quite unlike the syrupy, medicinal or brackish tasting concoctions which gave home-made wines a bad name and prevented them being taken seriously. Modern recipes aim for wines on the dryish side, nicely rounded and characterful without being heavy, in short, a pleasant drink to accompany a good meal. Next time you are offered a glass of parsley, mulberry or elderflower wine, just try it. It could surprise you. The fact is, a properly made country wine based on fruit, flowers or vegetables is a drink of much fresher flavour and charm than the acrid, chemical tasting grape products which wine merchants offer in the lower price range. An exquisite elderflower wine is an interesting drink, and a simple blackberry wine, light, dry and red, answers as well to what one expects of an agreeable table wine as anything you could find.

Country wines do not taste, in a crude or literal sense, of what goes into them. Pea pods make a light, fresh hock style wine. Flower wines are fragrant, naturally, and a glass of one of these fine delicate scented wines on a hot summer evening is something to remember. The problem with all home-made wines is keeping them long enough to experience all the improvements which maturity confers in the way of smoothness, balance and subtlety.

I have deliberately emphasized the often impressive quality of home-made wines because I think the people who make them are apt to be too modest but, of course, the clinching fact in their favour, and the one which sets most people making their own, is their astonishing cheapness. Using the thriftiest means – wild or homegrown fruit say – one bottle of attractive wine costs little more than a pint of milk.

Bowls of fruit and vegetables ready for fermenting with yeast, water and sugar: parsnips for one of the best and strongest white wines, elderberries for a medium sweet red wine that improves with maturity and freshly picked blackberries for a light, fruity, dryish red wine.

235

Wine making

Equipment

For an experimental 5 litres (1 gallon) of wine, you need only buy a length of plastic tubing for siphoning purposes, as you will almost certainly have a plastic bucket, and several large empty bottles in the house, and these will serve, well cleaned and sterilized, to ferment the wine in and store it later.

If you want to make wine seriously, buy the largest size fermentation bins, and several 5 litre (1 gallon) glass jars. It is very little extra trouble to make larger amounts of wine, the fermentation usually goes better in bulk, and at the end of it you have enough wine to put by, and forget about for six months or a year. Two 25 litre (5 gallon) bins – white plastic, purpose made, with snap on lids – plus ten jars is enough to make two batches of flower wines in spring, which will be ready to bottle by the time the next bout of wine making begins in autumn, with blackberries, elderberries, apples. Bottles are no problem, collect empties, wash and sterilize them and store in dust proof boxes, till needed. Wine must be protected during its stay in the gallon jars, from outside air and possible bacterial infection, but it must not be sealed off, or the carbon dioxide given off during fermentation cannot escape. The cheap solution is to fasten a polythene bag over the neck of the jar securing it with elastic bands to make a sort of balloon. Or buy proper airlocks: plastic ones with integral stoppers are handiest of all. Also needed is a length of plastic tubing for siphoning and 'racking off', a large plastic sieve for straining, a long handled wooden spoon for stirring, a long handled bottle brush to clean the jars thoroughly and a gadget for driving in corks or fitting metal crown caps. This equipment should be scalded or sterilized regularly and used only for wine. A hydrometer, which ascertains whether the wine has fermented out, is also useful though not essential.

Additives

Some chemicals are needed. Sodium metabisulphite is essential, for sterilizing the equipment, adding to the wine itself at various stages to protect against infection, or wild yeast ferments, and to stabilize and clear it. Most winemakers buy sodium metabisulphite in powdered form, which is cheaper, or you can buy it in the form of Campden tablets. For sterilizing purposes, dissolve it in water – one teaspoon or two tablets per 600 ml (1 pint) of water. Other chemical aids which are cheap and efficient are citric acid, sold in powder form, to use instead of the more expensive lemons, and pectolaze or pectozyme, which are used in some methods to prevent haze or clouding, caused by minute protein particles. All these can be bought from a chemist, or a specialist shop.

Definition

Wine is a fermented, flavoured liquid. During fermentation the yeast converts the sugar present into alcohol. To produce a drink which tastes nice as well as alcoholic, most country wines need supplementing in one direction or another – only wine grapes are naturally endowed with the right proportions of acid, tannin and sugar. Thus to some fruit or flower wines one adds acid (citric or lemon juice), to others tannin (cold tea or tannin extract, which is available from chemists) and to others extra 'body' in the shape of dried fruit. Some flower wines need all three. By setting up a ferment in this way almost anything, in theory, can be turned into wine – even plain sugar water with a dash of lemon juice. But some work better than others, and it is these reliable 'classics' I shall include in the recipe section.

Yeast

In the old days people spread brewer's or baker's yeast on a slice of toast and floated this on their open cask of 'must' – must, before we go any further, is the stuff in your fermentation bin before siphoning off, embryo wine. The old way, for once, was quite wrong. Neither of these yeasts is powerful enough to produce the alcohol content wine needs, they muddy the wine flavour, and the remaining unfermented sugar makes the wine sickly sweet. Fermenting without a lid, too, was an open-house to bugs, moulds, wild yeasts and off flavours. Today we use proper wine yeasts, a spin-off from the wine trade. You can choose between all-purpose yeast, which is cheaper, and named yeast types: hock, chablis, riesling. Wine yeast is more temperamental than beer yeast, and should be 'started' in the favourable micro-climate of a bottle of boiled water before being added to the must (see overleaf). This helps to start the fermentation.

A day before preparing the must, make up the starter. Half fill a clean bottle with tepid boiled water, add a tiny pinch of citric acid, sugar and yeast nutrient, then the yeast, and shake well. Plug the top with cotton wool, set in warm place and after 24 hours the fermentation should have begun. Look for tiny clusters of bubbles on top and a cloudiness in the water.

Sugar

This is the essential partner to yeast. Use plain white granulated sugar, bought in bulk if possible for cheapness. Yeast can convert roughly 1 kg (2 lb) sugar per 5 litres (1 gallon) of liquid into alcohol. For a dry wine add just this amount, for a sweeter wine, add rather more. For a 5 litre (1 gallon) batch of wine, add all the sugar at once, for larger amounts it is best added by stages, so as not to overload the yeast.

What can go wrong

It is rare for wines to go wrong if you take reasonable care. The worst that can befall is for a wine to be invaded by the vinegar fly, which turns it all to vinegar and this is rare. Off flavours – funny tastes – can happen, usually as a result of leaving the ingredients hanging about too long, or not being generous enough with the sodium metabisulphite. Off flavours cannot be hidden, though I would leave any wine for several months to make sure it *is* an off taste, and not just an awkward stage of development. If the ferment sticks, which means that the yeast gives up before the sugar is fermented out, leaving a flat, sweet mixture, correct it by standing the bin in a warmer spot or stirring hard to aerate the must, or adding a little yeast nutrient and acid to ginger up the yeast.

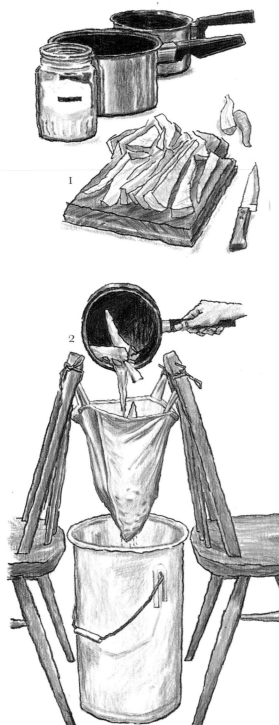

Making parsnip wine

1. Scrub $3\frac{1}{2}$ kg (8 lb) parsnips and slice lengthways. Place in a very large pan with 5 litres (1 gallon) of water and bring to the boil. Simmer until *just* tender – if you let them go mushy the brew will not clear properly.

2. Take a jellybag (if you do not have such a thing, a pillowcase is a good substitute) or hair sieve, and support it over a plastic fermentation bin. Tip in the parsnips and cooking water and leave to drip at their own pace. Do not press, squeeze or otherwise hurry things, or the result will be a cloudy wine.

3. Meanwhile boil up 7 litres ($1\frac{1}{2}$ gallons) of water, and then leave to cool until just tepid.

4. Add the tepid water to the parsnip liquor in the fermentation bin, with the juice of two lemons, and granulated sugar at the rate of $1\frac{1}{2}$ kg (3 lb) per 5 litres (1 gallon) of liquid. Stir well to dissolve sugar completely, then add the yeast starter. This should be made up the day before, by half filling a clean bottle with tepid boiled water and adding a tiny pinch of citric acid and sugar, 1 teaspoon of yeast nutrient and 1 packet of wine yeast. The bottle should be shaken, plugged with cotton wool and set in a warm place. After 24–48 hours the fermentation should have begun, shown by a cluster of bubbles on the top and a cloudiness in the water, and the starter is ready to use.

5. Cover the bin and leave in a warm spot for 10 days, stirring well each day.

6. The fermentation should have slowed down after this prescribed time and the 'must' should be ready to move on into large glass jars. Using a jug and funnel, transfer all the must into as many jars as you require, and fit custom-built air locks. For a first attempt at wine making, it is not essential to buy all the tailor-made equipment. Any large bottles you have will do instead of the proper fermentation jars. However, the latter are, of course, preferable, 5 litre (1 gallon) being the optimum capacity. Instead of commercial air locks, you can improvise a simpler non-return valve system to release carbon dioxide with a polythene bag or rubber balloon tied securely to the neck of the bottle or jar.

7. Slowly the active fermentation in the jars will cease, and the debris and yeast will settle in a solid layer on the bottom of the jar, and the wine will appear clear. To prevent 'off flavours' the wine must be siphoned off the sediment. Take a short length of plastic tube, place one end in the jar taking care not to disturb the sediment, and put the other in your mouth and take a sharp swig at it. This will bring the wine rushing down the tube. Stop it with your thumb, before directing it into waiting, sterilized bottles. Insert corks (you will need a special gadget for this) and store in a cool place for six months or more.

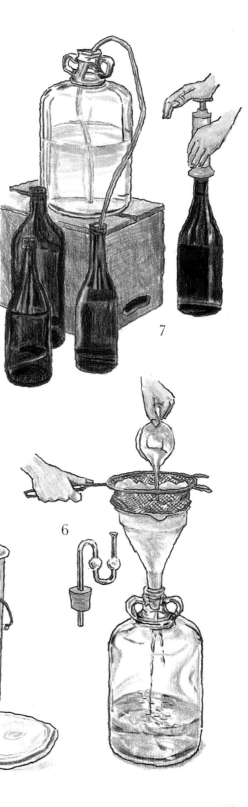

7

4

5

6

Preparing the must

The must is the flavoured liquid base of the wine, made up mainly of water. To extract as much flavour as possible the ingredients can be steeped in cold water for a day or two, with sodium metabisulphite added to prevent any natural ferments starting up. Or they can be simmered briefly. The cold water method is said to give a fresher taste, but it is not suitable for all ingredients. Flower wines use a combination of the two as a rule.

Ingredients should be sound, ripe and as fresh as possible – flowers in particular should be fresh, otherwise their scent fades. Hard ingredients – vegetables and apples – should be peeled, cored and chopped small to extract the maximum flavour. Use an electric blender where possible – metal should never come into contact with a must *after* adding yeast, but before will not hurt.

To make the must, simply combine the prepared ingredients and any other additions in the way of cold tea, citric acid or pectolaze, with the correct amount of water, stir in sugar, and then add the yeast from the starter bottle. After stirring well for a couple of minutes, press on the bin lid, and leave at room temperature. Within a day or two the ferment should have begun. A thick 'cap' on the liquid, composed of all the solids in the must, audible bubbling and a strong smell will confirm this. The must should be stirred vigorously at least once a day to aerate the yeast and any extra sugar added at the same time.

Fermenting the wine

After the prescribed time, when the ferment has slowed down, the liquid wine must be siphoned off – get a helper for this if you are tackling a large quantity of must. The quickest, easiest way to part liquid from solids is to tip the must into a large strainer, sieve, loosely woven cloth or jellybag, suspended over another fermentation bin. Wring out as much liquid as possible, pressing the pulp by hand, spoon or whatever serves best. Now lift the full fermentation bin onto a table and stand the sterilized glass jars below on the floor, or a chair. Dip one end of the polythene tube into the bin, put the other in your mouth and suck sharply. This will bring the wine rushing down the tube. Stop the end up with your thumb, place it into the neck of one of the jars and let it fill to just above the shoulder of the jar, stop it up again, and move onto the next jar. Continue till the jars are full, then fit airlocks or plastic bags over the necks, and stand them in a slightly cooler place for the second phase of fermentation.

The jars will ferment busily at first then, when the activity ceases, the debris and yeast will settle in a solid layer on the bottom of the jar and the wine will 'fall clear'. When clear, it is a good practice to 'rack' it, that is siphon off the yeast layer into a clean jar, or sterilized bottles. If left on the sediment, the wine can become musty. The siphoning is done as before, but be careful not to disturb the sediment. Add a little sodium metabisulphite as a precaution and stabilizer (1 half teaspoon per 5 litres/1 gallon). The racked wine can now be stored in a cool place to mature – with every month that you leave the wine undrunk it will gain in character, subtlety and distinction.

Wines

For convenience I am giving quantities for making five litres (1 gallon) of wine. The recipes are nearly all for wild flowers and fruit and they follow the order in which you would make them through the year.

Gorse wine
Difficult to pick, because of the thorns, but the coconut scented yellow flowers make a wine of beautiful colour and fragrance. Use a plastic jug for measuring, and do not squash the flowers.

3 litres (6 pints) gorse flowers
5 litres (1 gallon) water
1 kg (2 lb) sugar
225 g (8 oz) sultanas
2 oranges
2 lemons (or 7 g/¼ oz citric acid)
150 ml (¼ pint) strong tea or 8 drops tannin concentrate
2 rounded teaspoons all purpose yeast
1 level teaspoon yeast nutrient

Put the flowers into the fermenting bin immediately. Boil up half the water, half the sugar and the chopped sultanas together for a minute or two, then pour over the flowers. Thinly peel the rind from the oranges and the lemons, and add to the bin. Squeeze out the juice and add that too. Add the cold tea, or the tannin, stir thoroughly. Make up to 5 litres (1 gallon) with cold tap water, or cooled boiled water if you prefer. This should give you a tepid mixture, about right for adding the yeast from the starter bottle. Add the yeast and yeast nutrient, stir well, cover. Ferment for one week, stirring daily. After two or three days, when fermenting well, add the remaining sugar, stirring to dissolve. Strain through a hair sieve or cloth (as explained on page 240) and siphon into a 5 litre (1 gallon) jar. Fill up to the neck of the jar with cool, boiled water, if necessary (the less surface area exposed with all wines the better), fit an airlock or secure a plastic bag with an elastic band over the neck of the jar. Rack when clear, bottle and keep for six months.

Dandelion wine
Another flower classic. Pick the dandelions on a hot day, and use *only* the petals, pinching them off and discarding the centres and the stalks.

2 litres (4 pints) dandelion petals
5 litres (1 gallon) water
1 kg (2 lb) sugar
225 g (8 oz) raisins
3 oranges
1 lemon (or 7 g/¼ oz citric acid)
150 ml (¼ pint) strong tea or 8 drops tannin concentrate
2 rounded teaspoons all purpose wine yeast
1 level teaspoon yeast nutrient

The method is exactly the same as for gorse wine.

May blossom wine
Do not confuse may, or hawthorn blossom with the white blossom of the blackthorn or sloe, which comes out a month earlier, before the leaves. Both bushes have thorns but may blossom is always out with its leaves.

2 litres (4 pints) may blossom
5 litres (1 gallon) water
1 kg (2 lb) sugar
2 lemons (or 7 g/¼ oz citric acid)
150 ml (¼ pint) strong tea or 8 drops tannin concentrate
2 rounded teaspoons all purpose wine yeast
1 level teaspoon yeast nutrient

Method as for gorse wine.

Rhubarb wine
Use the first young sticks of rhubarb to make this fresh, fruity medium sweet wine. Rhubarb needs no extra acid.

1 kg (2 lb) rhubarb
450 g (1 lb) sultanas
1 Campden tablet or ½ teaspoon sodium metabisulphite
1 kg (2 lb) sugar
300 ml (½ pint) strong tea or 16 drops tannin concentrate
5 litres (1 gallon) water
1 packet of Sauternes yeast
1 level teaspoon yeast nutrient

Fruit and vegetables

Wipe and trim the rhubarb sticks, chop them small and crush or blend to a mush, saving the juice. Put this into a bin with the chopped sultanas, crushed Campden tablet or sodium metabisulphite, half the sugar and the tea or tannin. Add enough water to make the contents up to 5 litres (1 gallon) (a little hot will give you a tepid mix) add the yeast and the yeast nutrient, stir well and cover. Ferment for eight days, adding the remaining sugar after three. Stir well daily. Strain into a gallon jar and cover, or fit an airlock. Rack when clear. This wine can be drunk after a few months.

Elderflower wine

1 litre (1½ pints) elderflowers
5 litres (1 gallon) water
1 kg (2 lb) sugar
2 lemons
150 ml (¼ pint) strong tea or 8 drops tannin concentrate
2 rounded teaspoons all purpose wine yeast
1 level teaspoon yeast nutrient

Strip the flowers from the stalks as soon as possible after picking, as they are much looser then. The method is the same as for gorse wine.

Gooseberry wine
Green gooseberries are one of the best wine fruit, and they make a clean, crisp wine which resembles a good hock. Use hock yeast.

1¼ kg (3 lb) green gooseberries
5 litres (1 gallon) water
1 kg (2 lb) sugar
1 packet hock yeast
1 level teaspoon yeast nutrient
1 Campden tablet or ½ teaspoon sodium metabisulphite

Top and tail the berries, put them in the fermentation bin and crush them with the end of a rolling pin. Add the water and sugar – to make sure the sugar dissolves boil up some of the water and stir it in. Add a crushed Campden tablet or sodium metabisulphite dissolved in a tablespoon of water. Stir. Add the yeast and the yeast nutrient. Ferment for one week. Strain. Rack when clear. Bottle. Drink after six months.

Blackberry wine

1 kg (2 lb) blackberries
5 litres (1 gallon) water
225 g (8 oz) raisins
1 kg (2 lb) sugar
1 lemon
½ teaspoon Pectozyme
2 rounded teaspoons all purpose yeast
1 level teaspoon yeast nutrient

Put the berries into a pan with about 2½ litres (4 pints) of water, and bring just to simmering point. Put the chopped raisins and the sugar into a fermentation bin, add the blackberries and the water they were simmered in. Stir well to dissolve the sugar. Add another 2 litres (4 pints) of boiled water and mix. When cooled to just warm, stir in the lemon juice and ½ teaspoon of Pectozyme. Add the yeast and the yeast nutrient, cover and ferment for eight days, stirring daily. After eight days strain the contents through a large hair sieve into another bucket and press the pulp in a cloth to squeeze out any remaining juice. Return to a clean fermentation bin. Then siphon off into a 5 litre (1 gallon) jar, leaving behind as much sediment as possible. Fill the jar with cool, boiled water to the neck, fit an airlock till fermentation is finished. Ready after six weeks.

Elderberry wine
Elderberries are so strong on tannin that they make a harsh wine, unless well matured – one to two years. Best made medium sweet.

1¼ kg (3 lb) elderberries
225 g (8 oz) raisins
5 litres (1 gallon) water
1 kg (2 lb) sugar
1 packet Burgundy yeast
1 level teaspoon yeast nutrient
½ teaspoon Pectozyme

Heat the berries and the chopped raisins in water till simmering. Tip them into a fermentation bin, add the sugar, stir well. When cooled add the yeast, the yeast nutrient and ½ teaspoon of Pectozyme. Ferment for five days, stirring daily. Strain into jars. Rack when the wine has cleared, and again after three months.

Liqueurs and cordials

Very attractive liqueurs can be made by the simple method of steeping fruit in spirits with sugar. Not cheap, alas, but worth making in small quantities for gala occasions to drink with the after dinner coffee.

Danish blackcurrant rum
(Solbaerrom)

1 litre (2 pints) white rum
1 kg (2 lb) blackcurrants
6 bitter almonds
675 g (1¼ lb) sugar

Pour the rum into a wide mouthed crock, add the crushed blackcurrants and blanched almonds, cover and stand in a cool place for one month, stirring daily. Then drain the liquor off the currants, pressing out all juice, add the sugar and stir to dissolve. Bottle, corking well, and leave for at least six months.
Note: the remaining fruit can be used in pies.

Sloe gin
The best use for sloes, those tiny wild plums of the hedgerows. Made in the autumn it will be ready by Christmas.

1 litre (2 pints) sloes
1 litre (2 pints) gin
375 g (12 oz) sugar

Prick the sloes, and pack them into a wide mouthed crock with the other ingredients. Cover tightly. Shake from time to time to dissolve the sugar. After three to four months strain, bottle, cork tightly and keep as long as you can.
Note: Use the left over sloes to flavour pies, pasta sauces and casseroles – they keep for ages in a screwtop jar.

Raspberry cordial
Russians make this with wild berries. Use an equal volume of fruit to vodka. Combine them in a crock, leave for about a week, then strain the fruit out. Dilute the liquid with water, in about equal amounts, and add 450 g (1 lb) sugar per 5 litres (1 gallon). Stir well, bottle and keep for several months.

This is another Russian method, which can be made with mulberries, loganberries and strawberries as well as raspberries. The berries are fermented in sugar. Half fill a 5 litre (1 gallon) jar or plastic bucket with berries then fill to the top with sugar. Cover and leave for six to eight weeks to ferment. Strain through a sieve, pressing out the juice. Strain the juice through a jellybag to clear it. Then add alcohol – vodka, brandy or rum, to taste – at least one part alcohol to three parts fruit juice.

Noyau
This dates from the 18th century, and is a potent liqueur made with beech leaves. Pack a glass jar full of young beech leaves, then fill up with gin. Cover and leave for two weeks. Strain off the gin and to every 600 ml (1 pint) allow 250 g (9 oz) of sugar which has been dissolved in 300 ml (½ pint) of boiling water. Mix well, add a tablespoonful of brandy per bottle, and cork tightly.

Raspberry vinegar
Fruit vinegars are diluted with water or soda water before drinking.

1 litre (2 pints) raspberries or blackberries
1 litre (2 pints) white wine vinegar
sugar

Pour the vinegar over the fruit and stand for four days. Strain, adding 450 g (1 lb) of sugar per litre (2 pints) of liquid. Heat till just simmering. Cool. Bottle, cork tightly and store in a cool dry place.

Cherry shrub
Pick ripe Morello cherries, set them in a crock and set the crock in a pan of water (or cool oven) till the juice runs. Turn into a jellybag. Squeeze out the juice, sweeten to taste and add 1 part brandy to four parts shrub. Shake. Cork. Will keep all summer in a cool place.

Index

Recipes are in Italics
Step by step instructions are denoted
by numbers in bold